THE
GREAT CHRISTIAN THEOLOGIES

EDITED BY
Rev. HENRY W. CLARK, D.D.

LIBERAL ORTHODOXY
A HISTORICAL SURVEY

LIBERAL ORTHODOXY

A HISTORICAL SURVEY

BY

HENRY W. CLARK, D.D.

AUTHOR OF "THE HISTORY OF ENGLISH NONCONFORMITY," "THE PHILOSOPHY
OF CHRISTIAN EXPERIENCE," ETC.

LONDON
CHAPMAN AND HALL, LTD.
1914

RICHARD CLAY & SONS, LIMITED,
BRUNSWICK STREET, STAMFORD STREET, S.E.,
AND BUNGAY, SUFFOLK.

PREFATORY NOTE

NOT very much prophetic insight is needed to foresee one of the criticisms which may be made in regard to this book. " Liberal Orthodoxy is still in the transition stage," it may with plausibility and indeed with justice be said. " Indeed, the book itself closes with what is practically a statement to that effect. With what right can it be classed among the ' Great Christian Theologies ' ? " Well, one may say at least these two things by way of reply. First, that the story of Liberal Orthodoxy presents (at any rate in Germany) more than one theological construction which amply deserves the title " great." And next, that since part of the book's purpose is to show some of the reasons why Liberal Orthodoxy has failed to achieve that theological reconstruction whereto it has sometimes come so near and after which it has all the time been striving, the study, after all, is just on the border-line of the territory, if not quite within, indicated by the general name. If, in view of these points, one cannot altogether plead " Not Guilty " against the criticism mentioned above, perhaps one may at least ask that judgment shall make its sentence light.

If the writing of a book like this is begun with considerable apprehension—both on the score of the writer's own limited capabilities and on that of the further disadvantages under which smallness of space will set him—it ends in keen realisation on the writer's part that the initial apprehension has been more than fulfilled. So much has been left out, and so many men on whom one would have loved to dwell have been dismissed with a scanty line! I should not like it to be supposed that I am unconscious of this, or that I have wantonly slighted any claims. Probably I am as fully aware of what is *not* here as any reader can be. Yet I am not quite without hope that though these pages cannot provide a full meal for the mind hungering after this kind of food, they may at least form a temporary provision not altogether without its pleasantness and its use. Indeed, when the field is so large, no single writer—unless he confine himself to one corner of it, which would have been inconsistent with the present design— can expect to do more than indicate its general outline and the principal spots in it where digging will yield gold.

The greater part of the Epilogue is extracted from an article of mine which appeared in the *London Quarterly Review* for July 1913, under the title *The Christian Idea of Revelation*. I have to thank the editor of the *Review* very cordially for his kind permission to reprint the extracted portions.

HENRY W. CLARK.

Harpenden,
February 1914.

CONTENTS

CHAPTER I

CHAPTER II

CHAPTER III

CONTENTS

CHAPTER IV

CHAPTER V

free—Effect on other doctrines—Instances of the writers' methods
—Worth and limitation of their work—Arnold's spiritual
passion—The second school—Preliminary description—Need of
harmony between truth and the inmost self—Coleridge—Erskine
of Linlathen—Similarity and dissimilarity of the two schools—
In what way the second was more positive than the first—
Relation between the Coleridgean method and that of the
Cambridge Platonists—Comparison of the British method with
the German—Unlikeness in the British lack of system—Likeness
in readiness of surrender—And in that both remained a system
of ideas—Erskine on the way in which religion affects character—
Channing in America—"Liberal Orthodox" in spite of his
Arianism—His affinities with the second school of British
Orthodoxy.

CHAPTER VI

Characterisation of the period—Hegel and Hegelianism—Attempted
Liberal Orthodoxy on the Hegelian foundation—Marheineke,
Daub—Failure of the attempt—Biedermann—Destructive consequences of Hegelianism—Strauss—Bruno Bauer, Feuerbach—
The Tübingen school—Baur—New Testament criticism—Baur's
theory of "tendency"—Effect of this—Was the historic Christ
sufficiently guarded by Schleiermacher's system, in face of all
this ?—How the question was dealt with—The extreme orthodox,
Twesten, Nitzsch—The Erlangen school—Hofmann—The truer
Schleiermacher succession—Dorner and Rothe—Their super-
adding of speculation to the witness of the Christian consciousness—Dorner's system—Rothe's method—Schleiermacher's
influence—Other names of the period—Other countries—
Martensen in Denmark—The Groningen school in Holland—
Schweizer and Vinet in Switzerland—Pressensé in France—Summary—Even now it was felt that the historic Christ was not
sufficiently secured.

CHAPTER VII

The period—The background—Conservative Orthodoxy—The
Oxford Movement—J. H. Newman—Influences which were to
affect the future—Changes in geological science—Lyell—Pye-
Smith and Hugh Miller—Herbert Spencer, Darwin—Attacks
on Christianity, Hennell, Francis Newman, Greg—Progress of
Biblical criticism—Stanley, Jowett, Davidson's edition of Horne
—Theological development—The Coleridgean school—Hare—
Erskine's later books—Doctrine of salvation—How affected by the

CHAPTER VIII

The point at which we left German Liberal Orthodoxy—Ritschl
—His likeness to, and difference from, Schleiermacher—Starts
from Christian experience and the "historic Christ"—What
this means—Insistence on the "record"—Natural religion,
mysticism—How is all this an apologetic?—It provides a safe
retreat—"Fasten yourself down upon the one patent fact"—
But then what can we say and what can we not?—The theory of
"value-judgments"—Difficulties of it—Julius Kaftan's modification of it—The exact meaning of a "value-judgment"—We
carry back into the confronting reality what is given in its
effect upon us—This does not mean that we are only framing a
hypothesis—The charge is often made—"Equivalent-judgment"
—What then can we say and what can we not?—As to God—As
to Christ—As to miracle—The charge of denying the miraculous
sometimes brought against Ritschl—His real attitude—Ritschl
and the Resurrection—Philosophy as incompetent as theology
for ultimate explanations—How all this makes theology safe—
The price—No knowledge of ultimates—Dualism—Is it a possible
position?—Certain difficulties in it—And the history of the
Ritschlian school shows that the position is impossible—Two
paths of divergence—Some called on theology to explore ultimates,
some on philosophy—The consequences of each course—Those
who called on theology and became more conservative—Julius
Kaftan, Häring—The "positive" school—Seeberg, Kähler,
Theodore Kaftan—Those who called on philosophy and became
more radical—Greater attraction of this method—Lipsius,
Tröltsch, Harnack, Drews—Recapitulation—Addendum on the
rest of Europe.

CONTENTS

CHAPTER IX

LIBERAL ORTHODOXY

CHAPTER I

THE ANTECEDENTS

LIBERAL Orthodoxy—the effort to marry, or
at least adjust, Christian faith to progressive
thought, the effort to preserve the essentials of
the Christian religion, as Protestantism under-
stands them, while yielding all due deference
to the claims of advancing mind—is of course a
comparatively modern movement. It is in fact
not till the second decade of the nineteenth century
that the movement's real stirrings are to be discerned. But for the conditions which govern it
we have to look a good way back. The direction
of the movement—the precise points at which its
directors or would-be directors called a halt—the
reason why they failed to call a halt at others—
the further reason why, when they did call it,
the movement did not always obey, but sometimes flowed on to consequences unexpected and
undesired—all these things depend upon fundamental conceptions of Christianity which were
settled long before the movement itself began;
and to understand the movement we must
understand first of all what these fundamental
conceptions were. If we wish to know, over and

B

above the facts of the progressive movement, the why and the wherefore of them, their animating soul as well as their external shape, we must grasp the essential character of that religious system which, because it was what it was, held determined within itself, and supplied when the hour struck, the governing forces whereby the movement was controlled. It is back among these antecedent conditions, and therefore at a point whence we may be able to discern some of the consequences to which they gave rise, that this first chapter is intended to set us down.

The fundamental and primary fact is that the Reformation left the main stress of obligation upon correctness of intellectual belief. What Principal Workman has said, with much truth if with some over-emphasis, of Luther himself— that " as he grew older his conception of faith became more and more intellectual, till at last it comprised little beyond the assent of the mind to certain articles of an orthodox creed "— may be fairly said of the Reformation movement as a whole. This is not to deny that the original impulse which gave birth to the Reformation contained within itself much more than a recognition of the falseness of the dominant creed and a demand for a creed new and true : it is merely to deny that all the contents of the original impulse were drawn out. Nor is it to deny that the new creed was, as a matter of fact, much more correspondent to the truth than the old had been : it is merely to say that the new creed did not emphasise as it ought to have done the existence of a living and permanent spiritual dynamic, issuing out of a living and permanent Christ, in contact with which dynamic, rather than in acceptance of the creed itself, the secret of religion really lay. Least of all is it to deny value to the Reformation as an intellectual and religious re-birth : it is only to declare that in this instance, as in others, the very greatness of a forward step, or the realisation of its greatness, led to sudden paralysis of the advance, and that the good was to some extent the enemy of the best. When the rush and roar of the tremendous upheaval had died away, what had been accomplished was the substitution of a fresh for an old reading of certain doctrines which professed to convey the significance of a revelation given long ago and to declare the methods whereby the benefits of that revelation might be appropriated for men and women of later times. And however the underlying motive of the Reformation may be interpreted—whether we take the movement, with Guizot, as having been chiefly an uprising against priestly authority, or as an outburst of moral disgust against corruptions and abuse, or as the substitution of an infallible Book for an infallible Church, or as an emphatic assertion of the Protestant doctrine of justification by faith, or indeed as all these things combined—the statement just made holds good. For, in any case, it was upon the support of a bygone revelation that the reformer flung himself; and his summons to men was a summons to join him in that return upon a system of ideas delivered long ago and delivered

once for all.   Doctrine had been corrupted; and
pure doctrine must consequently be restored.
A supernatural revelation—and a supernatural
revelation of *doctrine*, of *truth*, in the sense of
propositions to which men must say " Amen "—
given in and by a supernatural Person, either by
direct statements or by implications which came
to the surface if the waters of direct statement
were stirred, must be released from the heaped-
up piles of rubbish wherewith the destructive
centuries had overlaid it, and presented once
more to claim the assent of the human mind.
But that the advent of Jesus Christ had been
the introduction of something new, not only
into the sphere of truth, but into the sphere of
reality—that Jesus Christ had brought with Him,
had in fact constituted, a new influx of creative
or re-creative life—that, because He had never
really quitted the world again, this re-creative
life was still dynamically operative for whosoever
would establish contact with the Christ who
held it—that in the establishment of such contact
the essential conditioning act of the Christian
life consisted—that not in what Christ had said,
not even in what He had been, but in what at
every successive moment of the world's history
He *is*, lies the supremely important thing—these
ideas did not emerge.   Needless to say, these
ideas would, like all other ideas, have made their
first appeal to the mind, and would have had to
prove their claims in the mind's open court;
but by their very nature they would have pointed
on to something beyond themselves which acceptance of them involved—to the need of such

an adjustment between the personality of man
and the Personality of Christ as would make the
creative life of the second available for, and
operative upon, the first; and they would thus,
in the very act of demanding acceptance, have
proclaimed that *not* acceptance of them, but
the " something beyond," was the supremely
important and decisive thing. But they did not
emerge; which is to say in other words that the
mystical element in Christianity did not assert
its rights. The accent was not shifted from
belief over to a direct relation between personality
and Personality, a relation wherein human personality is given up to, and re-made out of, the
Personality of Christ; but only from wrong
belief over to right belief. It is quite true, of
course (although the *rationale* of the thing remained
obscure), that the ultimate results of right belief
were held to stretch far beyond the region of the
mind : men could not, so ran the contention,
have a right belief in Christ without being morally
and spiritually transformed; and in the presence
or absence of this transformation the test of
belief's sincerity was taken to lie. And of
course the life of Christ Himself, under the new
system as under the old, supplied the standard
whereby the extent of the transformation was
to be gauged. No one can question that a very
real, indeed a very passionate, desire for holiness
lay beneath all the reconstruction of the Reformation time : to attempt any proof of this would
only be to buttress a proposition self-evident to
all who have eyes to see. And it was in the
interest of this desire that the connection between

right belief and moral regeneration was affirmed.
But, nevertheless, right belief was the essential
thing. Even the faith whereon the cardinal
doctrine of " justification by faith " insisted
was an acceptance by the individual of the truth
that Christ's atoning work had been all-sufficient
for *him ;* and although the warmth of emotion
which often accompanied the realisation of the
truth, and the glow of joy which often resulted
from it, might disguise the fact, the decisive
act was really an act of the intellect, and no more.
It is scarcely correct to say, as is often said, that
the doctrine of justification by faith substituted
a direct contact between the disciple and Christ
for an indirect contact mediated through priest
or Church. It provided for the mind a point
of attachment lying immediately upon the saving
work which Christ had wrought, and by so much
nearer to Christ Himself : but that is not quite
the same thing. It was still the mind and its
attitude that were in question. And whatever
consequences in the way of spiritual transformation might follow from the decisive act, they
would be not so much mediated through that
intellectual act of faith, would not result from it
as effect results from cause, but would be found
to have mysteriously taken up their abode in
him by whom the act of faith had been put
forth. The decisive, conditioning act of Christian discipleship was essentially an act of an
intellectual kind, a mental acceptance of certain
things as true. It was not the submission of the
entire human personality to the direct action of
life issuing dynamically from the Personality

of Christ, as the two stood face to face. Which is to say that under and after the Reformation movement Christianity was taken to be a doctrinal system still,[1] though a system whose doctrine had been corrected and made pure—a supernatural revelation given in and vouched for by a supernatural Person, who was also the pattern and example of what assent to His pronouncements would cause His disciples to be.

To treat this error from the purely theological standpoint, to indicate the grounds on which it must be considered an error, and to adduce evidence in support of the truer view, to show how the idea of a veritable life-dynamic in Jesus Christ is the heart of Christianity as Jesus Christ proclaimed it and as those who understood His inmost mind received it, is outside our present range.[2] What we have to do is rather to note how the prevalence of the error affected the method of that change in doctrinal belief which was in any case bound to come. For change was indeed inevitable. The progress of general enquiry and the enlarging results to which that enquiry led; the development of the scientific spirit and the addition of discovery as the years went on; these things would necessarily

[1] Quakerism, at any rate as represented in Fox, is a striking exception; and it is one of the saddest misfortunes of religious history that a constructive theology was not developed on the basis of the original Quaker idea. I have tried, in the *History of English Nonconformity* (the index of which will supply the necessary references), to explain why Quakerism thus failed.

[2] Perhaps I may be allowed to refer the reader to my book *The Philosophy of Christian Experience* for some treatment of the idea and certain related ideas.

have compelled orthodoxy to revise itself and to
re-draw many of the contours of its creed.   For
Protestant orthodoxy, like Catholic orthodoxy
before it, touched upon secular and scientific
fields at many points : the conception of the
Bible as an authoritative deliverance upon such
topics as the creation of the world (to name
but one of the most familiar) remained after
the Reformation as firmly in possession as it
had been before; and the new system, notwithstanding the greatness of its break with the old,
filled many of the rooms in its intellectual edifice
with furniture and equipment of the accepted
style.   Be it remembered, also, that this would
still have been done even if, on the main point
as to the decisive and conditioning act of Christian
discipleship, the idea of a directly-operative
life-dynamic in Christ had been substituted for
the idea of assent to a revelation given in Christ
long ago.   The established items of the generally
accepted religious creed, outside of those with
which the Reformation was immediately concerned, would still have kept their place; and
intellectual assent to those not challenged would
have been looked for as the natural accompani-
ment to the performance of discipleship's decisive
and conditioning act, though that act itself had
been no longer taken to be of an intellectual
kind. The Reformation, in short, simply took over
from the older system—and would in any case
have done so—everything with which it did *not*
disagree, not conceiving that the contents of the
scheduled creeds could be questioned from any
other standpoint than that which on its own

account it chose to take up. But this means that, as was said before, change in the orthodox Protestant beliefs was bound to come. Of course in saying this one remembers that Protestantism contained from the beginning an ultra-conservative school which steadfastly refused to abate a single jot or tittle of the first-received beliefs, whatever opposition to the march of thought such refusal might imply, and that in fact such a school persists, though in diminishing numbers, to our own day. But it is only with that section of Protestantism which bowed to the legitimate rights of mind, or which at any rate admitted that mind *had* legitimate rights, that we are here concerned; and of this section it is correct to affirm that changes in its beliefs were bound to come. Some such thing as Liberal Orthodoxy must of necessity grow up. The claim of science to have its boundaries respected and its territory reserved—the demonstration that many statements upon extra-religious themes, made in the Bible or in the formularies of the Churches, shrivelled as advancing knowledge flung upon them its cold and searching light—the activities of historical and literary criticism by way of showing that literalism had taken up many an untenable position and must retreat—these things and kindred things lay ahead, biding the hour when orthodoxy must make its reckoning with them and admit that their gage was not causelessly thrown down. Also, by mere growth of the spirit of toleration, by mere softening of controversial moods, by mere recognition of the fact that intellectual errors need not necessarily

involve moral offence, some of the earlier articles
of belief, unquestioningly accepted by men who
had not felt the blowing of these milder airs,
were to be robbed of their hold. Some were to
become simply impossible : some were to be
toned down so far that transformation became
virtual abolition in the end. Of course all this
was hidden from the shapers of the Reformation
creeds; but we, looking back, can see that they
could not but befall. It was in the nature of
things; and in a progressive world religious
belief could not be the one thing permitted to
stand with its feet immovably planted in the
ancient prints.

But the special conditions indicated above,
the taking of Christianity as being primarily
a revelation of truth supernaturally guaranteed,
imposed a special character upon the inevitable
process of change. Had the " direct dynamic "
idea stood central, it would necessarily have
been regulative of the process from beginning
to end : round about the doctrine that Christianity meant the submission of human personality
to a life-giving Personality constantly present
upon the world's stage since the advent of Jesus
Christ, and re-creative upon every individual by
whom submission was made (in other words,
round about the doctrine that acceptance of
Christianity meant *more* than the acceptance of
doctrine) all other doctrines would have been
gathered and grouped; and the function of all
other doctrines would have been to illuminate
that supreme doctrine, to draw out its implications, to declare why the adjustment of human

personality to such a re-creative Personality was
required, and how it had been rendered possible,
and in what manner it might rightly and success-
fully be made. This means, among other things,
that Christianity would have been a philosophy
as well as a religion; for it is involved in the idea
of a creative life-force in Christ that at Christ's
coming something actually *happened* to and in
the world-process; and the conception of that
world-process as a whole—the conception entertained by those accepting the " life-dynamic " idea
—would have had to be so shaped, so changed if
need be, as to make room for this " happening "
as one of its constituent elements; so that every
Christian doctrine, being in intimate relation
with the " life-dynamic " idea, would also *ipso
facto* have had its roots in a philosophical scheme.
By so much, therefore, the task of those who,
under the assaults of a philosophy definitely anti-
Christian, sought to find a philosophical basis
for the Christianity they did not wish to lose,
would have been simplified. Precisely in that
form, indeed, the task would never have come
upon their hands; nor, with a Christianity
essentially philosophical already, could any question ever have arisen of putting a philosophical
platform underneath a doctrinal edifice which
to philosophical scrutiny seemed to be hanging
in mid-air. It would have been as between
philosophy and philosophy that the battle would
have been fought out; and Christian doctrine
would have been spared the reproach of having
become philosophical under stress, and the suspicion, after it had so become, of resting upon a

philosophy unsound because constructed with
the exigencies of the doctrine in view. The
application of this, however, will be seen later
on. We return at present to the influence which
the dominance of the " life-dynamic " idea would
have exercised upon doctrinal change as the
necessity for change grew plain. All changes
made in other doctrines as time went on would
have been governed, out to the remotest edge of
the doctrinal circle, by the recognition that the
doctrine of life-dynamic in Christ and of human
personality's submission to it, and this alone,
was the doctrine vital to Christianity's con-
tinuance, that whatever was involved in it,
whether as necessary antecedent or concomitant
or consequent, must be clung to, and that all
else might go. This one doctrine would have
been held as giving Christianity's supreme dis-
tinctiveness; and this one doctrine would have
constituted " orthodoxy's " positive and negative
test. Whatever change, suggested by the accu-
mulations of enlarging general knowledge or by
the suspicions and findings of growing intellectual
power, left this doctrine unassailed and unim-
paired, would have been admitted if upon
examination its credentials were found good :
whatever change challenged this central doctrine
would have had its call refused; or, if obedience
to the call had been yielded, it would have been
with a confession that essential Christianity was
thereby given up. This is indeed the point to be
stressed and to be kept in mind in view of what
will presently be said—that the holding of the
" life-dynamic " conception for the central one

would have provided a standard to which all
possible changes might be referred, and would
have prevented anything like an unguided
" drift." For let it be remembered that acceptance of that conception points on to a " something beyond " that acceptance itself—to a
movement of the whole personality toward
Christ, an adjustment of the whole personality
to Christ's, to a something *practical*, in short
(none the less practical that it is a matter of soul,
and not of hand or foot), which must be done if
acceptance be sincere. It would have been
impossible, therefore, for the conception of " life-
dynamic " in Christ, having once occupied any
standing ground, merely to have glided out of
sight without being missed : if it had gone at all,
it must have gone openly and not surreptitiously,
at once and not by degrees; for immediately
upon its departure, the absence of that " something beyond "—that movement and adjustment
of personality—which it had previously called
for and created, would have been the patent
witness that it had gone. With that conception
for the central one, " drift " there could not have
been. As has been said, the central conception
would itself have had to be defended against
attacks from one quarter and another; but so
long as the conception held its ground Liberal
Orthodoxy, as the general movement of things
forced change in the religious sphere and thus
brought Liberal Orthodoxy into being, would
have known where it was, how far it might go,
where, if it was to remain " orthodoxy " at all,
it must pause. Its task would have been to

defend that central conception—to ask for no
more fixity of belief than successful defence
required, to yield no more change in belief than
successful defence allowed; and, if successful
defence proved impossible, to admit that Christianity's great cause was lost. One may venture
to put it that if Protestant Christianity had been
more mystical, it would have faced more rationally
the necessity of rational change. It would at
least have known where the limit of change must
be fixed—would have been able with unerring
instinct to mark the moment at which the sword
of change swung itself threateningly into position
for an attack upon Christianity's heart. And
it may be added that the Christ of Liberal
Orthodoxy could not, under these conditions,
have become less than " supernatural," since
His supernaturalness would have been given in
the very fact that He was, and must remain, the
communicator and creator of a veritable divine
life to and in man.

But with Christianity taken as a revealed
doctrinal system supernaturally guaranteed,
things ran differently. The main purpose of
Liberal Orthodoxy, in view of the general development of thought and criticism, came to
be the harmonising of the revelation with the
findings of these things, or, as hostile pressure
upon particular doctrines speedily grew so sharp
that this general programme had to be more
clearly visioned, the surrender of those once-
credited parts of the revelation which could not
be so harmonised—with this for the limiting
consideration, that there must be a sufficient

residuum, clearly supernatural in its source, to permit the continued assertion of supernatural knowledge (supernatural *knowledge* rather than supernatural *nature* in the strict sense, at any rate supernatural *nature* only as supernatural *knowledge* demanded this) in the Christ by whom the revelation had been brought.[1] The supreme enquiry, as each fresh challenger struck with his lance-point against the shield of faith, was not, " Does the alteration or reduction of Christian belief now demanded affect belief in the direct action upon man of a re-creative life-force issuing out of Christ ? " but, " Does it leave us still with sufficient warrant for ascribing to Christianity's Founder an understanding of divine facts and realities beyond that possible to ordinary members of the human race ? " The point of vital import, as each new crisis approached and some hitherto unassailed doctrine had to submit itself to the testing fires, was this—if the doctrine fails to pass, is there still enough of *any* doctrine remaining to justify acceptance of Christ as the revealer of a supernaturally-given system of religious ideas ? In other words, could that act of the mind which had been taken to be the decisive and conditioning act of Christian disciple-

[1] It must be borne in mind that it is with *Liberal* Orthodoxy we are concerned. *Conservative* Orthodoxy has always looked on the supernatural Book rather than the supernatural Christ as the citadel—not, of course, that it held the second of minor account, but that it deemed it impossible to keep the second if the first should go. Liberal Orthodoxy's very first movement, as we shall see, involved a looser holding (to say the least) of the " supernatural Book " idea—in the sense of a Book whose every word must, on supernatural authority, be taken precisely as it stands.

ship still be performed? The *sum* of ideas in
respect of which it was performed might be
modified, but was the act itself, notwithstanding
that, feasible still? Particularly as a sort of
" rational " religion presented itself alongside of
orthodox Christianity, claiming that the essential ideas of Christianity really beat up spon-
taneously, at a given point of development, in the
human mind, would the assertion of this supernatural *residuum* come to be Liberal Orthodoxy's
feverish concern. With Christianity looked
upon as assent to a system of supernaturally-
given ideas, Liberal Orthodoxy naturally took
for its task the adjustment of these ideas to the
imperious necessities of intellectual evolution,
guarding the process from going too far, or
seeking to do so, by repeating under its breath
that a *residuum* of supernatural ideas, enough to
justify the ascription of supernatural knowledge
to the Christ who brought them, must and would
remain.

From the carrying through of any such process
great gains must assuredly be, and have been,
won. True, it cannot of itself bring about a
correction of the initial error we have noticed,
the error of looking upon Christianity as a system
of truths supernaturally revealed and guaranteed
rather than as the introduction of an actual
new life-force upon the stage of the world. Even
in respect of this it cannot be quite without
effect; for once you begin to admit that a body
of doctrine, formerly deemed irreducible, can
after all be reduced without imperilling salvation,
you have come near to raising the question

whether salvation depends upon the acceptance of doctrine at all; and it is matter of history that Liberal Orthodoxy has frequently justified its surrender of one doctrine or another by a negative declaration on the point, though without seeing that by merely substituting a smaller for a larger amount of doctrine as necessary it was perpetuating on a more limited scale the error against which it had protested. We may put it, perhaps, that by the carrying out of the process just sketched correction of the error is suggested, but not made. Still, in spite of this failure, many of its results must be counted as all to the good. The harmonising of religious ideas with ideas in other than religious spheres, or at least the removal of contradiction between religious ideas and the verdicts of scientific and general research, the placing of religious doctrines as truly-fitting elements in the mosaic of the general intellectual construction, the banishment of theological opinions which unprejudiced thought and developing moral sensitiveness declare untenable—all this is for the profit alike of religion and of the world at large; and any criticism of Liberal Orthodoxy must be made with full acknowledgment of the fact that all this has been done. But over against this a consideration charged with serious import must be set.

The danger is that the process, as described— the process of adjusting religious ideas to the claims of advancing knowledge, under no other limiting consideration than that a certain supernatural *residuum*, in justification of continued belief in a supernatural Revealer, must be left—

c

that the process may easily, but unconsciously, be taken so far as to involve the elimination of even the supernatural *residuum* which it is avowedly desired to keep, and in the end may thus defeat itself after all. It was said that the holding of the " life-dynamic " conception for Christianity's central one would have prevented Liberal Orthodoxy from anything like an unguided " drift " : it must be said now that it is precisely upon such an unguided " drift " that Liberal Orthodoxy was launched when it conceived its task in the terms just named. Superficially, indeed, it may appear that the proviso which demands the perpetuation of a supernatural *residuum* sufficient to necessitate a supernatural Revealer behind it—that this supplies for all possible theological change a standard definite enough. And, theoretically, doubtless the case is so. But in actual experience the standard may easily fail to make its authority press. Liberal Orthodoxy, under the given circumstances and with its task conceived in the stated terms, is to go as far in the direction of change as general intellectual progress compels it to go, so long as a not very clearly defined *minimum* of doctrine is preserved. That is what it soon comes to. Very clearly defined the indispensable *minimum* cannot be; or, if a definition be attempted at first, it will not hold good for long. Liberal Orthodoxy speedily finds it impossible to spread its doctrinal possessions between two compartments, from one of which it may make its surrenders to the demands of intellectual progress, while the contents of the other constitute the *minimum* which is to remain inviolate. The first impulse will naturally be toward making such a division : indeed, Liberal Orthodoxy will tend more and more to purchase the safety of its untouchable *minimum* by enlarging the size of what it is willing to give up; and when criticism demands the coat, will offer the cloak also, hoping that this generosity will successfully stave off further demands. But the " general intellectual progress " with which it has to make terms will consent to no such bargain as that, and, let Liberal Orthodoxy attempt to rail off what territories it may, will break down the fences whenever it feels so disposed, refusing to recognise any doctrine as finally reserved. If, therefore, some belief hitherto supposed to be impregnably lodged in the supernatural *residuum* be challenged by advancing mind, and if advancing mind justifies its challenge to its own satisfaction, Liberal Orthodoxy must either surrender the challenged belief or admit that the task it has proposed to itself cannot be performed : rather than make the confession, however, Liberal Orthodoxy will fall back upon the inviting refuge presented by the sudden discovery that the impugned doctrine was not really part of the indispensable *minimum* at all, and ought to have been placed in the other " compartment," the one from which subtraction can be made without serious loss; and thus in the net result, the supernatural *residuum* is by so much the less. A few repetitions of this process, and Liberal Orthodoxy—finding that its list of beliefs is being abbreviated as it were at both ends, at the end it wished to keep intact as well as at the end where it did not object to the application of the knife—has to admit, what the other party to the procedure has quietly assumed all along, that the partition into "dispensable" and "indispensable" cannot be maintained, and finds itself resting, not upon a categorical assertion that certain specified doctrines *do* constitute the supernatural *residuum* justifying faith in a supernatural Revealer, but upon a much more vague declaration that, when the progress of mind has done its best or its worst, *some* such *residuum* will still be left.

Thereafter, the " abbreviating " process goes on. Moreover, it goes on with accelerated speed; for, since Liberal Orthodoxy's *minimum* is now so vaguely seen and expressed, the antecedent presumption is always on the side of " progressive thought " whenever this chooses to summon some doctrine to its bar; and the position has become such that practically all beliefs are only tentatively and provisionally held, are, indeed, almost suspect. Criticism objects to this and to that : revisal, modification, abolition, are humbly, at its command, repeated and repeated again : beliefs are stripped of supposedly supernatural sanctions, or deprived of their supposedly supernatural origin, or reduced to terms which leave them with no supernatural quality at all and make them to be no more than echoes of what ordinary human voices might have said without any supernatural revelation whatever. Let this reduction and diminution be carried far enough, and presently Christianity comes to be

merely a matter of two or three great ideas—
such as the Fatherhood of God, the brotherhood
of man, the ennobling influence of Christ's self-
sacrifice on the Cross—which, it can still be
affirmed, lie upon the surface of Christ's own
teaching, together with a summons to men to
live by whatever inspiration these ideas may
offer, and a pointing of men to Christ Himself
as the perfect Exemplar of the effect which a
perfect apprehension of these ideas and of their
value can produce. And on the fact that He
proclaimed and incarnated these ideas Christ's
claim to be of special heavenly birth is now based.

But then (and here the more serious consequences of the initial error begin) there inevitably
creeps in a feeling—only a feeling, for as a categorical statement, clamouring for acceptance, it would
have no chance—that for a Christ whose message
has been so cut down the term " supernatural "
is too large, or that, if the term be still used, its
connotation cannot be quite what it once was
taken to be. Meanwhile, the advancing critical
movement, in pursuance of its policy of holding
no doctrine whatever exempt from its question,
has been fastening upon the one supreme doctrine,
the doctrine of a supernatural Christ, which
through the whole battle it has been the hope of
Liberal Orthodoxy to preserve : criticism has
long since, after making its way through the
outer courts of the temple, begun to knock loudly
at the door of this innermost shrine : at any
moment it may select for the final attack, the
vague feeling just alluded to must constitute an
ally on the inner side; and at the end of the

day, Liberal Orthodoxy will find itself employing such words as " ideal man," " Head of the race," and the like (these phrases, in fact, came quite early into Liberal Orthodoxy's vocabulary) in place of the more stringent words and phrases in which its conception cf Christ was formerly cast. And this may mean that Liberal Orthodoxy has, without knowing it, ceased, even on its own original account of itself, to be " orthodoxy " at all; for it may mean that the really " supernatural " Christ has gone, having as it were slipped away unnoticed when the *residuum* of revelation became so small as not to call for Him any more. In brief, the first intention—the intention of preserving such a *minimum* of doctrine as could only be accounted for by the doctrine of a supernatural Revealer—has broken down. And it has broken down, or may easily have done so, unknown to those principally concerned. It is quite possible to employ such terms as those quoted just now, because they seem most appropriate in the intellectual atmosphere of some given period, and to think that they bear the same significance as the stronger terms abandoned; and it is not until some unevadable challenge rings out—whether from that same criticism which has already forced the change cf terms and now, become impatient of self-deception in those who use them, desires to enjoy the fulness of its triumph, or from that conservative section of the Christian world to which Liberal Orthodoxy and all its works are anathema—that the users find they have changed, not words alone, but ideas as well.

All unconsciously the transition from Liberal
Orthodoxy has been made to something which
is certainly not " orthodoxy," liberal or other,
whatever else it may be. It must be remembered that the final disappearance of the idea of
a supernatural Revealer need not immediately
announce itself by its practical consequences,
as we have said the disappearance of the idea
of " life-dynamic " in Christ must do. This
last-named idea points on to something beyond
itself, to a definite movement and adjustment
of human personality, to something practical, in
short, which must follow upon the idea's acceptance; and the non-appearance of the practical
consequence hoists the flag in token that the idea
is gone. With the idea of a supernatural Revealer
the case stands otherwise; and human nature
being what it is, it is possible for the idea to
become debilitated, and even to be utterly lost,
without the mind which once entertained it
observing its increasing weakness or its empty
place. By some such process as that sketched,
Liberal Orthodoxy—having started with the idea
that Christianity may be summarised as a revelation supernaturally guaranteed, and having
sought to go as far as possible in adjusting
revealed truth to the claims of advancing intellect
so long as the *residuum* of revealed truth is great
enough to justify faith in the supernatural
character of the Christ who brought it—may
easily defeat its own purpose, and in its very
effort at self-preservation compass its own death.
It is not meant that in every instance the journey
just sketched can be traced step by step, or that

all its steps are always *consciously* taken, or that in the case of every country and every individual we can decide without difficulty what point of it has at any moment been reached. Sometimes a distance taking two or three paces, according to the programme, may have been covered in one : sometimes ways round a given point may have been discovered : least of all must it be supposed that the different companies of Liberal Orthodoxy's army are always or often marching with fronts equally advanced. Also, the sketch as it stands undoubtedly applies more exactly to Britain than to other lands, owing to the particular characteristic of the British mind and its working which will be noticed by-and-by. But, roughly speaking, the sketch holds good. The process on which, from the indicated starting-point, Liberal Orthodoxy embarks is one of constant diminutions and reductions, contains within itself nothing that can at any point of the series transform it into a process positive and constructive, and really amounts to a continued slipping down the slope without having any barrier set up for safety's sake at the lowest edge.

Much of this, admittedly, is only realised in the light of experience; and only because we can sweep our glance backwards from things which have happened can we affirm that these things were implicit in some initial thing which happened long ago. But any student who has arrived at this conviction may be permitted to offer it—as a sort of hypothesis to be tested,

though certainly not as a mould into which facts
are to be forced—to those entering for the first
time, or afresh, upon a survey of the happenings
themselves. They may at least, without pre-
judice and with judgment duly suspended, ask
themselves, " Did Liberal Orthodoxy become
what it became, succeed where it succeeded, fail
where it failed, because, while recognising, as
Conservative Orthodoxy did not, the necessity
of change, it still considered Christianity, as
Conservative Orthodoxy considered it, to make its
primary appeal to the mind, to be a system of
ideas, though ideas supernaturally communicated
and supernaturally guaranteed, and the decisive
act of Christian discipleship to be an intellectual
acceptance of those ideas ? " For each event,
as they come upon it in the unfolding of the tale,
will acquire deeper significance for them, and
will be the more likely to be rightly appreciated
in all its bearings, if it be looked upon as a possible
link in a chain of sequences all more or less
dependent from an initial fact, than it could
have if it stood unrelated and alone. And the
keeping of the question alive in their minds,
however they may answer it at last, will at any
rate serve to remind them of the fundamental
fact whence enquiry into the matter must set
out—that Liberal Orthodoxy took for its task
(if previously-used phrases may be repeated)
the adjustment of a set of supernaturally-given
doctrines to the imperious necessities of intellectual evolution, with the proviso that such a
residuum of supernatural doctrine must be preserved as would justify calling the doctrines, and

the Christ who taught them, supernatural still. Which is to say that Liberal Orthodoxy represents a process legitimate and necessary in itself (for nothing that has been said, and nothing that will be said, has been or will be said in the interests of a reactionary theological conservatism), carried on without adequate reference to a proper standard, and apart from a central conception whose magnetism, while permitting all needed change, would at once have drawn it back when change lured too fast and far.

CHAPTER II

THE FORERUNNERS IN THE CAMBRIDGE PLATONISTS

IT would be a study certainly interesting, and probably not uninstructive, to show how in many cases intellectual, religious, social, and other movements have made two appearances upon the world's stage, on the first occasion hurrying themselves on to their ultimate consequences and to their end, on the second proceeding with slower pace. When in our study of history we see some movement forcing its way gradually to a front place before the eyes of men and by slow degrees pushing itself through from its first beginning to its glorious or inglorious close, we might find, if we took our study still further back, that the movement had once been heralded by a sort of prophetic epitomised movement (so long before, perhaps, as to be entirely forgotten) wherein the same fundamental idea was worked from a similar first suggestion to a similar close, only not gradually, but as it were at express speed and in a flash. Perhaps even in regard to many of the programmes now unfolding themselves before us—though to give instances might carry us into fields of controversy far removed from our present theme—the statement holds good. And it might be possible in at least some cases to foretell what the end will be—whether the ideas of the programme will succeed or fail, and whether, if they succeed, success may not after all be worse than failure would have been—by turning back a good many pages of the historical record and learning from some scanty paragraphs how once upon a time a few years or decades sufficed to achieve results and demonstrate consequences which are being reached and comprehended by slower methods now. Only, of course, if that paragraph were once read, and repetition of the previous results and consequences were felt to be inevitable at the movement's end, the movement in its present edition might at once receive its arrest. However that may be, it is a fact that in many instances a movement in thought or in practical life has appeared, rushed swiftly through its self-unfolding, died in the act, because the swiftness of its self-unfolding has meant the equally swift triumph of some radical unsoundness at its heart, and has re-appeared, when that first meteor-like passage across the sky has faded from memory, for a more gradual development later on. Why the second self-unfolding should thus be slower than the first is a question to which more than one reply might be given. Perhaps, if the interval be long, the fact that the idea has to make itself seen and heard and felt against a larger mass of accumulated scientific knowledge and law, even against a more thronged background of established conventions both just and unjust, may have something to do with it; or perhaps a voice mournfully reciting the earlier failure may after all haunt the halls and passages of the sub-conscious human mind, and send up its warning hints from there. At any rate, evidences of what has been said, both as to repetitions in history and as to the greater slowness with which on its second appearance a movement runs its course, may easily be discovered by all who search for them with open eyes.

What has been said in this general fashion may introduce the particular fact that Liberal Orthodoxy had its forerunner in Cambridge Platonism and the Cambridge Platonists—the Latitudinarians or "Latitude-men" as by their contemporaries they were styled [1]—in that movement (Benjamin Whichcot, Henry More, John Smith, and Ralph Cudworth may at once be given as its greatest names)[2] which in the later seventeenth century traced the edifice of its thought in lines of light across the intellectual sky, only to see the vision speedily dissolve again and leave scarce a wrack behind. The movement may be described, subject to qualifications and additions which will presently be made, as an effort, and a spontaneous one, to show that in a true philosophy the divineness of human reason [3] must be the primary article of belief; and to show also that once the harmony between

[1] The name "Latitudinarian," however, was used with reference to their tolerant attitude towards Nonconformists rather than with reference to their theological or philosophic views.

[2] Whichcot, 1610–1683; More, 1614–1687; Smith, 1618–1652; Cudworth, 1617–1688.

[3] Which really means human *nature*—but human nature conceived chiefly as intellectual rather than moral, the divine nature, correlatively, being conceived in a similar way.

the human reason and the divine is realised, or rather experienced as an operative fact, Christianity in its turn is seen to be harmonious with both, or rather *with the idea of their harmony*; so that Christianity becomes the natural religion for man, with his divine-human reason, to accept. The essential harmony, or rather unity, between man's reason and God's, the derivation of the first-named from the second, was the governing idea; or, to put it another way, human reason was the divine reason working its way along valley-roads where cramping hills blocked out the infinite view. Christian doctrine was either a re-statement in specifically religious language of that divine-human unity whereof true reason was already conscious; or, in so far as it added a supernatural revelation to reason's consciousness of itself as divine, it was either a larger extension and application, not hitherto perceived as possible, of what was really involved in that self-consciousness, or at the most the addition to the originally-involved content of something which, though it had not grown out of reason's native possessions, could at any rate be linked on to them without leaving any noticeable maladjustment at the junction-point. (These statements will receive clearer explanation presently; and we shall see that they point to more than the mere adjustment of Christianity in such wise that reason was conscious of no shock. For the moment, let them suffice.) In either of the given cases, Christian doctrine could easily enough be translated back again from specifically religious to philosophical terms.

But this is the barest outline, and filling in of details remains to be done. It is worth while to note, however, before passing on to closer examination of the movement itself, that in respect of their insistence on the oneness of human reason with the divine as the first article of valid thought the Cambridge Platonists were far in advance of certain thinkers who had to some extent prepared their way; while in respect of its spontaneity (in the sense to be presently explained) the movement was marked off both from what had gone before and from the later Liberal Orthodoxy—formed under pressure and, as sketched in the previous chapter, moving from one defensive position to another as circumstances compelled—which was afterwards to come. As to the point first named, men like John Hales of Eton and William Chillingworth had certainly championed with all manfulness the claims of reason against an arbitrary theological and ecclesiastical authority which declared that in its own august presence reason must meekly fold its hands and bow its head. The former, to quote but one of his striking observations, had declared that " they that come and tell you what you are to believe, what you are to do, and tell you not why, they are not physicians, but leeches; and if you so take things at their hands, you are not like men but like beasts." [1]   And the latter, who, though perhaps no greater man, bears a name more widely known, matches Hales when he says that " God hath given us our reason to discern between truth and falsehood; and he that makes

[1] *Of Enquiry and Private Judgment in Religion* (*Works*, iii. 150).

not this use of it, but believes things he knows
not why, I say that it is by chance he believes
the truth, and not by choice; and that I cannot
but fear that God will not accept the sacrifice of
fools." [1] But vigorous as are these utterances, and
the whole range of utterances whence they are
taken, they point to not much more than a conviction on the part of their authors that a Christian
believer should be able to render a reason for
the faith that is in him, and to a coincident
conviction that the great doctrines of the Christian
religion would be vindicated if they were sub-
jected to reason's tests. It was not so much
to construct doctrine as to judge it that reason
was called by these earlier champions of the
human mind : reason's function was not so
much to find truth as to find justification for
accepting truth already upon the field; and these
distinctions, which, if somewhat subtle, nevertheless became clear enough upon close examination, show how far the earlier champions were
from the methods of the Cambridge Platonist
school, to which reason was an actual divine
constructive power, on whose working man
might fling himself with unquestioning trust.
Verification as contrasted with discovery, a
reason that countersigns rather than promulgates,
sanctions rather than creates—so the antithesis
might be framed. As to the spontaneity of
the Cambridge movement, and its contrast in
this respect with anterior and posterior movements alike, it has to be said that it was not

[1] *The Religion of Protestants a Safe Way to Salvation* (ed.
Bohn), p. 133. Many other pages echo the idea.

with a specific antagonist in view that the Cambridge Platonists for the most part did their work. Before the men of the middle century, Chillingworth and the rest, the figure of despotic authority, speaking either from Rome or speaking from Canterbury—when Laud was seated there—in accents equally provocative and harsh, had loomed large; and it was at the challenge of that aggressive and hated figure that those men had girded themselves for their fight. When in later times—in the eighteenth century and onwards—assaults upon religion became multiplied and fierce, it was necessarily with these assaults in view that much theological thinking, indeed all theological thinking directed along new lines, was carried on : anything else than apologetic and defensive it was hardly possible for efforts at religious reconstruction to be. But with the Cambridge school, things stood differently. Its leaders were borne upon a high wave of speculation which owed its existence to something else than being flung up by the clash and contact of opposing tides, and which was rather a sign that somewhere or other a new gathering together of the waters had taken place. It is true that in their day the philosophy in Hobbes—a philosophy which, while doing lip-service to " a natural seed of religion " in man, and to immutable moral laws, nevertheless placed all religious and moral sanctions and inspirations in the *fiat* of the civil power, so that religion's " natural seed " could have no " natural " growth, and the finger pointing to morality's " immutable laws " might veer all round the compass as the

D

proclamations of the civil power changed—was parading as an energetic claimant for the votes of men. It is also true that such a philosophy, involving the denial of anything divine, within man or without man, save what the State chose to label with that epithet, involving in short the denial of anything *essentially* divine, was in direct antagonism to the fundamental ideas of the Cambridge thinkers, and that the majority of them—although John Smith takes no account of Hobbes at all—recognised the fact. Not even the profusion of Scripture quotations wherewith Hobbes garnishes his pages, thus murdering religion with a weapon supposed to be its chief defence, could throw a mist across eyes so far-seeing and penetrating as theirs. Yet it was not with the special object of confuting Hobbes that the Cambridge Platonists wrote and talked and preached. Some, indeed, have read the matter otherwise; and Principal Tulloch, from whom one can only disagree with diffidence, says of Cudworth and More that " both writers are only to be understood in the light of Hobbes's theories." Had this statement been made of certain allusions, paragraphs, and arguments in Cudworth and More, it would have been strictly accurate; but as it stands, it surely goes too far. A better view is that the philosophy of Hobbes had marked an attempt at checking the influence of the philosophy of Descartes—who had sought to show that the path of speculation must lead the true enquirer to spiritual conclusions at last, and had thus given to morality and religion a far deeper basis than Hobbes would

admit them to possess—and that the Cambridge
men transcended the controversy rather than
entered into it, though of course conscious that
it was going on and often sending down voices
from their upper air to mingle with those which
rose up from below.   They came *to* Hobbes as
they did their work, rather than started *from* him
to do it, though naturally they knew him for a
foe when their path and his crossed : they dealt
with him, though vigorously, as it were by the
way;   and one may assert that their message
would in its main outlines have been the same
even though Hobbes had not been known.
Cartesianism and Hobbism represent the action
and reaction of spiritual and materialistic tendencies respectively :   the Platonists represent,
not a reaction, but a new and independent start.
For as one reads these men one realises that they
had not, with painstaking effort and anxious
picking of their way through difficulties, found
a philosophy which would bear the weight of a
religious faith;   that they had not, on the other
hand, started from a philosophy as to whose
religious or anti-religious implications they were
at first uncertain;   but that through a sort of
spontaneous and buoyant up-leap of their minds
they had come upon both philosophy and religious
faith, and also upon a conviction that the faith
thus given was in all essentials the Christian
faith, in one and the same act.   It is less true to
say that they had found a method of reconciling
philosophy and Christianity than to say that an
already reconciled philosophy and Christianity
had found them.   They represented, so far as

they themselves were concerned, rather the breaking-in upon the world of thought of a new inspiration whose immediate source was not apparent than the opening of an escape (though, of course, for those caught in the toils acceptance of the inspiration became an escape) from a philosophico-religious *impasse* at which thought was blocked. This is not to say that they were wholly detached from or insensitive to the mental influences at work in their day; for no thinkers can ever be that. But it means that not from any single point in the line of such influences did their own mental processes definitely branch off. In brief, as was previously said, it was not with any specific antagonist or antagonists in view that the Cambridge Platonists for the most part did their work. And this fact, while interesting in the first place simply as a fact in the history of thought, and a lonely one—for the process of events made its subsequent recurrence practically an impossible thing—has a further interest still. Since it was not to specific defence of some specific religious truth that the Cambridge Platonists felt themselves primarily called, they were under no temptation to become, and did not become, specialists along some one theological line : the whole circle of theology, not a limited segment of it or a particular doctrine lying upon it, would be viewed by their minds as constituting the rightful sphere of their influence and work; and men whose dominant impression concerning philosophy and faith was that philosophy and faith had come to them *together*, not as reconciled after threatened divorce, but as partners in a marriage solemnised once for all in the secret temple of eternal truth, might well hold that *all* questions of faith (whether particular questions were asked or not would not matter) could be answered in the light which that apprehended unity threw out. To the possibilities herein contained, and to the reason why they failed to mature, further reference will by-and-by be made.

It is time, however, to fill up the previously-drawn outline of the position occupied by the Cambridge school. On the philosophical side, it was, as their name implies, from Plato that the Cambridge Platonists professed to start. " Professed to start," for as a matter of fact, their relation to Plato would not be correctly described by saying that they reproduced Plato's philosophy, or even that they drew from Plato's philosophy deductions and enlargements logically contained therein. In the last resort, what they really derived from Plato was a certain philosophical spirit rather than actual philosophical doctrine, a method rather than a theory, perhaps one might almost say a direction for mental movement (this direction running from particular facts back to eternal ideas whereof they were the expression and then round to the particular facts again) rather than definite conclusions on any formulated themes. It is not necessary, in order to support this, to enter upon any lengthened exposition of Plato's philosophical scheme. Enough for our purpose can be condensed into a few lines.[1] It will suffice to say here that for

[1] The best very condensed exposition of Platonism with which I am acquainted is in Erdmann's *Grundriss der*

Plato not particular objects, but " universals "
or " Ideas," alone possessed reality : it is, for
example, not individual animals, but the generic
Idea " animal," that actually exists; or, to
state the case from the other end, the real thing,
the Idea, is " the common essence and true being
of the individual existences comprised under
it," the ultimate Being above all " becoming "
and all change; while to make the summary
complete, it must be added that these Ideas in
their multiplicity are themselves subordinated to
one Idea back of them all, the " Idea of the Good,"
the " Idea of Ideas, the absolute Idea." And
philosophical investigation necessarily (since it
is with particular objects that man first of all
finds himself in contact) takes its course from
individual things to that which is the last ground
of them all. But though in philosophical *investigation* the process thus runs, and can do no
other, from particular objects to the " Ideas "
and thence to the " Idea of Ideas," the process
is all the time going *backward* and *upward* along
a path which has been constructed *downward*
before; for while the Good, the " Idea of Ideas,"
is the last thing at which exploring philosophy
arrives, it is itself the all-inclusive Reality wherein
everything is held; and as a matter of fact,
the ultimate Reality has simply " thought itself
out " (the phrase is Martineau's) into the system
of things we know. Further, in the realisation

Geschichte der Philosophie, §§ 74–82. There is an English
translation of this, edited by Williston S. Hough. A
somewhat less condensed and very admirable summary is
in Martineau's *Types of Ethical Theory*.

of this is given also the realisation that the all-inclusive Reality must be, just because it is all-inclusive, inclusive also of the mind which at the long last reaches and perceives it : not only the things we know, and the knowability of them, but our power of knowledge also is produced by and out of the " absolute Idea." So, with his task achieved, the thinker stands in the end, and stands consciously to himself, with all particular objects duly related to their " Ideas," with all " Ideas " duly related to the " absolute Idea," and with his own mind duly related to all three : he can move freely from particular objects to the ultimate Reality, and can return from the ultimate Reality upon particular objects; and he knows that as he performs the return journey just named, he is repeating the original " dialectic " of Reality once again, this *secondary* dialectic, so to call it, being itself but a part of Reality's *original* dialectic, and being possible only because the human mind partici-pates in the ultimate " Idea of Ideas." For our present purpose, this is all of Platonic doctrine with which we need trouble ourselves. Even the non-philosophic reader, to whom much of this may be darkened counsel, will be able to under-stand how Platonism is fitted to give " a direction to mental movement," and how it implies the participation of human reason in a reason higher than that of man. And if the actual debt of the Cambridge Platonists to him whom they called their master is to be estimated, it is under these two heads that the reckoning will fall.

The Cambridge men themselves undoubtedly

supposed that they were from beginning to end
of their thought in much more exact correspondence with Plato—perhaps it would be more correct
to say that they supposed Plato to be in much
more exact correspondence with them—than
this rather general statement makes out. But
that was because they did not distinguish between
Platonism properly so called and the later " Neo-
Platonism " from which certain features of their
thinking, and what must be termed certain
extravagances of their speech, were derived.
Of Neo-Platonism not much need here be said.
The claim to affiliation with Plato implied in
its title is so far justified that it holds with Plato
to an Absolute Being in which all things live,
to a procession of existences pushed by an
internal dynamic out of an Absolute Existence,
and that it makes it the business of all finite
existences, as they have flowed out of the Absolute,
to flow back to the Absolute again; though
even on these fundamentals it differs from the
pure Platonic word in various points.[1] But the
important thing to note is that Neo-Platonism
was really a philosophico-religious eclecticism
or syncretism, endeavouring to construct, on
the indicated Platonic basis, a religion tenable
by philosophic minds, and endeavouring to
do so by abstracting different elements from the
different extant religions and then stirring them
into a fresh compound. It was entirely natural

[1] The article on Neo-Platonism in the *Encyclopædia
Britannica* will give the general reader all the information
he requires. It mentions also the authoritative books for
more extensive study.

that a system which came at the end of the long
process of Hellenic philosophy, and at a time
when Christianity was thrusting its challenging
doctrines upon the attention of the world, should
seek to bring religion within its embrace, and
should do so, if only to combat more effectually
Christianity's claim to exclusive authority, along
the syncretic line. It is easy to understand,
also, that a system which for its very first activity
planted itself with a leap upon the conception
of the Absolute Existence, instead of reaching
it by the patient backward-tracing " dialectic "
of Plato himself (and it is here, in the search
for ultimate *Truth* as against the search for
ultimate *Being*, that one of the outstanding
differences between Platonism and Neo-Platonism
is found), would easily open the doors of its court
to the eclectic spirit and give it a welcome to
the bench. The primary assumption with Neo-
Platonism, no qualification being made, was that
all existences were derived from one primal
Source by a sort of natural " flowing down ";
and this general principle would necessarily
seem to apply to existing *beliefs* among existences
of other kinds; so that in adopting the primary
assumption you would appear to have deprived
yourself of power to pronounce any belief absolutely wrong, because by doing so you deny that
it has been carried down to you upon the bosom
of that stream whereon you have previously
declared all things to be borne along. If, on
the other hand, you credit a suspected belief
with at least partial truth, the difficulty, if
not altogether escaped, is at any rate glossed

over. This, however, is not meant to be taken as an exposition of actual Neo-Platonic doctrine on the point, but only as a hint which may help to account for the eclectic character which Neo-Platonism assumed; and it may be added that the hint is perhaps applicable to other and later systems besides that of the Neo-Platonists of long ago. Neo-Platonism, at any rate, be the hint sound or not, took the eclectic line. Plotinus, who in the third century formulated the doctrines of the school, and who is said to have been a one-time Christian fallen away, had a Trinity of his own : he found a place for the myths of popular religion, or for an expurgated and spiritualised rendering of them, in his scheme: he ran Stoic ethics in strange company by coupling them with magic and prayer; and he talked of self-discipline and of a practice of virtue, and of mystic ecstasies at last, whereby the soul could recover its perfect union with " the One." Later Neo-Platonism naturally enough exaggerated the curious catholicity of the earlier, till in some of its representatives respect for " the gods of the nations " became actual polytheism, and philosophy—a medley of genuine Platonism, astrology, alchemy, incantations, and many other things—degenerated into sheer superstition and nothing more. The system, having begun by keeping open mind for anything and everything that could by any possibility be crammed in, had finished by turning the said mind into a rag-bag of miscellaneous scraps. By the end of the fifth century Neo-Platonism as a separate philosophy was virtually extinct—

Proclus, its last great teacher in its school at
Athens, having sought to systematise it, and
having in the very act helped philosophy to
a method too sane and scientific to let Neo-
Platonism endure. But though Neo-Platonism
died, that Christianity which, along with other
religions, had been an unwilling contributor
to the Neo-Platonic faith was to be willing
recipient from it instead of unwilling contributor
to it now, and was to show Neo-Platonic influence
in a good many quarters as the years passed on.
Christian thought in the East had, of course, been
influenced by general Hellenic culture from the
beginning, the " Greek theology "—whose dis-
tinctiveness from the " Latin theology " of the
West is a commonplace of the history of doctrine,
and of which Clement of Alexandria and Origen
may be considered chief exponents—thus receiving its shape. But at first, even while drawing
from the wells of Greek thought, Eastern Christianity refused to have part or lot in the Neo-
Platonism which marked Greek philosophy's
last delusive outburst of strength. Yet it was
perhaps natural that a deeply-engrained tendency
to accept Hellenic influence should triumph over
a particular reluctance in the end : indeed,
Origen himself is usually taken to have been
under the Neo-Platonic spell in some degree;
and just when Neo-Platonism itself was dying,
the Church of the East was becoming willing to
take over no small part of the heritage it had to
bequeath. Of course a complete acceptance of
Neo-Platonism would have involved the denial
of God's incarnation in Jesus Christ, since no

such fresh emergence of the divine, in addition to the one " flowing down," could be admitted in the original scheme. And this the Christian Neo-Platonists knew. But the union of their Christian faith with their Neo-Platonic philosophy produced, notwithstanding this reservation in the deed of partnership, results that were grotesque enough. In the case of one great theologian and saint of the West—practically the only *early* case of a Christian thinker in touch with Neo-Platonism that the West has to show—the Neo-Platonic influence was, it is true, altogether for good, or was at any rate checked before it had gone too far. Augustine was helped by his study of Neo-Platonism to realise that God was one, an eternal and changeless spirit, the very life of all that is; and though the system could not satisfy nor hold him, he made full acknow-ledgment of his debt.[1] In other instances, how-ever—for example in " Dionysius the Areopa-gite " and those who followed in his track—the effect of Neo-Platonism upon Christianity was simply to burden the second with the super-stitions and absurdities of the first so heavily that the true shape of the second was almost indiscernible beneath the load; and not seldom, even when it inspired a mysticism whereof in pure form the Church has never had enough and could not have had too much, it went on to spoil with its excesses the very mysticism it had inspired. But the story must be read elsewhere : here this cursory reference must suffice.

The Neo-Platonic coat of many colours the

---

[1] See his *Confessions*, Book VII, chaps. ix–xxi.

Cambridge Platonists were content and happy
to wear. They all quote Neo-Platonic writers
as of equal authority with Plato himself; while
in Henry More spiritualism, thaumaturgy, and
all manner of fantasies, become actually rampant
at times. Their attitude towards all such things
was uncritical in the extreme. Yet one must not
over-emphasise their indebtedness to the Neo-
Platonic cults; and Coleridge's assertion that
Plotinus rather than Plato was their master puts
it far too high. Particularly in respect of their
theology is it necessary to insist that Neo-
Platonic eclecticism was not the platform on
which they came to rest. Many of the Neo-
Platonic absurdities, as we should term them,
threw a spell upon their minds; and they dallied
in those enchanted gardens for many and many
an hour. Also, in that their philosophising had
a distinctly religious end and aim did they follow
in the steps of the Neo-Platonic school—for which,
however, they may well be praised rather than
blamed. But when they came to actual dealing
with religion, and to actual summing up of their
religious conclusions, it was not at all a Neo-
Platonic contents-bill that they displayed, and
it was for the most part to tolerably orthodox
views of doctrine that they settled down. Necessarily, as one would expect from men steeped in
philosophy, they had their own special ways of
stating them; and in the arguments with which
they sought to make their fundamental theological position good the Neo-Platonic influence
frequently comes out. But they professed themselves to be loyal members of the Church of

England, loyal adherents to her faith; nor is
there any reason to suspect the profession false.
Neo-Platonism, as it surged round their minds,
found many an open gate, and entered in to
occupy large stretches of the ground; but before
it reached the definitely theological tract, they
had put it through such a process of reduction,
stripped it of so many of its gay and gaudy
trappings, that whatever it might do in the
outlying mental regions it effectively occupied,
it had to comport itself soberly there. In the
end, the Cambridge Platonists, standing face
to face with religious problems, borrowed from
Neo-Platonism's armoury little more than a
conviction that philosophy must be religion's
servant; borrowed from purer Platonism a
conviction of the divineness of human reason;
and added a last conviction that Christianity,
fitting easily as it did with its pronouncements
into the moulds which divine-human reason
had ready, was the natural thing for man to
believe.

When they came to theology, the Cambridge
Platonists adopted an attitude consonant with,
and following from, their philosophical views.
They construed both God and man, we have
seen, chiefly as mind. As might be expected
from this, they can scarcely be described as
religiously enthusiastic : so far as they were
enthusiastic at all, they were enthusiastic about
philosophy rather than about religion; or perhaps it would be more exact to say that they were
enthusiastic about the union of the two. They
do not mark, as has sometimes been asserted, a

revival of that " Greek theology " to which
reference was made a little while ago—such a
revival as did actually accompany some later
up-risings of the Platonic spirit in Liberal Orthodoxy's career; for the Greek theology had been
predominantly moral in its interest, had been
concerned with the immanence of the divine
nature, conceived as *holiness*, rather than with
the immanence of the divine *mind*, and had above
all laid special emphasis upon Jesus Christ as
the perfect manifestation of that divine immanence which possessed all humanity in its degree.
The Cambridge men, although, as has been said,
bent upon making philosophy the servant of
religion, and in that sense exalting religion to
the first place, did so rather with pride, by no
means illegitimate, in the process itself than with
ardour for specifically religious results; nor does
one do them any injustice in saying that it was the
intellectual aspect of religion as related to philosophy, not the moral and spiritual impulses it
might impart, that captivated them most. True,
they speak often of holiness and conformity to
God; but, consistently with their basal philosophy, which views both God and man chiefly
as mind, it is in thinking as God thinks, sharing
God's estimates, making the moral distinctions
He makes, and ordering life's external practice
in such wise as logically follows from all this,
that the content of such ideas would seem to be
summed up. An inward wisdom and its opposite
—hardly that inner purity and foulness which each
in its turn allures and shames the spiritually
sensitive soul—is what they know. They show

little of that spiritual passion, of that eager desire
for large spiritual and transforming consequences
to be enacted in the world, which have always
been the marks of the most vital Christianity,
even when those desiring the large consequences
have inconsistently expected them to follow from
mere correctness of belief. The Cambridge Platonists, notwithstanding that religion was their
final interest, satisfied themselves with satisfying
the mind on religious themes. Beyond that they
were conscious of no call.

The work they actually performed upon
religious doctrines was, as to its character (of
its extent we shall speak immediately), what we,
remembering their spirit and standpoint, might
look for it to be. Let it be recalled that the
divineness of human reason, the participation
of man's mind in God's, was their governing idea.
It was the thought of this oneness by which they
were obsessed. Not the inference which, once
the fact of oneness is accepted, leaps immediately
upon the thought of most—the inference that
a doctrine which contradicts human reason
cannot be true for God—not that, but the fact
itself, dominated their minds. Their conviction
of the divineness of human reason was, of course,
their warrant for setting reason to work as
a theologically constructive or reconstructive
force; but one must go on to say that it was not
so much reason *per se* as reason's *consciousness
of being divine* that, after all, constituted the
constructive or reconstructive force with which
they worked. With regard to theological doctrines, accordingly, their business was to translate

them into language which suggested oneness—
not merely terms which were in *harmony* with it,
but terms which actually *suggested* it.   The phrase
is clumsy, perhaps; but it must be pondered till
its meaning is grasped; for it is here that the
Cambridge Platonists are differentiated from
later thinkers to whom they carry a superficial
resemblance, thinkers who, also believing in the
divineness of human reason, have argued that
what contradicts human reason cannot be true.
To the Cambridge school the final question
concerning any doctrine was less the question
whether or not it came into conflict with reason's
findings than the question whether it bore upon,
emphasised, revealed itself as one aspect of,
the doctrine of unity between man's reason and
God's—the question whether, in accepting it,
man was making that unity more clear.   That
is, once again, its business in regard to theological
doctrines was to translate them into language
which was not only in *harmony* with, but actually
suggested, the participation of man's mind in
God's, the in-dwelling of God's mind in man's.
Each doctrine, in fact, had to become a version
or an application of that idea.   In one way the
task of the Platonists, as thus described, had a
narrower range than that of the later thinkers
alluded to; for each theological doctrine had
but one test to meet; and, moreover, the question
of its *absolute* truth—the question whether some
alternative doctrine might not profitably take
its place, or whether in the descent from original
premisses the true path might not have been
missed—was hardly faced.   In another way,

E

however, the task represented a greater enter-
prise; for it was at any rate philosophical in
that it pointed to the comprising of all theological ideas under one master-idea, the idea
of God's mind in man. "Open the shell of
every doctrine," said the Cambridge Platonists
in effect, "and you find that kernel lying within :
listen closely to all the strains drawn from the
theological instrument, and through all changes
of key and variations of time and tune you catch
the same *motif* beneath." And thus the Cambridge thinkers manifested in the theological
sphere that "direction for mental movement"
with which their Platonism had furnished them;
for as they touched upon this particular doctrine
or upon that, they drew back from it upon the
true "idea" of it as that true "idea" was given
in their all-inclusive "Idea," to return upon
the particular doctrine thereafter with understanding of its lineage and therefore of its real
significance and its real content.

At a first glance, it would appear that a movement like this looked promisingly in the direction
of theological construction; and it is disappoint-
ing to confess—what must be confessed nevertheless—that little came of it in the constructive
way. Yet perhaps on a closer scrutiny this
affords small reason for surprise. The movement had, as we have seen, the promise implied
in its spontaneity—the spontaneity which left
it free to deal with the entire range of religious
truth rather than with some specialised segment
or section of it. And it had, as has just been
said, the promise implied in being a philosophy

which desired to gather all theological ideas
under the sheltering wing of one master-idea.
But it is precisely this last statement, notwithstanding that at first it seems to speak of constructive promise, which shows that of constructive impulse the movement had practically none.
For it was a philosophy of *ideas*. Its purpose was
to deal not so much with facts and actualities,
or even with truths in respect of the " thing in
itself " they stood for, as with the *mental representation* of all these. Its programme was not
set towards relating together the *ultimates* en-
closed in religious doctrines—sin, salvation, and
any " acts " of God or man these might imply—
or towards relating all of them as a whole with
some *ultimate* divine " act " or " will " begun
and decreed from the foundations of the world;
but rather towards showing that when you are
thinking of any religious doctrine, you are really
thinking of the central doctrine of the divine
mind in man, and that if you turn the doctrine
you are thinking of a little round from its present
position, shift the angle slightly, let the light
fall upon it from the proper direction, you will
find this to be so. This is not theological construction in any true sense. In fact, in what was
previously said as to the business of the Cambridge
Platonists being a mere translation of all theological language into the standard language
which the standard doctrine of the " divine mind
in man " provides, it is implied that a real work
upon the essential material of theology could
hardly be looked for from their hands. They
were prepared, so to say, with the dictionary

necessary for the translating work; or, to change
the metaphor, they were prepared to give the
nearest value, in the coin of their own philosophical gold, for whatever ideas, cast in inferior
metal, might be put into their hands; or, to
change the metaphor again, they were prepared
to dress all ideas uniformly in a garb made in
the workshops of their own supreme idea, so
that the membership of all ideas in that supreme
idea's retinue might be made plain. But then
all this is essentially a process of *reduction*, not
one of *construction* at all, and moreover a process
of purely *mental* reduction; for when you re-state
in pounds a sum of money previously stated in
shillings (a fair analogy, as has been suggested,
to the work of the Cambridge School) you have
simply altered your manner of viewing a given
fact, the mental language wherein you embody
it, and you have not attempted, or suggested
the need of, an alteration in the fact—*i. e.* the
actual sum—itself. The work of the Cambridge
men could result in nothing more (whether it
might not result in something less is another
question which need not here be raised) than
providing " thought-equivalents," so to call
them, the substituted " equivalent " being in
each case taken from the deep reservoir whose
containing walls are those of the " divine mind
in man " idea.   There is therefore nothing to
surprise us in the fact that of actual constructive
work in the religious sphere the school accomplished so little in the end. The promise apparently implied in the philosophical character of
its standpoint failed because its philosophy was

a philosophy of ideas, concerned less with the essential substance of a doctrine than with the mental representation of it, and therefore did not aim at altering or re-shaping a supposed truth in such wise as to make it truer and bring it into conformity with ultimate truth; but only at showing that if you looked at a doctrine intently enough and long enough, the mental picture before you dissolved, outlines changing and colours melting together, till presently that of the " divine mind in man " idea stood upon the screen. And the promise apparently implied in the spontaneity of its up-rising, and in the free range over the whole theological field which that spontaneity permitted, failed because men engaged in the indicated process of exchange, translation, transformation of mental pictures, would naturally be engrossed in the process itself, in the assertion of its validity, in the proclamation of the fundamental idea which justified it to their own minds, would touch or take up any doctrine for no other purpose than to illustrate how the process worked out, and would therefore be comparatively heedless of the wide theological tract they might have occupied if they had willed. Certainly the mere fact that it *was* wide would for such men have no inviting charm at all. A real theological construction it was not in the nature of Cambridge Platonism to make.

In fact, of dealing with specific Christian doctrines there is comparatively little in the Cambridge men; and it is with the " fundamental idea " just alluded to—the idea which justifies the process of " mental interchange " or " translation "—rather than with the doctrinal applications of it, that they are mostly concerned.[1] We find Whichcot affirming in many modes of speech that " reason is the divine Governor of man's life, the very voice of God," that " when the doctrine of the Gospel becomes the reason of our mind, it will be the principle of our life," that " there is nothing so intrinsically rational as religion is, nothing that can so justify itself, nothing that hath so pure reason to recommend itself "; that " reason is not a shallow thing, it is the first participation from God, therefore he that observes reason observes God." We find John Smith saying that " to seek our divinity merely in books and writings is to seek the living among the dead; we do but in vain seek God many times in these, where His truth often is not so much enshrined as entombed; no, *intra te quære Deum*, seek for God within thine own soul; He is best discerned, as Plotinus phraseth it, by an intellectual touch of Him." We find Cudworth, whose work is so vastly conceived and so minutely worked out that almost any quotation, torn from the many threads of thought which have gone to the weaving of every

[1] Whichcot is represented by his *Select Sermons*, first published in 1698, fifteen years after his death, and by his *Moral and Religious Aphorisms*, edited by Dr. Jeffery early in the eighteenth century. From John Smith we have the *Select Discourses* published in 1660. Cudworth's chief works are *The True Intellectual System of the Universe*, which appeared in 1678, and *A Treatise on Eternal and Immutable Morality*, which was issued by Bishop Chandler in 1731. The second is really a part of the first. More's writings are numerous, but the *Divine Dialogues* (1668) are the most significant, and are sufficient for most readers to-day.

sentence, is liable to be misunderstood if taken alone—we find him visioning at the back of all things an eternal Mind in the very existence of which the distinction between good and evil is given, so that good is good and evil is evil, not because God's will has chosen to proclaim them good and evil when it might have chosen differently, but because God's own nature, as it were automatically, by a sort of inner compulsion, reads them so; and we find him asserting that in the nature of man the substance of this eternal Mind is reproduced and its voices echoed, so that in man's judgment and conscience you really have the eternal order asserting itself once again. We find More, consistently through all his strange visions and dreams, through all the ecstatic transports and mystic up-liftings which befell him, contending for a spiritual existence above and yet in the material fabric of the world, and for a spirit above and yet in the material body of man, and for the close relation, as between the larger and smaller parts of one great whole, between the two. By all of them the essential unity of the human mind with the divine, though never in such wise as to rob human personality of its separateness or to strike the pantheistic note, is emphasised on almost every page. But all this is merely repeated affirmation of the fundamental conception of the Cambridge Platonists, not an application of that idea by way of modifying definitely Christian truths. When we set out on a quest for this, it is but little that we find. Cudworth, indeed, has some limited dealing with the doctrine

of the Trinity; but the dealing makes no more
than a sort of digression, and has the special
purpose of showing that the Christian Trinity,
rather than Arianism, is consistent with Platonic
ideas. But with all the writers the theological
range is small. Whichcot remarks, as to atonement and reconciliation, that Christ's work
must be recognised as " not only something
without us but also *within* us . . . to the effect
of taking away all our enmity and making us
godlike "; and as to heaven, that it " is *first*
a temper, and *then* a place." The sermons of
John Smith are largely devoted to rebuke of
merely legal and mechanical ideas of salvation,
which must not be looked upon " as a pertinacious
imagination of our names being enrolled in the
book of life, or of the debt-books of heaven
being crossed, or of Christ being ours while we
find Him not living within us," but as " a true
compliance with the divine will, which must
render us such as the Divinity may take pleasure
in "; and he objects to the idea of the verbal
inspiration of the prophets on the characteristic
ground that to think of them as having had a
" symbolical and hieroglyphical shaping forth
of things in their imaginations " gives a more
exalted view. From Cudworth and More these
utterances may be easily paralleled as often as
a reader may desire. But if we search for any
systematic treatment of the doctrines which fill
the various compartments of the evangelical
creed, we search in vain. The Cambridge Platonists were not theologians in that sense : they
did not painstakingly hew out the stones for a

theological structure of their own, or even trim
and dress the stones which others had hewn :
what they did was now and then to lay a frag-
ment of existing theology alongside of their own
" fundamental idea," and call attention to the
perfect match made by the two. What theologising they did is almost casual, and is done
only by way of providing samples of the method
under which all theology would—as they assume
without seeking to prove—yield its inmost meaning up. Particularly is it noticeable that of
Jesus Christ Himself, in the sense of Christological
statement, they have little to say; nor is their
system in any wise " Christo-centric " as Liberal
Orthodoxy of a later age sought and claimed to
be. This was not because their view of Jesus
Christ dropped at all below that held by the
Church in general, but because the doctrine of
Christ as divine Revealer lay easily for them upon
or within the circumference of a circle drawn
from the centre at which they stood, and accordingly neither required to be itself made a centre
nor offered any special help if it were so made.
Christ as supernatural Revealer, Christ as the
supreme instance and expression of the " divine
mind in man," was altogether in harmony with
their main primary conception : at least, whatever difficulties there might be in the way of
so accepting Him were not yet being very
energetically proclaimed by any adversaries;
nor was there as yet any suggestion on an
extensive scale, such as in the following century
a loud-voiced Deism was to make, of a religion
in which the supernatural Christ could be dis-

carded while God was kept.　For the time being
religion meant to practically all Christianity
with its supernatural Christ.　The Cambridge
Platonists, therefore, starting from the idea of
the " divine mind in man " as the primary idea
of both religion and philcsophy, would pass
swiftly, unconscious of the intermediate obstacles
which later thinkers were destined to confront,
to the idea of the divine mind *specially* dwelling
in Christ; and their fundamental conception
would, in this respect, tend naturally to the
strengthening of the orthodox view.　Perhaps,
indeed, they came to the idea of the supernatural Christ *too* easily—as we may presently
note again.　Easily, at any rate, they came to
it; so easily that it scarcely appeared to them
as demanding affirmation or stress.　And in
fine, we may say of them that what they did,
so far as distinctively Christian truths are concerned, was to take a few of the most familiar
Christian formularies—perhaps those which enter
most frequently into Christian preaching and
Christian appeal—and translate them into the
philosophical or philosophico-religious language
they loved best to use.

Nor, if the specifically theological changes
attempted by the Cambridge school were small
in quantity, were they in quality (so one would
suppose) such as need cause any alarm.　That
is, they scarcely appear so important as to make
the most orthodox view them as dangerous
assaults upon vital parts of the Christian faith.
Certainly no one in our own time, except possibly
those in the extreme rearguard of religious

conservatism, would hesitate to employ such
language as that quoted above, or if he did not
care to employ it himself, would fling any accusation of " heresy " against those who did.   It all
seems little more than a transference of emphasis,
a slight alteration in the dip of the doctrinal
curve.   It is true that the Cambridge Platonists
did not escape the rain of reproachful voices,
for we find Tuckney, Master of Emmanuel
College, and Whichcot's close friend, writing to
Whichcot various letters in complaint of " a
vein of doctrine which runs up and down in
many of your discourses, and in those of some
others of very great worth " ; and on the publication of Cudworth's *Intellectual System of the
Universe*, its author found himself pelted with
charges of Socinianism such as are in some form
or other flung at the heads of nearly all who
swerve from the high roads whereon at any given
time religious speech is wont to walk.   It may
be that the explanation, covering both the
Cambridge men and many wrongly arraigned
for " Socinianism " or " Unitarianism " in later
times, lies in that tendency to an ultimate
lowered view of Christ as supernatural Revealer
which, as was said in the previous chapter, is
from the beginning implicit in any process of
theological change when Christianity is taken as
a system of beliefs supernaturally guaranteed,
and in a vague consciousness of that tendency in
the accusers' minds.   But this is a very different
thing from admitting that in the case of Whichcot
or Cudworth or their brethren such charges are
just.   As a matter of fact, they are not ; and

so far as Socinianism is concerned, we have
already seen that to accept Christ as the perfect
example of the divine mind in man would come
easily to the Cambridge school. In their theologising they laid no rough hands on any Christian
truth in such wise as to leave it, after their
handling of it, unrecognisable by those who
loved it : nothing was there that could justly
have sounded like a shattering of the priceless
and cherished heirlooms of the faith in ears most
sensitive and alert; and a fair summary of their
work upon distinctively Christian doctrine could
put it no higher than this—that as they hung
their own representations of Christian truth
beside those which the gallery of Christian truth
already contained, there was to be found in
theirs a deepening or lightening of colour here
and there, a slight shifting of perspective, in
many instances no more than a change of frame.
It must be confessed that Liberal Orthodoxy,
anxious to point to these men as its pioneers, has
in some cases exaggerated the theological dis-
placement they brought about. Yet there is
the less need to do this, since apart from any such
exaggeration it is certainly as pioneers of Liberal
Orthodoxy that they must be ranked. They
were liberal in method rather than in doctrine,
in spirit rather than in their actual theological
verdicts, but liberal they were—more so, in the
essential point, than many who afterwards
travelled further from the stereotyped ways.
For all we have said of them proves how with
them the principle that between religious and
general thought there must be no warfare was

accepted enthusiastically, not reluctantly and
with pain and with hesitancy in applying it
even after a nominal acceptance of it has been
uttered, as so often by later Liberal Orthodoxy
it has been : the principle was, in fact, the
fount of all their day, the master-light of all
their seeing : so far were they from requiring
to have it forced upon them that they actually
possessed it for their own uses in a more positive
form; and they insisted that their Christian
faith must come to them, not as something which
general thought had spared, but as something
which general thought had either given or at
least endorsed. They did not merely submit,
as under protest, to be drawn out from the
shelter of ecclesiastical authority or tradition,
covering themselves from the chill winds of
criticism outside with what garments of religious
belief those winds were kind enough not to blow
away. They went boldly forth, confident that
they would meet in another region the same
Christian faith which dwelt in the tents of
authority and tradition they left behind. And
they represent Liberal Orthodoxy, therefore,
without the falterings and fears whereby in
later times Liberal Orthodoxy—driven forth from
the shelter whence they voluntarily departed,
and unable by reason of its special circumstances
to call up the confidence which accompanied
them in their going—was to be so frequently and
so sorely beset.

But this first of Liberal Orthodoxy's voices
speedily sank to silence; and in the early years

of the eighteenth century the movement died.
Nor are some valid reasons for its extinction
difficult to discover. Circumstances were not
favourable : upon the intellectual field there
sprang to arms anti-orthodox forces which by
its very nature Cambridge Platonism was incompetent to foil. It soon became impossible
for any mind to affirm contentedly that the idea
of " the divineness of human reason " and orthodox Christianity were given to it *together ;* and
that examination into the *ultimate* truth of
Christian doctrine—which, as we have noted,
the Cambridge school did not make—was pressed
upon every thinker as at the sword's point.
For it could not but be recognised that the reason
so much exalted by the Cambridge men was
working in many quarters in a direction they
had not contemplated, was working, in fact, to
discredit the very Christianity which in their
eyes had been so to say borne upon its native
breath. Socinianism had been present alongside
of Cambridge Platonism from the first; and as
in the new century its appeal grew stronger and
its votaries more numerous, it flaunted itself—
even though the Socinianism of the time did not
involve a denial of essential supernaturalness to
Jesus—as an instance of readiness to assail
orthodox Christian views. It may be noted in
this connection that some of the later followers
enrolled under the Cambridge flag deserted early
in the century to the Socinian ranks. And if
at first this appears inconsistent with what was
said as to the ease with which the Platonists
found themselves able to accept the full doctrine

of a special divineness in Jesus Christ, yet if
another thing previously noted be also recalled,
the seeming inconsistency disappears. The
Cambridge men, it was remarked, came to the
doctrine *too* easily. That is, in the very fact
that they found no difficulty in harmonising it
with their fundamental position there lay a
snare, if not for themselves at any rate for some
who trod in their tracks. For it meant that
they built no defences round it, that it was taken
for granted rather than asked to produce its
testimonials and its guarantees, and that against
a specific attack upon the doctrine no preparation
was made. When, therefore, some later men—
less permeated with that Platonic philosophy
which had for their masters put the doctrine
beyond the need of verification, at least holding
the philosophy more nominally and in much less
of a Platonic spirit, followers not so much in
the deepest things as in the mere " translation "
of conventional theological language into more
general speech, Latitudinarians in short rather
than Platonists of the true order—when these
found the doctrine assailed, it was as easy for
them to give it up as it had been easy for their
predecessors to receive it. In the absence of
an apologetic on the doctrine's behalf, the very
exaltation of reason to which they were committed by their membership in the school—all
the more that the spirit of their homage was
colder far than that which had animated Whichcot, Cudworth, Smith, and More—would make
reason's assault, as in this particular case it
developed before their gaze, at the very least

interesting, and would tend to draw their sympathy to the attacking side. But apart from any question of secessions to Socinianism, the fact that the reason so acclaimed by the Cambridge school was now turning against one of the chief doctrines which the Cambridge school had held was bound to discredit the school itself, to rob it of its power, and to cut short its days. Its chief foe was of its own household. In respect of Deism much the same thing may be said. Deism, like Socinianism, was an older thing than Cambridge Platonism itself; for it was to a time well back in the seventeenth century that Lord Herbert of Cherbury, the " father of English Deism," belonged. But it was in the eighteenth that its full force was attained; and from the deistic quarter, as from the Socinian, the reason which Cambridge Platonism had taught many to hold as sacrosanct was seeking to overthrow much that Cambridge Platonism had loved. In fact, from east and west voices were calling to those who had learned Cambridge Platonism's chief lesson, " You want to obey reason? —then follow her *all* the way ! " There was no room, in such a condition of things as this, for a school which thought that in the idea of " the divineness of human reason " the established system of Christian doctrine was involved, and looked upon idea and system as if they were two sides of one coin. For the school's primary assertion could be overthrown by any observer, not by argument—that was quite unnecessary—but by a single glance upon the facts.

So the movement had to die. Nor could

Liberal Orthodoxy ever appear in that particular form again. The circumstances which killed it perpetuated themselves in such increasing strength as to make it impossible for any resurrection to take place. And the movement, interesting as it is in itself and great as were its leaders, stands out as the first example of Liberal Orthodoxy's failure, starting from the conception of Christianity as a system of supernatural truths rather than as a dynamic of life, to effect a reconstruction of truth which could stand in the evil day.

F

CHAPTER III

THE INTERVAL

It was long before Liberal Orthodoxy had its second birth—not till the nineteenth century's years of infancy and early youth were past. If, indeed, Channing may be counted, as we shall by-and-by venture to count him, in Liberal Orthodoxy's ranks, this statement requires some qualification, since it was quite early in the nineteenth century that Channing's work began; but on the whole it may stand. We must take a rapid glance across the interval, in order that we may see how circumstances and conditions changed, and how the changed circumstances and conditions both made Liberal Orthodoxy's reappearance necessary and to some extent prescribed the forms under which it should reappear. And as it was in England that we saw Liberal Orthodoxy first appear and die, it is with England that our survey of the period intervening before its re-birth had best begin.

Of England there is indeed in this connection but little to say. It is on the deistic controversy that the observer's gaze rests, as upon the event which, so far as religious thought is concerned, looms largest in the eighteenth century's annals.[1]

[1] The authoritative English book on the topic is Leslie Stephen's *History of English Thought in the Eighteenth Century*.

As has already been said, it is back in the seventeenth century that the commencement of Deism is to be found; but it was from the beginning to the middle of the eighteenth century that the stream of deistic argument ran most strongly; while that same century was near its close before the waters dried. Deism may be briefly characterised as a system which sought to depreciate the idea of " revealed religion "—that is, Christianity—in the interests of " natural religion," and which, while affirming the existence of a God by whom the world had been made, denied that the Deity had, subsequently to the Creation, interposed in the world's history in any such wise as Christianity declares Him to have done. The world had been put forth, a finished product, from the Creator's workshop; and thereafter the Creator had withdrawn His hand, averted His gaze, and allowed things to go on as they might. Religion was no more than the observance of those moral ideals and precepts which God had originally implanted in the nature of every man, together with a recognition of the fact that it *was* by God's will and through God's implanting that they had come; although it should be said that belief in future rewards and punishments—this belief being, as was supposed, native to the human mind—characterised the majority of the school. As for Christianity, while it was of course impossible for those occupying the general position just described to accept the supernatural elements which the Christian religion contains, the precise attitude taken up and the line of attacking treatment adopted varied greatly with different men. Tindal held that the object of Christianity was merely to re-publish that " natural religion " whereof man had been possessed from the beginning of time, declared that Christianity's claim to be a new and special revelation was sufficiently discredited by the fact that the alleged " revelation " was made to only a small portion of the race, and resolved into legends many of the Bible narratives both in the Old Testament and in the New. Collins concentrated chiefly on difficulties and contradictions in the Bible, and on the impossibility of maintaining that occurrences recorded in the New Testament were really fulfilments of supposed prophecies in the Old. Bolingbroke introduced the idea of fraud, suggesting that much of the received Christian doctrine was invented by the clever and imposed upon the dull in order to exploit the last-named for the benefit of the first. And Woolston, employing violently corrosive language which excited the admiration of so good a judge as Voltaire, dissolved the miracles into " allegories " which could not be accepted in their literalness by any sane mind.

But it is needless to construct a complete or even a lengthy list. What is necessary to note, for our purposes, is this—that both parties to the deistic controversy helped on the reappearance of Liberal Orthodoxy, though neither party intended or knew it, and although the defending or Christian side occupied strictly conservative ground. The controversy itself ended in Deism's defeat; for so one is entitled to conclude from

Deism's disappearance by the century's end. One must remember, however, that the main contention of the Deists had been on behalf of the superiority of " natural " religion over " revealed," and the substitution of the former for the latter, and it was on this contention alone that issue was really joined. The attacks made by the deistic writers upon the contents of Scripture, acute as they were, were not much more than incidental after all. And the Christian apologists—Butler and Paley are, it need hardly be said, the two greatest names among them—addressed themselves, not so much to the direct attacks upon Scripture which the Deists made, as to the ultimate proposition for whose sake the Deists had entered the arena. Of course, the detailed difficulties and objections brought forward by the challengers necessarily came into debate; but they were considered less on their intrinsic merits than under a consciousness of their bearing upon that ultimate proposition itself. Butler's great work, the *Analogy*, in fact bases itself upon, and is an expansion of, the single idea that natural religion has as many difficulties as has revealed, and that notwithstanding difficulties, therefore, the latter, no less than the former, may stand. And Paley, arguing that even the " natural " religion advocated by the Deists as sufficient could not have maintained its authority unless additional revelations and sanctions had been bestowed, defends miracle mainly on the ground that, once the need of such additional revelation has been seen, it is only to be expected that attention should be won

for the revelation, and the authoritativeness of
the revelation confirmed, by miraculous events
such as Scripture records. One has only to
glance over some of his chapters—for example,
the one on " Discrepancies between the several
Gospels " [1]—to see how perfunctory much of his
dealing with detailed difficulties and objections
really was. In short, the untenability of the
general idea of revelation, and its untenability
mostly on abstract grounds, was the doctrine to
which the Deists stood committed : it was
against this doctrine that the Christian apologists
fought; and it was on the claims of this doctrine
that a negative verdict was returned.

But after the actual deistic controversy had
died, the problems which the Deists had more
or less incidentally raised were found to remain;
and the crumbs which they had scattered were
taken up by some who came after and kneaded
into something very substantial indeed. When
men like Hume, with a historical feeling and
instinct far greater than any of his predecessors
had owned, made a direct assault against miracle
on the ground that human witness could never
be strong enough to sustain it, and against the
idea, never questioned by earlier Deists, that
monotheism was the primitive belief of mankind
—when Gibbon, politely scornful, and insinuating
rather than asserting, flung out his famous " five
causes " as being so amply sufficient to account
for Christianity's spread that no actual supernatural divine driving force behind it need be
assumed—when Paine, appealing to the un-

[1] *Evidences of Christianity,* Part III, chap. i.

learned masses, poured ribaldry upon the central
Christian doctrines of incarnation and atonement,
supporting his ribaldry, however, by scientific
argument of a by no means despicable kind—it
was clear that the time had come for a new
defence movement on the Christian side. It
was clear, that is, or slowly grew clear, to some;
for then as always, there was much Conservative
Orthodoxy which refused to shift its ground by
an inch. But some there were who saw that,
exaggerated as criticism of the Bible might be,
exaggerated, at any rate, as the supposed destructive effect of it upon Christianity might be,
by an attitude of mere obstinacy before it more
would be lost than saved. Very naturally, the
closer examination of the Scripture records into
which Christian apologists were driven by the
fierceness of their enemies' attack, the quickening
of the historical instinct caught by the Christian
apologists from those on the other side (and the
influences acting at home were, moreover, reinforced by others wafted over, though at first
only in small measure, from abroad)—very
naturally these things brought not a few to see
that the conventional estimate of the Bible as
inerrant in every line must be revised. And we
shall presently have to note how in the nineteenth
century this conviction proved its presence and
set about its work. The Deists, in fact, had
built better than they knew : although their own
main contention failed, they had started lines
of critical investigation which afterwards did
much to mould Christian thought; and the
Deism which, as we saw in the previous chapter,

made Liberal Orthodoxy of the Cambridge
Platonist type impossible, really made inevitable
the reappearance of Liberal Orthodoxy in another
form.

As for the part of the anti-Deist apologists in
similarly preparing the way for Liberal Orthodoxy's return, this was necessarily played along
other lines. None the less, it was played. For
the general method of Christianity's defenders
in the deistic controversy had made it clear to
those who had eyes to see (and if these must be
small in number they would nevertheless be the
spiritual elect, the spiritual salt, of the Christian
community) that the God and the revelation
for which they contended were altogether too
external, too remote—that, in fact, the God of
their system was, after all, only the Deists' God
somewhat improved, different only in that He
had come out of His absenteeism a little oftener
than the Deists had been willing to allow, had
emerged at a few outstanding points in history's
progress, had emerged particularly in Jesus
Christ. There was in their method no suggestion of God *in* man, God communicating to
man anything more than could be communicated
by a bare word of instruction or by a redemptive
act displayed upon the stage of time. The whole
relation between God and man remained, on the
apologists' reading of it, one between a God
outside the world, though of course interested
in it, and man within it, contact being established chiefly as man's reason led him to accept
the probability of God's existence and of those
manifestations of interest which God was declared

to have given. The apologetic was as purely
" rationalistic " as the attack—on which ground
it was to come under Mark Pattison's censure
later on in *Essays and Reviews*. Religion was
not taken as a matter of inward experience, as
speaking of a God with whose nature man's
nature was kindred and with whose nature man's
nature, its original harmony with God's having
been impaired, was by Christ's redemption to
be made truly kindred again. It could be said,
certainly, that the Christian apologists met the
need of the hour, confronting the Deists on the
latters' own chosen ground. But the very fact
that they could take this ground, and that there
they appeared so thoroughly at home, would for
some make their whole conception of religion
suspect. It is easy to believe that souls of
intenser quality, as they surveyed the position,
would react against the very method whereby
religion had been defended, would at least find
it poor and cold, and would seek for some richer
wine of religious thought wherewith to fill the
vessels of their thirsty minds. The entire deistic
dispute, on its Christian no less than on its anti-
Christian side, would force such souls to enquire
whether the whole conception of religion, of God,
of man, of redemption, it involved did not fall
far short of the true. And, once that enquiry
wakened, they would—besides adopting the
changed attitude on the question of Scripture
inerrancy just now spoken of—search for clues
toward some view of religion which should bring
God in from His distance, set Him from the
beginning to the end of history in a more vital

relationship with His children, and so answer
to the inner call they had been roused to hear.
And just as we shall presently see Liberal
Orthodoxy coming upon the nineteenth century
in an altered attitude towards the Scripture
records, so we shall see it coming also in a
deeper appreciation and a revised statement of
the essential relation between God and man,
both as to the original aspect of that relation
and as to the rehabilitation of it which the term
" salvation " implies. So that, to sum up, we
find the eighteenth century in England preparing
the way for Liberal Orthodoxy's second advent
along two lines—first by the new attitude towards
the Bible which the Deists' attack upon it
(incidental more or less when Deism made it,
but afterwards becoming capital and primary)
forced upon those who would in any wise save
the Bible for faith, and second by the new conception of religion in general after which the
anti-Deist apologetic caused spiritually sensitive
souls, if only by way of reaction, to aspire. The
actors in the century's events did not, indeed,
know who or what was to come along the road
they made : the following feet were too far
behind for any echoes prophetic of their advance
to be wafted on. But the following feet stepped
swift and sure; and along the prepared way
Liberal Orthodoxy came in its due time.

Passing from our own country to Germany,
we find that there, during the eighteenth century,
an accumulation and interplay of forces had by
the coming of the nineteenth thrown Christianity

upon a more pronounced defensive than even in England, and had compelled the appearance of a revised theology if defence was to be successfully maintained. It was through the spread of Kant's philosophy, or rather through the application to Christian faith of Kant's philosophic method in one of its aspects, that the great battle was at last forced on; but before Kantianism finally gave the signal and drove the opposing hosts to engage, there had been preliminary movements whose significance had been by degrees growing clear. The " rationalistic " spirit—which in the more general sense of the epithet is so character-istic of German intellectual processes, and which always manifests itself so clearly in the German passion for systematic thoroughness, even when the system built up is opposed to " rationalism " usually so called—the rationalistic spirit had been giving signs of its future activity ever since the eighteenth century began.

It is necessary to say, in order to an under-standing of the situation, that of religion which touched both the heart and the mind Germany had at this time little or none. It had a religion of the mind alone, in that Lutheran orthodoxy (or that orthodoxy calling itself Lutheran) which, founded upon the letter of Scripture, took the sacredness of the creeds as almost on a par with that of the Scripture itself, and cared only that all the established shibboleths should come in unclouded enunciation from Christian lips. And it had a religion of the heart alone, in that pietism whereof Spener had towards the close of the seventeenth century been the chief apostle, and whose adherents, while doctrinally as orthodox as the dominant school, nevertheless abandoned themselves to a merely emotional religiousness quite divorced from thought. But a religion both warm and intellectual was not upon the field. Evidently from neither of these schools was an effective opposition to an anti-Christian rationalism likely to come. The first might indeed be itself termed rationalistic, at any rate scholastic, in a quite valid sense; for a certain starting-point once adopted, the religious ultimates of God, revelation, and the Bible being taken for granted, its whole procedure consisted in the drawing out of logical consequences and the arrangement of a duly proper credal mosaic; so that the subsequent anti-Christian rationalism may be viewed as only another exercise of the same method, the starting-point having been pushed further back, and what had for orthodoxy been the ultimates consequently losing their status and being displaced from their place in the logical chain. But although Lutheran orthodoxy thus found the weapon with which it had coldly carved out its system wrested from its hands and coldly pointed against the very system it had carved, it was in no case, since its own ultimates had been left unguarded and were now, according to the new reading of things, lost, to make effective resistance in any effective way. And the pietistic school, less accustomed even than the other to dialectical fence, could in no wise step into the breach. The interests of Christianity, it would seem, must in a time of stress collapse between two stools unless an entirely fresh champion could be found. As the attack developed, it became plain that theology must make an entirely fresh start, must lay its foundations anew, and practically forget the things that were behind, if theology were to be saved.

But this is to anticipate. The seriousness of the assault, as has been said, showed itself only by degrees. The rationalistic *method*, as distinct from rationalistic *doctrine* in the sense of hostility to religion, was emphatically driven home upon the mind of the German world by Christian Wolff (1679–1754), who aimed at covering the entire field of human knowledge by the employment of the syllogism, contending that there was no question which reason, putting that weapon to its amplest uses, could not solve. It is, in fact, the form rather than the content of Wolff's philosophy (he was in the main a follower of Leibnitz) that gives him his importance in the history of thought—his conviction, and the daring wherewith it was applied, that everything which might be held for truth, be it in metaphysics, ethics, theology, or aught else, could be gathered within the embrace of reason most strictly defined. Philosophy, according to Wolff, was the " science of the possible "; and by this he meant, in brief, the discovery of what human reason could itself discover. By picking up, as it were, at the beginning of his explorations, the thread which hung from the mind of man and its logical categories, and drawing it as from a thickly-wound reel, he could roam, or thought he could, over all the fields of knowledge without for a moment dropping the thread, finding it, indeed, unrolling in his hand and so preserving the connection with his starting-point as he went on. This was, of course, the rationalist method *in excelsis*—and the rationalist method none the less that so far as religion was concerned Wolff held to the orthodox faith; for it was by stretching to its utmost the thread just spoken of, and by keeping his grasp upon it as he beat round the circle it permitted him to cover, that the orthodox faith was found. And the rationalistic method, taken up by other hands, soon led to other than orthodox results. It was to the Bible considered as a historical record that the method was at first principally applied; and Semler (1725–1791) earned the title of the " father of German rationalism " by putting the Scriptures under the same critical treatment as that which any other historical book must expect to face.[1] He was not doctrinally a heretic : in fact, he appeared as the antagonist of heterodoxy in respect of the *Wolfenbüttel Fragments* whereof we must presently speak; but he insisted that not every portion of Scripture was of equal value, that each part of it must be considered in relation to the circumstances of the time at which it was given, that many things ordinarily taken as " revelation " were in reality

[1] Jean Astruc, a French physician, published in 1753 a book putting forward the theory that Moses had compiled Genesis from two documents, in which two different names for God—Elohim and Jehovah—were employed. But Astruc put forward his idea only tentatively, and with no thought that it possessed any special, still less any revolutionary, significance.

" accommodation " on the part of teachers, or of Christ Himself, to the current notions of their age, and that it was accordingly the business of later study to separate the eternal from the temporary, the body of truth from its outward dress. Much of this is now the commonplace of what is known as the historic method; but the step which Semler took, and after the taking of which he stopped, was made the beginning of a longer journey for some to whom that one step of his had indicated the existence and direction of a road. In Eichhorn (1752–1827) the rationalistic spirit reached to what were rationalist conclusions in the full sense, to a denial of the possibility of miracle, and consequently to something more than the mere " accommodation " theory with which Semler had been content. Working upon both the Old and New Testaments, but mainly upon the Old, Eichhorn found a perfectly natural explanation for every event which at the first blush seemed to be outside natural law, getting rid of all such events with ease by dissolving the statements of them into Oriental hyperboles and metaphors and figures of speech. And Paulus (1761–1851) —though the mention of his name carries us, as also does that of Eichhorn's, beyond the strict limits of the ante-Kantian period—pushed similar methods to their furthest, apparently revelled in a sort of reversed conjuring which, instead of producing marvels, showed how easily marvels could be explained away, and fell upon the New Testament miracles as if determined to rend to tatters the mysterious veils they wore. So, to take examples, the account of the transfiguration became the confused story of the disciples' half-recollected dreams, and the resurrection of Jesus Himself a legend growing up upon the fact that Jesus had not really died at all. Turning to other early influences which gave some push to rationalism's career, the name of Lessing (1729–1781) calls for mention; for he published the famous *Wolfenbüttel Fragments*—really the work of Reimarus, by whose daughter they were given into Lessing's hands—in 1774 and subsequent years.[1] The attitude of Reimarus himself was frankly and thoroughly rationalist; and in his insistence on Bible discrepancies, and in his general belittling of Christianity and its ideas and ideals, he recalls the English Deists at whom we were looking a little while ago. Lessing disclaimed concurrence in the actual views of Reimarus—at least, he did not defend them; but in the controversy which ensued on the publication of the *Fragments* he declared that not upon Scripture must the truth of Christianity be considered to rest, but upon its demonstrable adaptation to human nature and human needs. Once again we come, as we meet this assertion of Lessing's, upon an idea which, with little qualification, is a commonplace to many ardent defenders of the Christian religion to-day; but in a time of transition such ideas are apt to be used only as platforms whereon men stand for a moment before leaping to ideas yet further removed from the original base;

[1] Lessing was librarian at Wolfenbüttel, under the hereditary prince of Brunswick, at the time—hence the name.

and one must reckon the publication of the *Wolfenbüttel Fragments* with the weight of Lessing's name behind them, together with the dispute they stirred, as one of the undoubted influences preparing full-fledged rationalism's way. In connection with Lessing, also, his later work on *The Education of the Human Race* —in which he maintains that every stage of development must have its own religion, and that as a matter of fact every historic religion has been on the one hand born out of, and on the other hand fittingly adjusted to, the wants of its age—must be named. The idea, once more, is by no means inconsistent with an acceptance of the established Christian faith, as countless minds since Lessing's day have proved : whatever danger to Christianity arises from it arises, not from the idea itself, but from the inference sometimes drawn that because every religion is relative to its own age, therefore no religion can claim to be final and supreme; but coming at the time it did, it would stir the waters of enquiry, not to say those of doubt, to higher and stronger waves. And with the mention of one other influence—that of English Deism—the list of preparatory forces, of forces which as it were laid down the train which Kant's philosophy was fated to fire, may come to an end. How far the direct influence of English Deism extended it is impossible to say; though we know that some of the English writers— Tindal, for instance—were translated into German; and in Semler, Reimarus, and a few others, the touch from England is plain to see. The

G

frivolity which distinguishes a certain number
of the English Deists is, perhaps, found among
German theologians only in Bahrdt (1741–1792),
the extraordinary controversialist who delighted
in giving offence, and who for a good while acted
in the afternoon as proprietor of a beer-shop
after lecturing on moral philosophy in the earlier
part of the day. Yet, on consideration, one is
inclined to think that Bahrdt's frivolity and
vulgarity in theological controversy smacks less
of England and Deism than of France and
Voltaire. However that may be, contact with
English Deism there certainly was, more or less
close, more or less direct; and the England
which has received so much theology—as some
would put it, so many heresies—from Germany,
may enjoy whatever satisfaction is derivable
from the recollection of an impulse administered
to German destructive thinking long ago.

But all this was only the preface to the more
pronounced rationalism which derived directly
from Kant. We must remind ourselves, however,
that chronological exactitude cannot be altogether
observed in dealing with such a series of events
as that wherewith we are now in contact : movements overlap instead of arranging themselves
in a precise succession; and the Kantian influence—for Kant died in 1804—was permeating
theological circles before the work of some whom
we have already named was done. Indeed, the
critical rationalism which applied itself principally
to the Scriptures, and the doctrinal rationalism
which operated principally upon the contents of
religion and Christianity as a whole, make two

distinct streams traceable henceforward across
the map of German, not to say of general,
theological thought. It is in Kant's philosophy,
or rather in one department of it, that the well-
spring of the latter lay. In one department of
it, for in point of fact Kant's system had two
departments very clearly differentiated; and if
by his work in one department Kant made for
rationalism pure and simple, by his work in the
other he sought to relieve the human mind from
having its wings crushed and broken under
rationalism's oppressive weight; to which we
must add that, however some may have taken
it, then or later, Kant himself attached as much
importance to the second department as to the
first. In fact Kant's system is not really a
rationalistic, but an idealistic, one : he is actually
against, rather than for, the current rationalism
of his time in maintaining that *not* reason *per se*,
but reason *acting upon experience*, is the true
source of knowledge, just as he is against mere
empiricism in holding that *not* from experience
flung down upon a passive mind, but from
experience *acted upon by mind*, does knowledge
come. Moreover—and more significantly for our
present line—his close examination of reason,
its possibilities and its impossibilities, is carried
through with the express purpose of showing
that, just because reason cannot pass beyond
the bounds of the sensible to a super-sensible
world, that super-sensible world must be sought
by other means; and it is one of the ironies
of philosophy's history that the concentrated
intensity wherewith Kant carried through his

survey of reason's constitution and reason's powers should have attracted so many and led them in the end to an estimate of pure reason's all-sufficiency which Kant himself would never have shared.[1] But Kant's searching enquiry into the laws of the human reason—his assertion that there *are* laws of cognition embedded in the human mind's constitution antecedently to all experience, and that all knowledge results from the application of these laws to the material which experience supplies—his consequent limitation of knowledge in the strict sense to that which, inasmuch as it is derived from the working of the mind *upon* experience, comes at least in part *through* experience—all this, and particularly the last, became, when some of Kant's half-disciples looked at Christianity in the light of its principles, a dissolvent upon a good many of the hitherto-accepted Christian facts and ideas. That Kant, while affirming in his *Critique of Pure Reason* (1781) that we could not get behind mere phenomena, could not know ultimate realities or " things in themselves," could not prove God, immortality, or the freedom of the will, had gone on in his *Critique of Practical Reason* (1788) to recover much of what he had seemed to lose, had declared that the reason which could not prove these things could not disprove them either, had justified a " moral " faith (because without it the world and the happiness of mankind must remain incomplete) in many things

[1] An exposition within moderate compass of Kant's system may be found in the volume on Kant, by Prof. Knight, in Blackwood's *Philosophical Classics.*

to which a purely " rational " faith could not be given, had taken this " moral " faith to be as sound and indeed as obligatory as any " rational " faith could be, and had thereby left an opening at which on his own general principles many other non-rational faiths besides those he himself mentioned might plausibly apply for admittance—all this sank with some quite out of sight. We are not here concerned with Kant's consistency or with the validity of his view, but only with the fact that some who called themselves his disciples were no more than partial disciples after all. And with some of these partial disciples, for whom strict " reason "— because Kant gave it in his system such definiteness of outline, such precision of working, such a plainly-written commission—came to be the beginning, middle, and end of all truth's tests, the supernatural element in Christianity was deprived of its savour. Reason had so lost its mysteriousness in the dry light which Kant had thrown into and round all its secret spots, that it could tolerate no mystery elsewhere. What happened was that the rationalistic spirit already abroad took prisoner a part of that Kantian system which as a whole was so hostile, and coerced its captive into service under its own flag.

Among the theologians who treated Christianity under the rationalistic impulse which Kant had unwillingly, at any rate unintentionally, rendered dominant in them, we naturally find differences in the intensity of their rationalistic mood, and in the consequences which it entailed

upon their Christian faith. Some, like Tieftrunk
(1759–1837), while pushing to the front the
assertion that pure reason could not justify
anything in the nature of a special revelation, endeavoured in more or less vague fashion to assert
the possibility of *some* sort of revelation without
explicitly defining either its message or its
accompanying historical setting, inasmuch as a
revelation having the ultimate happiness and
good of mankind in view was consonant with
that " practical reason " which must not be
despised. This was in a manner to found
nominally upon both sections of the Kantian
philosophy rather than upon one section alone;
and it might also appear as if within the borders
of the general statement just given the whole
Christian system could find room.   But in effect,
insistence upon pure reason's limitations came
to outweigh the gracious permission apparently
given to revelation to re-enter after having been
expelled : it was only in the narrowest sense
that the permission was to be understood : the
" practical reason " was not to set its doors
wide open in order that a procession of Christian
ideas, having started from somewhere beyond,
might come in, but only to put them ajar at
revelation's knock in order that what was already
within might slip out and show itself; and
revelation was after all not allowed to do more
than republish those ideas of love to God and
man which the " practical reason," when closely
interrogated, declared itself to call for. In
short, Tieftrunk appears to halt between two
opinions, anxious, one might almost say, to

save the *idea* of revelation while averse to much
of its actual *content*, and accordingly may be
said without unfairness to destroy the specifically Christian material in his very effort to
construct a Christian scheme. Others, among
whom Bretschneider (1776–1848) bears the best
known name, though equally fascinated by the
doctrine of reason's all-sufficiency, nevertheless
appeared to look on that all-sufficiency as for
the present potential only, and admitted a
revelation as imparting a provisional knowledge
of what reason afterwards came on its own
account to perceive as true—a position which,
though obviously allowing Christian orthodoxy
to hold its place for a while, as obviously gave
it no security of tenure against the time when
reason's light should have shone through as-
cending degrees of brightness to the perfect day.
Others there were who, with Wegscheider (1771–
1849) and Röhr (1777–1848), became, under their
half-devotion to Kant's system, so enthusiastic
in reason's cause that the very idea of a supernatural revelation grew, not only incredible, but
actually distasteful, to them, because it seemed
to imply a disparagement of man's native power
to live himself out to the fulness of his worth.
Whatever revelation was given in Jesus Christ
was, according to this school, nothing else than
a revelation of reason at its highest and best :
indeed, if we have in Tieftrunk a preservation
of the *idea* of revelation without its *content*, we
have here a preservation of the mere *term*
" revelation " without any real meaning being
attached to it at all : of course all the distinctively

Christian doctrines, the special divinity of Jesus,
atonement, miracle, were so much lumber to
be incontinently thrown overboard; and religion
was transformed into a morality rationally discovered, rationally satisfactory, and rationally
guaranteed, reason being at the same time the
sole creator and the sole judge. By the time
rationalist theology had reached this stage in
its progress, it had become a matter of very dry
bones indeed; but we conclude the present list
of representative names by mentioning that of
De Wette (1730–1849), who sought to breathe
across them some air of emotion and heat, and
so to make them live again. In his early days
De Wette had come under the influence of Herder
—the friend of Goethe and one of the greatest
figures in the German literary romantic movement, sensitive, highly-strung, jealous on behalf
of imagination's warmth as against cold reason's
dissective surgery—and from beneath Herder's
spell he never passed. He did not, indeed,
sympathise with Herder in the fierce attack
which the latter, in his *Metakritik*, made upon
Kant's system : on the contrary, he shared
Kant's view as to pure reason's limits and
power; and so far as constructive theology is
concerned (he was greater in Biblical criticism
and exegesis than in doctrinal construction, his
work in those departments having value still) it
is undoubtedly with the rationalists that he must
be classed. But he was passionately eager to
insist that man was more than mind, and that
even in holding the rationalist creed man should
so to say let himself go. Over and above the

intellectual acceptance of belief, there was an æsthetico-religious feeling into which the believer must rise; and whatever the intellect might say, the heart must be allowed to lift him into a feeling of enthusiasm and worship towards God and Christ which would perhaps only have been really warranted if the very things denied by rationalism had been true. Though he expelled the specifically Christian truths at reason's bidding, De Wette ran after them when he had cast them out, to bring them back again, not indeed as truths, but as poetic translations of truths; so that the ostracised doctrine of the atonement, for example, was implored to come back as a figurative way of saying that under the influence of Christ our peace of soul returns; and before the poetic beauty of this and other symbolic statements, not before their truth, De Wette would have men bow down, as he himself bowed down, in wonder and love. In the very fact that they are the exaggerations of poetic art, and in the skill with which they have been wrought, he finds their title to our reverence and their uplifting power. The picture is not without some pathos—the rationalistic thinker thus tearing the cords which his own chosen method has wound round him, and stretching the soul which has been so cramped; and not without significance, either, in that it shows how the supposed emancipation brought by rationalism was found to be bitter bondage by some of the finest and the best, how the fruit which hung so invitingly from the rationalist tree turned out to have the Dead Sea taste. And it is not without regret that

one finds oneself compelled to allot to a soul so
finely tuned as De Wette's a place in the rationalist ranks.   But so it has to be.   For all his
emotionalism, and for all the flaming border
which he ran round the scroll whereon he wrote
his creed, De Wette—when it comes to asking
him how far intellectual justification for Christian
truth existed—passes, albeit with downcast head
and reluctant feet, to the ground on which the
other rationalists stand.   With this placing of
him we may, as we said, close the list of
rationalist theologians properly so designated;
but it is, perhaps, well to cast a glance upon
that corner of the field where history was doing
its work—since views on present doctrine must
necessarily affect views on doctrine's growth—
and observe that the history of the Church was
written from the rationalist standpoint, though
in quite arbitrary fashion and without anything
of true historical feeling, and presented as the
mere development of superstition and error, by
two historians now probably left unread, Spittler
and Planck.[1]

The gathering of all these thunder-clouds
necessarily forced Christianity in Germany—as
we saw that the events of the eighteenth century
forced Christianity in England—to build new
shelters for itself if it would escape.   Let the
previously-given caution, as to the impossibility
of drawing precise lines of chronological division,
be recalled, however; for just as our reckoning
of the forces preparatory to Kantian rationalism
brought us over into the Kantian time, so our

[1] Spittler, 1752–1810; Planck, 1785–1831.

reckoning of the post-Kantian rationalism has brought us into the period of that theological reconstruction which post-Kantian rationalism compelled. The building of the new shelters began before the storm was at its height. And one has always to remember that some of the workers in the previous movements—Paulus, for instance, from the earlier critical school, and Wegscheider from the rationalist school at which we have just been looking—repeated the old cries long after the sounding of new cries had called the bulk of followers away, worked on so to say by dim candle-light after the sun had gone down upon them to rise elsewhere. This holds good, indeed, through the entire history of thought; and it is scarcely too much to say that every school of any account that has ever existed has its representatives down to our own time, many of them looking strangely enough in the intellectual dress of long ago. But speaking generally and roughly, we may say that the movements of which some account has been given created the necessity for a reconstruction of Christian thought. And the necessity was pressing. If attacks upon the established faith over-shot the mark and collapsed thereafter through their own excess, they nevertheless caused the adherents of that faith to realise that attack was possible. The failure of the un-regulated assault brought into prominence the weak places where a properly regulated assault might prevail. Of course, Conservative Ortho-doxy had its representatives who deemed them-selves sufficient for all the demands of the day.

Some of these fell very eagerly upon what seemed a way of killing rationalism with its own weapons; for Storr (1746–1805), Reinhardt (1753–1812), and others, belonging to what is sometimes termed the older Tübingen school—Storr was a Tübingen professor—contended that on Kant's own showing the Bible ought to be received on its own terms and its authority unquestioningly admitted. " Your philosophy confesses that reason cannot reach to ultimate realities, to what transcends experience "—so ran their challenge to the rationalist Christian school—" but it also confesses, through the lips of its master, that it cannot deny these things, and it receives on the authority of the ' practical reason ' what the ' pure reason ' cannot attain. In other words, authority is called in to say the final word. Why not let authority do a more perfect work ? Why not accept every Bible text as true merely because a supernatural authority—whose credentials your system admits itself unable either to pass or to repudiate— flings them at your feet ? " Of course the fallacy is obvious; for while, according to Kant himself, the test of what " practical reason " admits is given stringently enough in the " ultimate happiness of mankind," according to the theory of this school there was really to be no test at all; and the demand really was that anything and everything should be received if only a Biblical text could be quoted in support. The position is familiar enough; and those who wander contentedly round the circle involved in believing that the Bible is true because it is

authoritatively inspired and authoritatively inspired because it is true are with us still. But
then, as now, this doctrine could not prove a
Gilead with balm for faith's wounds to any one
who realised the fierceness and power of faith's
foes. The call for a re-statement of Christianity,
made after a fair and square facing of the situation, and after a proper estimate of what criticism
had done and of what it had failed to do, was
insistent. And, as we shall see in the next
chapter, the call was heard.

Over England and Germany, then, we have
seen the " interval " pass. Beyond these two
countries our gaze need not at present travel—
unless, indeed, it drops for a moment upon
France, allowing us to remark that from France
it was hardly possible for any reconstructed
theology to come. Need enough for it there
certainly was; for the wind of Voltaire's vehement
onslaught had swept over the fields of French
religion with results at which all who cared for
the faith might well take alarm. But, inevitably
under the circumstances, France being what she
was, it was by Roman Catholicism that the
defence, if defence there was to be, must be
made; and this—notwithstanding that Joseph
de Maistre, the unbending upholder of Catholic
authority, and Chateaubriand, defender (in *The
Genius of Christianity*) of Catholicism along
another and much more fascinating line, are
both of them surpassingly interesting figures
if we might linger with them—does not fall
within the limits of our theme. France, indeed,

though she is not to be wholly absent, will play
but a small part in our story; and for the moment
she has no part at all.   As for other lands which
were by-and-by to feel the effect of the German
and English movement or to make a contribution
of their own, they were for the most part unstirred
as yet by any keen prophetic sense of something
new to come.   To Germany and England, therefore, we may at once turn back.

CHAPTER IV

THE REVIVAL : GERMANY

It may be well, before taking up the actual narrative of Liberal Orthodoxy's re-start and development when the " interval " had gone by, to set out one or two points which must be borne in mind if the narrative is to be rightly understood. And chiefly, it needs to be said that both in Britain and in Germany, the two countries in which the development of Liberal Orthodoxy may be most plainly traced, the development itself drops into two periods, with the dividing-line between drawn fairly clear. In Germany the name of Schleiermacher stands at the commencement of the first period, that of Ritschl at the commencement of the second; while in Britain it is, roughly speaking, at the publication of *Essays and Reviews* that the division falls. Further, the two periods may be characterised by saying that in the first period Liberal Orthodoxy was prepared to grant much—and to grant it voluntarily and without reluctance—to Christianity's assailants, perhaps scarcely realising the seriousness of the position and certainly not realising the seriousness of the ultimate threats which the position held out : it was, in fact, possessed by that willingness

spoken of some time since, a willingness to
purchase the safety of its untouchable *minimum*
by enlarging the size of what it gave up; while
in the second period Liberal Orthodoxy, finding
that its previous concessions had not been taken
as final, and that what it had deemed safely
guarded was in danger of being snatched away
to keep company in the limbo of out-worn
beliefs with what it had readily surrendered,
moved more warily, stiffened its attitude somewhat, and abandoned more or less its previous
forwardness in agreeing with its adversaries
upon the way. It may superficially appear a
questionable procedure thus to credit Liberal
Orthodoxy with a more cautious spirit in its
later stages than in its earlier. Surely changes
in religious belief, even among those who held
fast to the Christian fundamentals, spread further
and struck deeper and carried an ever more
complicated multiplication of consequences, as
time went on ! For the moment, however, we
may content ourselves with making sure that
the statement, superficially questionable, is
properly understood, leaving its justification
to appear by-and-by. What is meant, when it
is said that Liberal Orthodoxy showed less
swiftness, less of what might be called abandon,
in the second indicated period than in the first,
is not that as to the *substance* of its faith it re-
verted to its more ancient ground (though in
some instances it did even this), but that its
mood became tinged with a more cautious hue.
One may put it that while it was of course
further down the road of change, it looked more

hesitatingly and suspiciously ahead and around
before taking the next step : it needed more of
a push or pull before the next step was taken,
instead of standing as it were poised and ready
before the call; and it was reluctant, whereas
previously it had been willing, to disburden
itself of what must be relinquished if the next
step were to be made at all—sometimes, indeed,
reaching back for what it now discovered it
had relinquished too soon. So much may be
set down by way of a right interpretation of
the statement made. For the justification of it,
we will, as was said, wait till the narrative
supplies it in due time. Meanwhile, the two
" periods " as mentioned, and the characterisation of each as given, should be registered upon
the mind.

It will make for clearness, besides, if we
occupy ourselves for a moment or two in conceiving correctly the main difference between the
British and the German minds, and the consequent difference in the working and the product
of the two. For although the broad statement
as to the two periods of Liberal Orthodoxy's
development holds good for both countries alike,
the actual history manifests, as we should expect
it to manifest, the special national character-
istics in each case. The German mind is predominantly systematic, and strives always to
see the parts of any problem *as* parts, which
means of course that it must see, not *only* the
parts, but the *whole ;* with the result that in
theological construction, as in other fields, each
worker of any account refuses in turn to rest

H

content with the making or trimming of isolated
bricks or buttresses or columns, but acts from
first to last as his own architect and builder,
putting his own building through from foundation to coping stone. German theological change,
in other words, proceeds for the most part by
way of a succession of systems, rather than by
way of discussion and modification of single
doctrines—not that such discussion and modification are not carried on, but that they are carried
on with an entire theological scheme, its harmony,
its symmetry, its completeness, kept full in
view. In England and Scotland, on the other
hand (in England perhaps with less qualification
than in Scotland), thinking is more broken up,
deals more with patches and parts, occupies
itself with departments rather than with wholes;
which means that in British theology it is by
treatment of special and isolated doctrines that
old things become new. Moreover, we may go
on, once this distinction is grasped, to note that
the difference in general mental working had
an effect upon the process whereby Liberal
Orthodoxy, in the two countries, passed from
its readily concessive to its more cautious stage.
In Germany, since a thoroughly worked out
theological system appeared under Liberal Orthodoxy's ægis from the first, that whole system
necessarily stood at once face to face with the
anti-Christian attacks which still went on:
Liberal Orthodoxy offered all the material necessary for a satisfactory test to the forces which
waited to perform the test; and the whole system
was revealed practically at once as to its qualities

and its defects, as to its power or its powerless-
ness to maintain its ground, and as to the degree
in which its concessions had been made in vain.
One may put it that the system knew itself,
and enabled both its adherents and its opponents
to know it, in all its parts, and that, at any rate
for the immediate hour, the issues as between the
system and its foes were therefore clear. Or
one may put it that the system stood with exact
understanding of its distance, not only from one
point, but from all points of the field of thought;
so that any subsequent movements which might
be necessitated would be made as in the light,
not gropingly as in the dark, would be each of
them as it were a real and deliberate change
of place, not a mere flurried shifting about of
bewildered feet. We have, accordingly, within
Liberal Orthodoxy's first period, a succession of
systems, each one—after the necessary working
of the German mind—complete in itself, although
raised upon a foundation similar to the foundation of the one before, and each one becoming
somewhat more restrained in the readiness of
its surrenders; and we are thus brought at last
to the inauguration of the second period, when
—upon a new *foundation* this time—system-
building begins again. In Great Britain, on the
other hand, we have at the outset Liberal Orthodoxy dealing with and compromising upon one
doctrine in chief, and because this dealing with
and compromising upon one single doctrine was
not systematically thought out as to its consequences for theology as a whole, having those
consequences thrust upon it to its own surprise;

realising, dimly at first, more vividly later, what had been involved in its own initial act; and awaking in the end to find that inasmuch as it had kept no watch and ward upon the stream of unfolding change, it had been carried into strange realms upon the rapid tide. The movement which was open-eyed in Germany was more or less blindfold in Britain : in place of what we find in Liberal Orthodoxy's first period there, a deliberate *making* of changes to suit clearly-visualised conditions, we find here a late *realisation* of changes following, though not known to be following, upon a change made at the start ; though of course the end of it all— the necessity of a new start, the inauguration of a second period less ready for compromise and surrender—was in both instances the same.   But of these things, as of the things previously noted, we may say that while an apprehension of them will help to make the story clearer, it is in the reading of the story itself that their justification will be found.

With Schleiermacher (1768–1834), as has been said, the first period of German Liberal Orthodoxy—and it is to Germany that the present chapter is confined—begins. Any account of Schleiermacher's system that can be given here must of necessity be condensed; [1] but even the briefest account must be prefaced by a recognition of the fineness of Schleiermacher's spirit, the nobility of his spiritual conceptions and ideals,

---

[1] For a thorough exposition see the volume *Schleiermacher* (in this series) by Rev. Principal Selbie, D.D.

the greatness of his services to theology, and—
this notwithstanding the obscurities and even
contradictions which a close scrutiny may find—
the marvellous intellectual skill wherewith he
designs and erects his edifice of thought. He
was, in fact, such a combination of brain and
sensibility as seldom appears in the theological
workers' ranks : in the make of him both these
elements were fitly framed together, each supply-
ing something toward the beauty of the resulting
whole; and if it was largely true of him that
the heart made the theologian, it was also true
that the heart's exercise was disciplined and
guided by an alert and self-watching mind.
The warm piety of the Moravians, in one of
whose schools his earliest education was received, imparted to his own religion a corresponding warmth it never lost; while his studies
at the University of Halle, where he heard
Semler lecture and came under the influence of
the Kantian philosophy, then in the ascendant,
balanced that inner warmth of religious emotion
by a mental habit at once critical and constructive. As to Kant, indeed, we may say
that Schleiermacher learned Kant's lesson so
well as to transcend it—not only Kant's first
lesson, at which we have seen the rationalists
stop, but his second lesson as well. Kant had
passed beyond the limitations of the " pure "
reason, and had recovered faith in God and in
a moral order by means of the " practical "
reason, since these things were needed for the
ultimate happiness of mankind. Schleiermacher
passed with Kant beyond the bounds which the

" pure " reason set, but passed further beyond
them, arriving not at a mere morality for which
the " practical " reason called, but at a religion
which " feeling " affirmed, and which, being so
affirmed and experienced, was to be accepted
as one of the world's basal facts.   But discussion
of the original formative influences which worked
upon Schleiermacher, and of the degree in which
he ultimately levied contributions upon each
and all, would detain us too long.   It is a brief
statement of our theologian's main positions
that we must at once attempt.

What has just been said—that Schleiermacher
leapt across to " feeling " after the limitations
of " pure " reason had been felt—may serve as
the point of start.   For in Schleiermacher's
dealing with religion, " feeling " serves as the
point of start to Schleiermacher himself; and
though at times a certain vagueness besets his
use of the term, so that if one confined oneself
to the phrases employed on such occasions one
might find it a little difficult to answer the
enquiry "Feeling of what or toward what ? ",
the whole run of his thought, as well as his
own most frequently-used words, settles it for
us that he meant the " feeling of dependence
upon God."   This, then, is essential religion as
Schleiermacher characterised it in his *Reden
über die Religion* (1799).[1]   When we are conscious that behind the action of the whole world
upon us—which action of the whole world is
of course effected through the agency of its
single and separate parts, we reaching to a

[1] This has been translated into English by J. Oman.

consciousness of the action of the whole through
our consciousness of the action of the part—
there is the working of something more, of the
Absolute and the Eternal, of God, and when we
recognise that while we can in our turn react
upon the world's single agencies and upon the
world as a whole, we cannot react upon that
final Something behind them all, then are we
in religion's grip. Schleiermacher pictures, so
to say, a consciousness in us running backward
over point after point. It lights first of all
upon the individual phenomenon as we are
affected thereby—but with the consciousness of
that individual phenomenon is mingled a consciousness that we not only receive, but give,
are not only acted upon, but act. It lights
next upon the total universe wherein the single
phenomenon inheres—but with this second consciousness, as with the first, there is mingled the
consciousness of our own reciprocal activity and
reply. It lights last upon the Absolute behind
all the single phenomena and behind the total
universe—and now consciousness is silent as to
anything in us save receptivity, passiveness,
dependent contact with the ultimate Source of
everything that is. Thus consciousness stands,
for Schleiermacher, gazing up the " great altar-
stairs that slope through darkness up to God ";
and past all the landings on which its eye may
linger for an instant it discerns the First and the
Last. If we probe ourselves, we find the sense
of dependence which all this implies to be a
fundamental constituent of our natures. And
it all involves—let it be noted—no *knowledge* of

God in the speculative sense. That must be
sought for afterwards if it is to come at all;
and if it comes, it must be, in order to have
validity and worth, knowledge found in and
drawn from the sense of dependence as its source.
In the primary religious experience no slightest
jot or tittle of such a thing as speculative knowledge is given. It is *feeling* from beginning to
end; and in the presence and the persistence of
this feeling religion's essential characteristic lies.

This, however, takes us no further than to
Schleiermacher's view of religion in the most
general sense. What of his definitely Christian
construction, his attitude towards the specific
Christian faith? It is to his later and most
outstanding work—*Der Christliche Glaube nach
den Grundsätzen der evangelischen Kirche* [1] (1821–
1822)—that we must turn when this is the
object of our search. As in his general treatment of religion Schleiermacher starts from the
experienced fact of dependence on God, so in
his specifically Christian system he starts from
the fact that through Christianity the feeling
of dependence is, if not perfected, at any rate
developed and deepened; and just as all you
can say about religion in general is an explication and drawing out of what is involved in
the sense of God-dependence, so all you can
say about Christianity is an explication and
drawing out of what is involved in the fact
that Christianity produces the effect described.

[1] This has not been translated into English. *The Theology
of Schleiermacher*, by G. Cross, supplies a summary. See
also Selbie's book mentioned in a former note.

Schleiermacher, that is, begins, not with *à priori*
reasonings, not with the Bible, not even with
the historical Christ, but with the Christian
consciousness. The necessity for an influence
which can raise the sense of dependence to a
higher stage results from the fact that the
religious consciousness is not supreme in our
living : within us the lower or sensuous consciousness and the loftier or God-consciousness are at
war; and in this abridgment of the sense of
dependence lies human sin. But in Christianity
we have, by the testimony of all the Christian
centuries, by our own experience if we like to
make the test, a power which corrects our
human failure and brings back the God-consciousness to its true and proper strength. And
Christianity works through the Church; and
the Church rests upon Christ; and thus Schleiermacher follows the river of Christian truth as it
were *up* stream rather than *down*, claiming to
use in his final investigation and explanation of
the ultimate fact at the river's head all the
knowledge he has gathered on the way, and to
use nothing more. He does not begin with
what Christ was, in the sense of beginning with
the written record of His words and works, and
argue to what His effects upon man ought to
be : he begins with Christ's manifested effects
upon man and argues from them to what Christ
must have been. These effects, we have said,
consist in a God-consciousness deepening toward completion, and mediated now, though at
first it was of course Christ's direct gift, through
the Christian community or the Church—Christ,

therefore (putting the matter the other way round or down), was One in whom the God-consciousness was perfect, who communicated His own God-consciousness to the Church He set up, and who through that Church communicates His own God-consciousness to men to-day. It must be remembered, however, that this rather bare formula contained a great deal; for Schleiermacher held fast and firm to the absolute sinlessness of Christ, and maintained that not even in intellectual conceptions did He originate or adopt any mistake. If we enquire next as to the how and whence of Christ Himself —how and why it came to pass that He, with His perfect God-consciousness, appeared when He did upon history's field—Schleiermacher's reply is that the thing was miraculous in a sense, miraculous in that it certainly involved a new initiative on the part of God, but that at the same time, inasmuch as Christ simply fulfilled and embodied what man had been intended to fulfil and embody, His sinless nature was only the working out of the forces which had been set into operation by God's first creative act and which had been arrested by man's failure and fault. Of course it is easy to criticise this position for inconsistency, for concessions which, while not yielding enough to satisfy Christianity's foes, yield too much for the comfort of its friends; but that it was a Christ of special divine greatness and power, a Christ who brought extra-human influences to bear upon the spiritual problem of man, a Christ consequently to whom all honour and glory might and should be ascribed, whom in the end Schleiermacher possessed for himself and left to us, there can be no manner of doubt.[1] For one sufficient proof, we may take these resounding words : " When, forsaken in the thought of being silenced for ever, without seeing any outward institution for fellowship among His own actually set up, when in the face of the solemn splendour of the old corrupt system that had so mightily resisted Him, when surrounded by all that could inspire awe and demand subjection, by all that, from childhood, He had been taught to honour, sustained by nothing but that feeling " (the consciousness of the singularity of His knowledge of God and of His existence in God) " He uttered without delay that Yea, the greatest word mortal ever spake, it was the most glorious apotheosis, and no divinity can be more certain than that which He Himself proclaimed." Naturally enough, having regard to his starting-point and his deliberately-adopted method, Schleiermacher sat loosely to some of the articles of the customary creeds; and yet it was not so

---

[1] " Aber als Er verlassen, im Begriff auf immer zu verstummen, ohne irgend eine Anstalt zur Gemeinschaft unter den Seinigen wirklich errichtet zu sehen, gegenüber der feierlichen Pracht der alten verderbten Religion, die stark und mächtig erschien, umgeben mit allem was Ehrfurcht einflöszte und Unterwerfung heischen kann, mit allem, was Er selbst zu ehren von Kindheit an war gelehrt worden, Er allein, von nichts als diesem Gefühl unterstüzt, und Er ohne zu warten jenes Ja ansprach, das gröszte Wort was je ein Sterblicher gesagt hat : so war dies die herrlichste Apotheose, und keine Gottheit kann gewisser sein als die, welche so sich selbst setzt " (*Reden über die Religion*, Ed. Pünjer, pp. 284, 285. The rendering in the text is from Oman's translation).

much to the spiritual truths and ideas these
articles were intended to enshrine as to the
expression of them—and not even to the expression of them so much as to the forcing of the
expression upon all and sundry as the only way
of affirming eternal verities—that he took exception.   He held to a doctrine of the Trinity, since
apart from the oneness of God and Christ the
experience of the Church cannot be explained;
but he could not attach supreme value to the
statements of the Trinitarian doctrine as given
in the usual formulæ : words about " eternal
distinctions " did not fetch or find him; and he
could only let them pass by unheeded, because
the religious consciousness neither called for
them nor welcomed them as things hitherto
unknowingly awaited when they appeared.
Miracles or what men deem such, may happen;
but each event may be examined on its merits;
and in any case, the miracles of Jesus must not
be regarded as magical acts, but as the effluence
of what was in Jesus Himself, natural as coming
from Him, and in so far as they were extraordinary, extraordinary only because He Himself
was so.   But it is not necessary to carry the
description further.   If we fix in our memories
these outstanding ideas—that religion consists in
dependence upon God—that Christ lived and
moved and had His being in that sense of dependence at its highest, possessed the full God-
consciousness without let or hindrance or any
such thing—that He was accordingly supernatural
in a very real fashion, though from another point
of view the crown of natural development too—

and that He communicates to His disciples, as
the ages pass on, His own unalloyed God-consciousness through the mediation of the Church,
so redeeming men into that complete self-hood
which loses itself and finds itself again in God—
we shall possess the salient points of Schleiermacher's epoch-making scheme.

An epoch-making scheme it certainly was.
An entirely fresh beginning in theological thinking
it certainly signalised. And perhaps the first
thing that strikes one in connection with Schleiermacher's method, and with the system he worked
out by its means, is the thorough divorce between
philosophy and theology which Schleiermacher
was prepared to concede—or, one should rather
put it, on which he was determined to insist.
For his starting-point, as we have seen, he went
right away from any general view of the universe
which might on scientific or philosophical grounds
be entertained, not seeking to relate religious
truth with truth as other departments of investigation yielded it, but planting himself upon the
feeling of dependence as upon a rock which
heaved itself up from the whole surrounding
seas of fact, and which, when religion was in
question, was to be taken as the centre of the
world. He did not care or try to be rational in
the sense of beginning with facts of sensible
knowledge and experience, or with theories
which could account for such facts—with the
material universe or with philosophical doctrines
of its origin and process—and then, by reasoning
onward and upward, inference after inference
being drawn and becoming premiss in its turn,

syllogism topping syllogism till the edifice was complete, reaching at last to God and God's relations with that world whence the mind had set out on its lofty journeyings; but, forsaking all such unifying endeavours, he built his theological system on a primary inward fact alone. There is not involved in this, however, any contradiction of what was formerly said about the systematic character of the German mind. Once Schleiermacher's basis in feeling was found, the whole business of theological construction was systematic enough, indeed rational through and through in a very real sense: *only* what was given in feeling or deducible from its presence, but *all* so given or deducible, was to find a place; so that although Schleiermacher does not fasten philosophy and theology together, or draw out the second telescope-wise from the first, his theology is, *within itself,* a compact whole with all its parts mutually dependent and framed together; and his readings of Christian doctrine radiate, so to say, from one common point as wheel-spokes radiate from a common centre, being inter-related at least through their common relation to that which supports them all. But he abandons philosophy, in the sense of a world-view, when theology begins, and, bidding it go about its business, fixes himself firmly upon his own.

It may be well to say at this point, with a view to what is to come later on (if a brief *excursus* may be allowed), that such a divorce as that which Schleiermacher makes between philosophy and theology will be found largely characteristic of German theological thinking on what may be called Liberal Orthodox lines from the beginning of our survey to the end.[1] Of theological thought which seeks to *reconcile* philosophy and theology, to make the latter a department or extension of the former, Germany does indeed present examples enough; but they are not, for the most part, within the Liberal Orthodox bounds, and find their place as a general rule within the Hegelian or the Neo-Hegelian or the derived schools. Two or three of the earlier disciples of Hegel may, it is true, be justly called Liberal Orthodox as well as Hegelian; but Hegelian theology passed swiftly into the destructive phase.[2] And to what was previously said concerning the difference between the British and the German minds, this other point may now be added—that, in contrast with the divorce between philosophy and theology which the German Liberal Orthodox school has as a rule maintained, it is at a reconciliation between philosophy and theology, at the lowest between science and theology, between religious and general ideas, that British Liberal Orthodoxy has usually aimed. Antecedently, perhaps, this is just the opposite of what we might have looked for. It might seem most likely that the German passion for system would mean a desire to fit all the pieces of thought into one homo-

---

[1] It is worth remarking that Schleiermacher had for a contemporary the designer of one of the completest philosophical theologies ever produced—Baader. And it was produced, somewhat strangely, by a member of the Roman Catholic Church.

[2] See below, pp. 154, 155.

geneous mosaic, and that to such a passion any fissure running up the middle and making two pictures instead of one would, however finished and well-fitting as to its various elements each picture showed in itself, be an irritating ugliness to be got rid of with all speed; while on the other hand the British method of dealing with single and isolated doctrines would appear to be more compatible with, indeed to lead to, a blindness toward philosophy's claims and toward the relations between special and general ideas. But a possible explanation may in each instance be found. In Germany, indeed, the influence of Kant, the suspicion which by his close analysis of reason's powers he had cast upon philosophy's ability for the loftiest flights, for any flight at any rate that should carry it to such ideas as Christian theology must deal in if it is to have any *raison d'être* at all, is explanation enough. Not even Kant's restoration to the " practical reason " of some of the strength he had compelled the " pure reason " to give up could, for any one who desired to save the Christian religion, be adequate compensation; and yet Kant's translation of his base from the " pure " to the " practical " reason when it suited him, gave a clue. Such extra-rational ideas as could be snatched at as they floated in the void, and safely brought down to earth, under cover of the permission which " practical reason " had received—limited as these ideas were to those of a merely " moral " make and flavour—were indeed far from affording material for a religious system deserving of the Christian name. But the obvious procedure, for

those desiring such a system and unable to free
themselves from the Kantian grip, was to quit
any hope of climbing, from a ladder grounded
upon the observable phenomena of the world, to
a point whence Christianity should be seen as
coming within the limits of the view; then,
accepting Kant's permission to take up a position
outside the " pure reason," as his prohibition
against expecting too much from " pure reason "
had been accepted before, but making that permission cover more than Kant himself had
intended, to move to a platform wherefrom the
Christian view could be taken in; and then—returning upon Kant's method after Kant's particular use and application of it had been exceeded
—to become systematic again, and to adopt and
justify the Christian ideas, as Kant had adopted
and justified his " moral " ideas, on the ground
that they had now come legitimately within
range of sight. The passion for system, while
it could not ward off the blow aimed at it in the
very name of system by the Kantian scheme,
recovered itself as soon as it was able and,
though bearing the mark of the struggle, went
on its way once more; and it is in the Kantian
touch which had been laid upon it that the
explanation of its lameness lies. So far as
Liberal Orthodoxy was concerned, Christian
thought had to become temporarily unsystematic
—at least had to accept, and just a little widen,
the gap across thought's expanse which Kant
had left—in order that it might afterwards become
both Christian and systematic again. As for
Britain, it may suffice to say that the very

I

absence of the systematic passion—the very fact
that thought habitually deals with single
doctrines, their fates and fortunes, alone—would
almost necessarily cause British theological
thought to take the line of reconciliation between
theological and other ideas. For to say that
thought deals with single and separate doctrines
alone is really to say that thought takes the line
of least resistance, rouses itself only when it
must, and, beset somewhat by sluggishness,
betakes itself to its task only under the whip
and spur; and it is only through an assault
delivered by thoughts ranked under some other
banner that the application of whip and spur
can come. The sole business of such a theological method as that indicated, accordingly, is
to save the threatened doctrine from the *immediate* danger, or, if full salvation be impossible, to
make what terms of compromise are possible
between the doctrine and its foe. It will be a
matter of agreeing with one's adversary while
one is in the way with him. The system-maker
has the standard of wholeness, of proportion—
the standard supplied by his central idea and
its permissions or requirements—to work to;
and though it may be under consciousness of
impending or even of actual attack that the
construction of his system is begun, it is the
health and soundness of the system, taken as an
organic whole, that will be his primary test.
The defender of isolated doctrines has only the
satisfaction of the momentary situation—his
one doctrine against a doctrine hostile to it—
before his eyes; and it is reconciliation, adjust-

ment, compromise on that one point, that he naturally enough turns himself to achieve. How much such a reconciliation, affecting only one point at a time in the relations between theology and philosophy or theology and science, and made without survey of the entire boundaries on which they meet—how much it may be worth, and to what extent it can be a genuine and permanent reconciliation at all, is of course another question. But at any rate it is to such isolated reconciliations that the method of dealing with isolated and special doctrines naturally leads. So, perhaps, the difference between the British and the German methods, and the paradox apparently involved in it, may be explained. And one has to add to it all that a combination of the two—of the method of " system " and the method of " reconciliation " —is perhaps the method whereby a satisfactory reconstruction of Christian theology will in the end be produced; for only through such a combination of methods can we hope for that perfect unity of all our thinking wherein alone mental content consists. But, however all these things may be, we have to note—bringing our *excursus* back to the point whence it set out— that we find in Schleiermacher that divorce between philosophy and theology which was through all the succeeding years to be so marked a feature of German religious thought.

As against the rationalist attack, Schleiermacher's system must doubtless be judged an adequate defence, or even a successful counter-attack. While accepting the restrictions under

which strict reason was now said to lie. and
abandoning any attempt to construct theology
upward from purely speculative foundations, it
nevertheless avoided the apparently inevitable
consequences (as rationalism's hasty and eager
verdict declared them) by making an entirely
new route to the most essential articles cf the
Christian faith, the route's starting-point lying
in a land over which rationalism's writs did not
run. Christian faith, if it could no longer be
buttressed against the east winds blowing upon
it as it occupied its old standing-ground, could
be removed into warmer and more sheltered
quarters for safety; and this was done. It is
quite true that Schleiermacher's method resulted, as we have seen, in the lighter holding of
certain doctrines which had been rigidly defined
before, in some blurring of their outlines, in a
transference of emphasis from the validity of
the words embodying them to the validity of
their inner content; and it is quite true that
under the conditions which have dominated
Liberal Orthodoxy's progress throughout (the
reading of Christian discipleship's constitutive
act as being the acceptance of certain ideas)
this stirring of crystallised doctrinal formulæ
might easily bring about combinations and dis-
integrations not anticipated at first. Nevertheless, so far as Schleiermacher himself is concerned,
his title to a place upon Liberal Orthodoxy's
roll cannot be questioned; for it was above all
things the supernatural Christ (and herein surely
lies the final test) that he sought to preserve. It
is at its Christology that any theological system

reaches the supreme decisive judgment-bar; and at the Christological judgment-bar Schleiermacher stands erect before the most searching eye. From his starting-point in feeling, and in the work which through the influence of His Church Christ has done to make feeling what it ought to be, he finds himself carried to a Christ who must have been in the main, after legitimate criticism has done its best and worst upon each recorded incident and word, as our written Scriptures portray Him. The " archetypal Christ " whom the Christian consciousness postulates must have had an actual existence in time, Schleiermacher declares. Whether a grip upon the historical Christ, stretched out upon Him from this direction and in this way, was sufficiently strong to detain Him when criticism sought by new methods to tear Him away, is a question which subsequent developments were to push to the front. Schleiermacher certainly thought the grip was safe. Some of his words of laud and worship toward this Christ we have already heard. He has passionate jealousy for the honour and glory of his Lord. Even against the idea that the discourses set down in the Fourth Gospel have been to the smallest extent " edited " by the writer—an idea which, with whatever qualifications, all except the most conservatively orthodox accept to-day—he protests with warmth.[1] He stands for the supernatural Christ; " Liberal Orthodox " he may be called with right; nor

---

[1] *Reden über die Religion* (ed. Pünjer), p. 297. Oman's translation, p. 262.

need the slightest faltering of emphasis come in upon the second word.

For the rest, however, and from the general standpoint whence in this book we are taking our survey, one has to sum up thus. Schleiermacher's system does indeed embody an effort to escape from the conception of Christianity as a system of ideas supernaturally guaranteed, but an effort which fails in the end. In his affirmation of a developed God-consciousness, of a transformed feeling toward the divine, mediated from Christ through His Church to the Christian of to-day, Schleiermacher is undoubtedly striving after the conception of a living influence exerted still upon men, and is drawing back from the notion that to assent to certain facts *about* Christ secures the good that Christ has to bestow. This is, indeed, Schleiermacher's permanent contribution to theology—this reminder that it is not to the mind exclusively, or even chiefly, that Christianity appeals, that Christianity is something more than an intellectual reading of the universe and its origin and its destiny, and that it is in other regions of personality than the brain that man's relations to the Eternal are settled for evil or for good. Schleiermacher did more for Christian thought by his flank movement in answer to rationalism's challenge than he could ever have done by a frontal resistance, however bravely carried through. And yet, his system came back, as it were in spite of itself, in spite certainly of his inmost impulse in framing it, to an acceptance of ideas about Christ after all. A feeling of dependence is produced, by Christ's influence acting through the Christian community, within those who stand ringed round by that community's borders. But what can the communication of a *feeling* be but the consequence, the emotional consequence, resulting from the communication of an *idea?* For although it is possible to have an idea without having the feeling to which it ought to give rise—the arrested process is indeed common enough—it is not possible to have the feeling without the causal idea. What we have, therefore, is really the man of to-day receiving an *idea* from the Christian community to which he belongs—admittedly an idea fitted to bring about a certain emotional consequence, and all the more fitted to do so because the man of to-day sees that the idea has brought the consequence about in the Christian community while the ages have passed on, but an *idea* all the same. What is this idea? Clearly, it must be an idea running back into the personality of Christ Himself, else the chain of mediation from Christ through the Church to the man of to-day is destroyed. Let us, however, withholding the reply for a moment, carry the thing a little further back. In the Christian community, the Church, there originally arose, according to the theory, the true feeling of dependence under the spell of Christ Himself. But this feeling, in its turn, must have been the emotional side, the emotional consequence, of an idea—and, once again, of an idea running back into the personality of Christ. What, then, was *this* idea? Not merely that dependence upon God *ought* to be perfect; for not by this would the given condition—that the idea must run back into the personality of Christ—be fulfilled. Back into Christ's *teaching*, indeed, it might run, but not into His *personality*. It must be something more. Evidently, then, the idea that in Christ perfect dependence was both advocated *and* exemplified; so that at the topmost point of the series Christ stands as both proclaiming and exemplifying perfect dependence upon God; next, the idea that He does both these things becomes in the Church the source of a dependence kindred with His own, in a very real sense the offspring of His own; and finally, since the Church gives out what it receives, the idea that He does both these things passes on from the Church to the Christian of to-day to become the source of a kindred dependence there. But if this reading be correct, the acceptance of a truth *about* Christ is the formative influence, the constitutive act, of Christian discipleship still. The fact that it is in feeling, not in the mind, that the final effect is wrought does not alter the other fact that out of the acceptance of an idea the final effect is supposed to spring. True, upon the individual Christian of to-day the idea and the feeling may come together, so that he may not pause, or may not be able, to disentangle within himself the two several movements of response to the Church's call; but since it was the feeling *as dependent upon the idea* that the Church received, so it is the feeling *as dependent upon the idea* that the Church hands on; and if the individual Christian of to-day comes to self-analysis, it is upon acceptance of an idea *about* Christ—in short, upon acceptance of the idea that Christ proclaimed and exemplified an idea—that he will find himself standing at last. There is after all no such direct life-dynamic from Christ to man as Schleiermacher, when he first carried us away from the speculative reason's chilly chambers to feeling's warmer rooms, seemed bent upon discovering. Taking the matter in its long and large range, it comes to this—that though when we are making a theology something may be believed because something has been felt, the historic *rationale* of Christianity is rather that something has been felt because something was believed. We shall note a little later on how the weakness inherent in this—in the fact that though Schleiermacher's system did not start, in his construction of it, from acceptance of an idea about Christ, it nevertheless did cause the Church's Christian experience, and therefore the individual's practical use of Christianity, when he seeks an impulse to such use before making it or a justification for such use after making it, to depend upon such an acceptance after all (for the *ultimate* to which we come in the explanation of a Christian experience must necessarily be the *primary* in the making of it)—how the weakness inherent in this was displayed, how it exposed the system to attack, and how in consequence Liberal Orthodoxy was compelled at length to take fresh ground once more. But that is for presently. Just now, the essential point is that Liberal Orthodoxy in Schleiermacher failed to free itself, notwithstanding that the yearning for freedom was manifestly felt and that a movement which had some promise of freedom was made, from the error of taking the constitutive act in man's right relationship to Christ as the acceptance of an idea *about* Christ, however disguised, or however drowned for the acceptor's own consciousness under the flood of its spiritual consequences, the act of acceptance may be.

CHAPTER V

THE REVIVAL (*continued*) : BRITAIN AND AMERICA

FROM Germany we turn homewards to our own land, where in the shape of Cambridge Platonism Liberal Orthodoxy had made its earliest, its preliminary appearance, to see how there Liberal Orthodoxy's renewed life began.

We noticed, as we surveyed the " interval," that the events of the eighteenth century in England prepared the way for Liberal Orthodoxy's reappearance there in two somewhat different forms, the one consisting chiefly in a freer treatment of the Bible (of course with certain consequences therein involved, consequences which as it were thrust themselves in once the door was set ajar), and the other, while adopting this freer treatment, passing on from this to formulate richer and warmer views as to the relations between God and man. The first form, we also saw, resulted from the pressure of the problems as to Biblical inspiration, as to the fulness and exactness of Biblical accuracy on other than capital spiritual matters, which the deistic controversy had left behind it; while the second form came largely by way of reaction from the coldness and dryness of the very apologetic wherewith the deistic attack had been met. It is with a consideration of the first form that this chapter may start.

" The early Oriel school " is the title under which the promoters of this order of Liberal Orthodoxy are usually grouped.[1] It does not, however, cover all the stars which shine within this constellation of religious liberalism; for Thirlwall and Milman had no connection with Oriel at all. Milman, though belonging to the same University, was a Fellow of Brasenose; and Thirlwall was a Cambridge man. But Whately (1787–1863), Hampden (1793–1868), and Arnold (1795–1842), were thrown together at the Oxford College; and in the new movement these men played a principal part. In any case, the accuracy of the conventional title matters little. It is the spirit of the movement, its method, its aim, with which we are concerned. And these are briefly but truly summed up by saying that the movement was designed to substitute attention to the large ideas of Scripture for attention

[1] The " Noetic school," or the " Noetics " is another designation. For the school in general consult the biographies of its various members; the relevant pages in J. Hunt's *Religious Thought in England in the Nineteenth Century* ; and Lecture 2 in Tulloch's *Movements of Religious Thought in Britain during the Nineteenth Century*. The *later* Oriel school is of course the Tractarian school wherein John Henry Newman was one of the chief figures. Newman became Fellow at Oriel in 1822 and Tutor in 1826, and necessarily came into contact with Whately, to whom he acknowledges a great debt. But Newman was the far from the position he subsequently reached. It is cu ious, having regard to the places which accuser and accused occupy in history, to learn that in 1827 Whately charged Newman with Arianising ! (See *Apologia*, ed. 1889, pp. 11–16.)

to its mere words, to induce readers to receive meanings *from* Scripture instead of forcing conventional meanings *into* it, to show the necessity of taking the historical setting and context into one's reckoning when interpreting the sacred Book, and, generally, to make the study of the Bible a contact of the modern mind with the minds which once lay behind what is written rather than a mere gathering up of detached letters, words, and texts. Necessarily, the implications of all this could only be discerned so far as the condition of knowledge and the amount of available information permitted at the time; so that for the Oriel men and their associates what has just been set down did not mean what it means for those who put forward a similar programme to-day. But, if this be understood, the indicated programme may be taken as that by which the Oriel men and their associates endeavoured to work.

The outstanding facts in the story are the publication of Whately's *Essays on Some of the Peculiarities of the Christian Religion* in 1825, and of his *Essays on Some of the Difficulties in the Writings of St. Paul* in 1828; the delivery of Hampden's Bampton Lectures on *The Scholastic Philosophy considered in its Relation to Christian Theology* in 1832; the appearance in 1825 (to pass away for a moment from the Oriel men properly so termed) of a translation by Thirlwall of Schleiermacher's *Essay on St. Luke*, with an introduction of Thirlwall's own; and the appearance in 1829 of Milman's *History of the Jews*.[1]

[1] Thirlwall, 1797–1875; Milman, 1791–1868.

In this enumeration Arnold has found no place; but Arnold's contribution, though no less valuable than that of the rest, was spread over a longer period, and consists not of one or two particular books, but of sermons and essays preached or written during his incumbency at Laleham and his headmastership of Rugby school. Indeed, while the other Oriel men did their work for religious liberalism as it were at one discharge and then retired—though their works sometimes followed them in unpleasant fashion, as when Hampden had to endure fierce attack on his appointment as Regius Professor of Divinity in 1838, and again on his elevation to the see of Hereford in 1847—Arnold went on with gentler but no less effective out-pouring of his ideas up to his death. It is as a Broad Churchman rather than as an innovator in doctrine that he is most widely known; naturally enough, since the Church question is much more living to-day than the more strictly theological matters on which he wrote, and the religious novelties of his time have become commonplaces now. Yet when one reckons up his various gifts, such as his *Sermons on the Interpretation of Prophecy*, his *Essay on the Right Interpretation and Understanding of the Scriptures*, and all the rest of the similar statements and arguments lying in such profusion upon the pages which enshrine his works, one sees the total grow large. For that matter, Arnold accomplished at least as much, reckoning quantity alone, for the common cause by his long-sustained pressure—put forth, as it was, more for the satisfaction and delivery of his own soul than for any other reason, and without any faintest trace of the slightly rough fighting spirit which we cannot but detect elsewhere—as was accomplished by the explosive bombs of his allies. And when we weigh the permanent effect of Arnold's work against the permanent effect of the work of the others, it is undoubtedly Arnold's scale that dips down.

As to the substance of these writers' witness, a glance over the works mentioned above will suffice to show any reader who cares to take it that the previously-given account of the " Oriel " programme is correct. In theology, it was simply for a freer interpretation of Scripture—and not for some *specific* interpretation which could only be reached under freer treatment, but rather for the principle that *interpretation should be free*— that these thinkers fought. That was their one contention, to which all other contentions were consequential and subsidiary. The Bible must not be made a fetish. It was not true that every word had equal worth. An interpretation might need revising, even though—or because—it had hoary years upon its head. In brief, it was verbal or plenary inspiration against which the school chiefly launched its darts. Of course, in the assertion of the school's general principle certain religious and theological ideas, holding their place only in virtue of Biblical views which it was now proposed to discard, came under review, and, since the Biblical view which had hitherto stood sponsor for them had lost its status, had themselves to accept notice and go. But these expulsions were made rather for purposes of illustration than for any other; and moreover, modification, rather than expulsion, would in most instances be the truly descriptive word. We find Whately dealing plangent blows against the usage of isolated verses as proof-texts, denying that passages which had been taken as teaching geology and astronomy were designed to do so, and protesting against reading St. Paul as if the apostle had kept a carefully catalogued and pigeon-holed set of technical terms which always bore for him, and must always bear for us, precisely the same sense. We find Hampden declaring that the aim of Scripture is practical rather than doctrinal, distinguishing between what the Bible really said and what scholasticism, obsessed by misunderstandings of the Bible's purpose and caught in the involutions of its own logic, had supposed or made it to say. We find Arnold taking a very similar line, and taking it with a sweet and gracious persuasiveness Hampden could not boast, emphasising the idea that it is the spiritual truth behind the words which must always be sought for; that while the words are necessarily and naturally the product of the time in which they were written, the spiritual truth is *of* no special time, and consequently *for* all time; that by making your handling of the Bible nothing more than a superstitious ceremony you may lose the Bible's best response to your appeal. We find Thirlwall, in that introduction to Schleiermacher's book which he wrote when he was still a layman, taking the position that the dogma of verbal inspiration must go, and that its going would be gain rather than loss. We find Milman, within whom something like the modern historical spirit was struggling to power, protesting against any supposed obligation to accept as literal fact all the Old Testament narratives—such, for instance, as those of the arrest of the sun and moon at Joshua's word or of the destruction of Sennacherib's host—asserting that at the far-back stage of moral development they occupied the Old Testament characters could not but be imperfect in moral instinct and moral knowledge, and generally treating the history of the Israelites as the history of any other ancient people would be treated. Of course Milman, being a historian, had another purpose besides that of impugning the traditional inspiration theories : indeed, he only did this last in order that his main objects, the telling of his historic tale as he conceived it, might be the more efficiently achieved; but as to the direction of his influence on theology, and as to the precise point at which that influence touched religious thought, he exactly matches the rest. But there is no need to labour the matter. Reference to the books of these men will show at once that this *was* their work—to assail the narrow and mechanical views of the Bible which had been in the ascendant for so long. What such a work is worth was their legacy to the world : under the limitations of such a work they were bound; and neither the worth nor the limitations need be denied. The worth of it will certainly not be questioned by a generation which can quietly assume what they, in the face of such obloquy and scorn, bravely declared.

K

As for its limitations, well, one confesses that as one watches members of the school at their labours, one gets no impression of large construction, finds the results to be negative rather than positive, though by no means exclusively so, and is not conscious of any very warm spiritual currents, set towards the latitudes where deeper conceptions of God and man waited for discovery, running through the labourers' souls as they toil. To this last statement, however, Arnold—one of the passionately aspiring saints of the world—is to a great extent an exception : the heat of moral passion which dwelt in him made many of his utterances sound as though it must be upon some conception of a profound ultimate unity between God's nature and man's that they were founded, as indeed it was out of an experience of such unity, an experience already real and longing to intensify itself, that they actually came; and in virtue of this he may be said to form a sort of bridge between the Oriel school and that other Liberal Orthodox school to which we shall in a moment turn. But on the whole, one sees in these men concentration upon one of the outer courts of religious thought rather than architectonic strength lavished upon and producing large conceptions of the central temple; and one hears in their working the hammer-blows of those who overthrow rather than the sound of the finer instruments which shape and plane and fit together. For touches of poetry or mysticism in them one looks mostly in vain. They served their day and generation well, and gave it one of the gifts it greatly required. But a fair reckoning has to say—not by way of depreciation, but as a mere matter of fact, and as fixing their place in the story of English theological growth—that they gave only the one.

We turn to the other school of thought which took part in the revival of Liberal Orthodoxy in Great Britain, the school whose activities marked a reaction against that hardness and dryness which had for long characterised religious thought, and which was only modified, not cured, even by the method of the Oriel men. By way of brief preliminary description, it may be said that the members of this other school abandoned, as did the members of the first, the mechanical usage of the Scriptures prevalent before, finding the value of the Bible in its eternal truths rather than in its words, and holding accordingly that an uncompromising literalism in reading and interpretation might easily lead astray; but also that they went further than this, feeling that they would not have reached the ultimate platform of truth even when they had built up such a system of ideas as a use of the Bible in the newer light might enable them to construct, but only when they had become conscious of a real harmony between truth and their own inmost selves. To put it another way, they held that God's nature and God's activities, as these were suggested by any proffered truth, must commend themselves to the spiritual constitution of man. To the Oriel doctrine that inspiration did *not* reside in mere words, but in the truth behind them, they gave a fuller and more positive content, declaring that it *did* reside in, and was

tested by, the self-commendation of the God
hidden within the truth to the divine hidden in
man.   It will spring at once to the reader's mind
that we are thus taken back to something very
like the position of the Cambridge Platonists of
a century and more before.   How far this is
true—and yet how far it falls short of the truth—
we shall be better able to understand when we
have briefly surveyed the facts to which we now
proceed.

The name of Coleridge (1772–1834) claims first
mention in the telling of the tale.   Much more
than mention of his name there cannot be; and
one has to keep back many things that are worth
saying, and that one would wish to say when
speaking of an intellect so acute and a spirit so
rare.   For indeed the scantiness of the space
one can afford him almost seems to imply pro-
fanation, and one must, while bowing to necessities, at least express one's regret.   Coleridge
was of course one of the outstanding examples,
in spheres quite outside religion, of that revolt
against eighteenth century aridness which the
early nineteenth century inaugurated, and which
in literature and in politics, as well as in other
things, came so quickly to its high tide; but it
is with Coleridge in respect of his influence on
religion alone that we have to do.   We need
not here trouble ourselves, fortunately, with a
minute examination of his general philosophical
ideas, nor with any reconciliation of the many
inconsistencies, some real and some imaginary,
in which he has been detected, nor with the
charges of pantheism which have been levelled

against him by some who wish to enlist so desirable a recruit on the anti-Christian side. Coleridge was unsystematic in his thinking, and certainly did not, when he wrote or uttered a sentence, look carefully north, south, east, and west, to see what echoes, along the curiously-configurated hills and valleys of the countries there, his words might chance to raise. But as to his essential Christianity, and his essentially orthodox Christianity, no one who examines his work without preconceived ideas can for a moment entertain any doubt. All we need do for our present purpose is to give some indications—the justification of which may be found chiefly in *Aids to Reflection*, published in 1825—as to Coleridge's line. It should be clearly stated, however—lest the number and variety of the points at which Coleridge touches religious thought should cause it to be forgotten, and so obscure the justice of placing him under the general description of the school as previously given—that Coleridge's dealing with Christian ideas was always performed as against, and as an alternative to, a dealing with them and a rendering of them based upon the traditional inspirational views; and, upon whatever religious topic he might tarry a short time or a long, it was always of this background that he was conscious. He had spent fourteen months in Germany, had heard Eichhorn lecture, had come home with the German influence as strong upon him as any influence ever could be upon so original and independent a mind; moreover, the German influence would act, not in opposition to, but in reinforcement of, his native tendencies; and

though the *Confessions of an Inquiring Spirit,*
wherein Coleridge's ideas on Biblical criticism
are given to us, did not appear till 1840, after
its author's death, the futility, and worse, of the
antiquated superstitious veneration of the Bible
had been present to Coleridge throughout. Not
that way could there be reached any permanent
establishment of Christianity for the mind of
man. But a more excellent way might be found;
and it was upon an exposition of the more as
against the less excellent way that Coleridge was
bent. The credentials of Revelation lay in the
fact that man found within himself, elsewhere
than in the mind, something which affirmed the
Revelation as true, and as true in the sense of
enabling him to be true to himself while, and by,
accepting the truth of God; and it was therefore
into the depths of his own personality, not to a
scroll of texts hung out before the face of the
world, that a man must look if he would know
how true Revelation is. By way of illustration
Coleridge shows that the idea of sin becomes valid
only, but inevitably, when you admit the existence
of a spiritual consciousness and constitution to
which man can be true or false; that the idea of
redemption becomes valid only, but inevitably,
when you make that same admission and view redemption's process as re-adjusting man's spiritual
constitution both to its own proper original
condition and to its proper relations with the
spiritual Source of all; that the idea of the Trinity
(to pass to more difficult matters still) becomes
valid only, but inevitably, when you look at it
from the standpoint of an experienced redemp-

tion such as that just described.[1] Still it is *only*
by way of illustration that Coleridge deals with
these things, even though one has to add that
the illustrations are so many and so thoroughly
worked out that the unsystematic Coleridge
comes near to being a real system-maker after
all. These things, his dealing with these things,
illustrate, and are meant to illustrate, the
superiority of Coleridge's method over the one
he antagonises : they sharpen the contrast, and
go on sharpening it, till the bankruptcy of the
older method shows stark and bare against the
abounding wealth of the new; and the dominant
purpose is always thus to put the older method
to shame. Coleridge, in short, answers to the
description of the school as previously set down,
puts fire under the Oriel doctrine that inspiration
does not reside in the mere words of the Bible
but in the eternal truth behind, and makes it
glow till its real brightness and colour appear.

Mention of Coleridge's direct disciples will
come further on, when we are considering the
growth of the seed sown in the nineteenth century's early years. For the moment, we have
to leave Coleridge and England and, travelling
in thought northwards, speak briefly of a Scots-
man in whose mind ideas very similar to those
of Coleridge were moving. Thomas Erskine of
Linlathen (1788–1870)—not a clergyman nor a

---

[1] " On the doctrine of Redemption depends the *Faith,*
the *Duty,* of believing in the Divinity of our Lord. And
this again is the strongest ground for the reality of that
Idea, in which this alone can be received without breach of
the faith in the unity of the Godhead. But such is the
Idea of the Trinity."—*Aids to Reflection* (ed. Bohn), p. 120.

professional philosopher or theologian, but a
barrister and a country gentleman whose delight
it was to meditate on the most sacred themes—
working from his own point of view and out of
his own experience, set forth in various books,
beginning with *Remarks on the Internal Evidence
for the Truth of Revealed Religion* (1820), Coleridge's central idea that whatever is believed
must commend itself to humanity's consciousness and humanity's inner life, must " find "
humanity and give humanity the sense of being
" found," and that doctrines prove their truth
only when they prove themselves possessed of
this self-commending and " finding " power.
Like Coleridge, too, Erskine touched—at first,
like Coleridge, by way of illustration, afterwards
for the sake of more definite theological revisal
and its results—upon various established doctrines : with the lighting of his new lamp came
a new vision of many things, a new appreciation
of their outline and colour; and Erskine could
not but tell what he saw. In his case, indeed,
we can easily understand that he, living where
he did, should carry actual revisal and reconstruction further than Coleridge had carried it;
for the moment he had kindled the light of his
new fundamental idea, and thrown it round the
circle of Christian beliefs, he saw how unbeautiful,
under Scotland's rigid Calvinism, these had been
made and left, and how much fairer under the
new illuminating glory they could be made to
appear. Erskine's more elaborate theological
writings, however, will call for mention presently
under the " development " head. Development,

it should be observed, started sooner in the case
of this second type of British Liberal Orthodoxy
—as one would have expected from the richer
and warmer soil of thought into which its roots
were struck—than in the case of the first : the
men whom we saw working on the " Oriel " line,
from Whately to Milman, hold themselves pretty
much within identical limits of ground; whereas
in the other case—indeed within the bounds of
Erskine's own life and labour—we much more
quickly find a movement, an unfolding, a larger
application of initial ideas. And as it is only
with beginnings, with the taking up of the initial
position, that this chapter deals, our time-limit
falls earlier in the present instance than in that
of the " Oriel " men, cutting in fact across the
record of Erskine himself. Beyond Erskine's
second book, the *Essay on Faith* (1822), we need
not now pass. Putting this alongside the book
previously named, and turning the pages of
both, we come again and again upon assertions
that no voice can be divine unless it awakens an
" Amen " in the human heart ; that mere authority
has no right to impose faith on man ; that the
case for Christianity cannot be exhaustively
tried by such processes as prevail in the courts
of human law—processes which seek to forge as
complete a logical chain as may be, and are
deemed satisfactory if a sufficiently large logical
probability can be shown ; that something always
leaps out from man to meet the in-coming truth
of God and that, if no such stirring takes place,
there has been no real divine approach. The
purpose of the *Remarks*, he informs us, is " to

analyse the component parts of the Christian
scheme of doctrine, with reference to its bearings
on the character of God and on the character of
man ; and to demonstrate that its facts not only
present an expression of all the moral qualities
which can be conceived to reside in the Divine
mind, but also contain all those objects which
have a natural tendency to excite and suggest
in the human mind that combination of moral
feelings which has been termed moral perfection." [1]
Elsewhere he says, " This, then, is the first
reasonable test of the truth of a religion—that
it should coincide with the *moral* constitution
of the human mind." [2]   It is all Coleridge over
again.   Not, of course, in any sense of plagiarism ;
for, as the dates given above show, Erskine's
books anticipated the publication of the *Aids to
Reflection ;* but Erskine and Coleridge had each
by his own independent route reached the banks
of the stream whose waters had this taste.   We
even find Erskine using Coleridge's illustration
of the doctrine of the Trinity to point his case.
The doctrine can be believed, because " the
doctrine of God's combined justice and mercy
in the redemption of sinners, and of His continued
spiritual watchfulness over the progress of truth
through the world, and in each particular heart,
could not have been communicated without it,
so as to have been distinctly and vividly apprehended."   So " it stands indissolubly united
with an act of divine holiness and compassion,
which radiates to the heart an appeal of tender-

[1] *Remarks on the Internal Evidence, etc.* (9th ed.), p. 16.
[2] *Ibid.*, p. 23.

ness most intelligible in its nature and object, and most constraining in its influence."[1] So did Erskine in the north, as Coleridge in the south—the former, indeed, a little in advance of the latter by the reckoning of time—throw over the appeal to a text-book whose minutest words were sacrosanct, and bid what claimed to be truth vindicate its title elsewhere.

Thus, from the two points we have indicated, did British Liberal Orthodoxy make its second start. Both the similarities and the dissimilarities between the two schools in which it was embodied stand out clearly enough. In both its manifestations Liberal Orthodoxy really based itself upon, and was practically constituted by, repudiation of a single idea, modification of a single doctrine—that of Scripture's mechanical or verbal or plenary inspiration, and of the necessity of such a mechanical acceptance of its statements as a Scripture inspired in that sense would obviously demand. But Coleridge and Erskine, as we have seen, went further; and the difference between these two thinkers and the men of the " Oriel " family lay here—that while the revolt from the traditional dogma was for the latter negative in the main, it was for the former a much more positive thing. The " Oriel " men broke the net-work of words which, under the old theory of inspiration, had been wound round the Christian mind, and of course moved more freely because of the rents they made : for Coleridge and Erskine the Bible, as they gazed upon it with the eyes of their

[1] *Remarks on the Internal Evidence, etc.* (9th ed.), pp. 95, 96.

enlightened understanding, became a transparent
screen behind which they discerned " eternal
ideas " moving to and fro and appealing to
something which, behind that other screen of
their own intellectual apprehension, moved out
in recognition and welcome. And if this be
understood, we are in a position to gauge that
relation, previously alluded to, between the
Coleridgean method and the method of the
Cambridge Platonists of earlier years. Certainly
a relation exists, and in Coleridge's case a conscious and deliberate one; for Coleridge expressly
affirms himself to be reproducing the ideas of
John Smith and Henry More. And for that
matter, one sees at once that for the older and
the newer thinkers alike man was as a mirror
reflecting the glance of God. But the theology
of the two later men goes beyond that of the
seventeenth century school : its underlying idea
was that of a moral and spiritual, rather than a
merely intellectual, correspondence between God
and man; and in fact, when we come to Coleridge
and Erskine, we have reached to that revival of
the " Greek " theology which we said, when we
were studying the earlier thinkers, was absent
in them but would be found in later up-risings
of the Platonising spirit in Liberal Orthodoxy's
career. God in His wholeness, and therefore
chiefly in His holiness, not merely God's *mind*
in man's *mind*—that was the note; with the
necessary consequent, that Christian truth was
at the same time an affirmation of this immanence
and a means of intensifying it still more. At
the time of which we are speaking, all this was

rather a spirit moving upon the face of the deep than a definitely-shaped idea; but the more definite shaping was soon to come, a little later on in the work of Erskine himself, still later in Maurice; and the second half of the century was to see the conception pushed to the full, perhaps indeed pushed somewhat too far. Here, in Coleridge and Erskine, we mark the place and time of its resurrection from the silence wherein it had lain so long.

So much for the two schools, and for the likeness and unlikeness between the two. If now, instead of comparing them with one another, we put them together and compare them both with the German method and movement at which in the previous chapter we looked, likeness and unlikeness again at once appear. Unlikeness—to take this first—in that the thinkers of our own country felt little or nothing of that impulse to a thoroughly systematic theology which drove Schleiermacher to his great task, and, as has been said, concentrated upon virtually one doctrine alone. Passing from Schleiermacher to Whately and his co-workers, or even to Coleridge and Erskine (although in the case of the two latter the impression is slightly toned down) we feel that we have passed to something smaller, to contracted walls, to eyes which penetrate and hands which stretch less far. Schleiermacher builds, while our own men touch up and repair. The British voices sound like half-sentences uttered in bated whispers beside Schleiermacher's organ tones. But that lies in the nature of the varying national moods and

methods, and need not detain us for more than
the above word. If the unlikeness between
Britain and Germany is so marked, the correspondence is marked as well. British Liberal
Orthodoxy at this period justifies, as we found
German Liberal Orthodoxy justify, the general
description previously given of Liberal Orthodoxy as a whole. It ran swiftly and readily in
its abandonment of whatever was to be abandoned, knew no hesitancies, was quick by large
concessions to secure itself in possession of what
remained. For, though it was but the one
traditional doctrine of Scripture inspiration from
which British Liberal Orthodoxy cut itself adrift,
that one doctrine stood so far in the position of
security for other doctrines that the act of
severance might almost seem to involve a general
farewell to them all : the cable wherewith
religious thought was fastened to other beliefs
was wound first of all, or was usually taken to
be so wound, round *this ;* so that to cut the
connection with *this,* expecting to make or pick
up some link with the other beliefs again, argued
a sort of careless courage as to winds and tides.
Of course the British thinkers recognised, as we
noted before, that abandonment of the traditional
inspiration theory involved *some* consequences
for other doctrines too; but they had an almost
gay conviction that essentials were safe. Why
then should they hold back? It was the time
when Liberal Orthodoxy, here as in Germany,
willingly made its surrenders in order that the
untouchable *minimum* might remain. Most of
all, this early British Liberal Orthodoxy is like

the early Liberal Orthodoxy of Germany in that
for both Christianity still remained a system of
ideas. How this holds good of Schleiermacher,
we saw. In the case of the " Oriel " men, the
accuracy of the statement is immediately clear.
The Christian ideas and doctrines were not to
be framed precisely as the first aspect of Biblical
words and phrases might suggest, but it was in
ideas, and in the acceptance of ideas, that the
essence of Christianity and of Christian discipleship lay after all. Such change of doctrine as
might under the new and looser handling of
Scripture come in could not hide the fact that
by assent to doctrine a man performed the
constitutive Christian act of his life, the act
which passed him into the Christian fold. As
for Liberal Orthodoxy of the other type, this
was indeed an instinctive effort—as Schleiermacher's basing of religion on feeling had been
an effort—to supplant intellectual assent to
truth by something else. But it was an effort
which, like Schleiermacher's own, failed. What
you ultimately came into contact with, when
you forsook the " plenary inspiration " ground
on which you formerly stood, was still *truth*,
just as truth had been the thing wherewith you
supposed yourself to be in contact there. You
had other and stronger reasons for concluding
that you were in touch with the revelation given
by God in Christ; but that was all. Of course
the knowledge of the truth was expected to bring
certain spiritual transforming consequences upon
you; and, while this expectation has always
characterised all true Christian men of every

school, it was to be expected that the main conceptions with which Coleridge and Erskine worked—their insistence on the " divine immanence " idea—would push it more forcefully to the front. Moreover, the assertion, the very heart and soul of their thinking as it was, that it was by a moral and spiritual element in man the revelation was recognised, and that recognition of the revelation reacted upon that moral and spiritual element in its turn, tended to disguise the fact that it *was* by the recognition and the consequent reflex action of " revelation," the result, in the way of spiritual transformation, was achieved. Yet when Erskine sets himself to expound the *rationale* of the process, he shows that this is the case. " The reasonableness of a religion," he declares, " seems to me to consist in there being a direct and natural connection between a believing of the doctrines which it inculcates, and a being formed by these to the character it recommends. If the belief of the doctrines has no tendency to train a disciple in a more exact and more willing discharge of its moral obligations, there is evidently a very strong probability against the truth of that religion." [1] With the latter part of the statement—indeed, with the statement as a whole—we need not quarrel. But, looking beneath its terms, and reading what it implies as to the fundamental process of Christian discipleship and the constitutive act of the Christian life, we find ourselves upon the old ground—that acceptance of truth is the decisive thing. The line of

[1] *Remarks on the Internal Evidence, etc.* (9th ed.), p. 59.

cause and effect runs from *believing* the doctrine
to *being formed* to the character it recommends.
In short, not even the second and richer type of
early Liberal Orthodoxy in our country, fruitful
as its suggestions were, reached to the conception
of a direct life-dynamic in Jesus Christ, or shook
itself free from the idea which has beset Liberal
Orthodoxy throughout, as indeed it has beset
nearly all Christian thinking from Reformation
days.

Far away from both Great Britain and Germany, Liberal Orthodoxy made an appearance
at which we must take at least a passing look—
and made it before either in Great Britain or in
Germany the movement had gathered strength.
The star of William Ellery Channing (1780–1842)
flamed out suddenly in the sky of American
religious thought; and it is not easy to say precisely what the causes of its rising were. We
know that rationalist tendencies made themselves
felt in the States when the eighteenth century
was dying; but there is no evidence that these
affected Channing to any considerable extent,
though of course he must have been aware of
their presence on the field, or that it was by
way of defence against them or compromise with
them that Channing's theological liberalism was
shaped. More probably it was by reaction against
the long Calvinistic controversy which had
wakened so many strident voices across the
continent that Channing became what he was.
The Calvinistic controversy itself—with its be-
wildering crowd of " Old School " men, " New

L

School " men, " modified New School " men,
" Edwardeans," " Hopkinsinians," and the rest
—need not trouble us here.[1] We need only note
that while it was the Presbyterian Churches
which were chiefly concerned in it, the slackening
of Calvinism's sternness affected other Churches
too; and the Congregationalists, to whom Channing at first belonged (he became minister of
Federal Street Church, Boston, in 1803), soon
had their own Arminian school. In America
Arminianism speedily led, as it had previously
led in England, to lowered views of the Divinity
of Christ—a definite severance between the
stricter and the more liberal Congregationalists
beginning about 1815, becoming more pronounced in 1819, and resulting in the establishment of a body which soon came to bear the
Unitarian name. Channing was on the liberal
side. It may appear strange, in face of these
facts, to label Channing as one of the " Liberal
Orthodox " : the first deduction suggested by
what has been said is that his liberalism had
gone much further than orthodoxy could ever
consent to go; and yet any fair scrutiny of
Channing's words and works soon fixes his right
to the name. For one thing, he was an Arian
rather than a Unitarian in our modern sense,
holding that Christ, though not eternally co-equal
with the Father in the Godhead, had been pre-
existent in heaven, had come down to earth for
the salvation of men, and had in some mysterious
way—though the usual doctrine of the Atonement

[1] The curious can read the tale in E. H. Gillett's *History
of Presbyterianism in America.*

was surrendered—secured for man the remission
of sin. The sinlessness, the miracles, the resurrection, of Jesus remained for him, as for the
most strictly orthodox, immovable certainties
of the Christian faith. But even Channing's
Arianism was an accident of the situation, at
any rate a subordinate feature in it, rather than
its essence or fulcrum. Channing's negations, in
fact, were picked up almost incidentally—because,
being the " opposites " already in evidence, they
offered themselves—as he sprang back from the
Calvinist point of view. His real spiritual affinities were with the second school of British Liberal
Orthodoxy spoken of above; and the necessity
and possibility of a response from the divine in
man to whatever appeal the divine without man
might make was the keynote of his thought.
One finds him using words which might well be
Coleridge's or Erskine's own. " A religion claiming to be from God can give no surer proof of
its falseness than contradiction of those previous
truths which God is teaching in our very natures."
" Reason must prescribe the tests or standards
to which a professed communication from God
should be referred; and among these none are
more important than that moral law which
belongs to the very essence and is the deepest
conviction of the rational nature." " God can
never contradict in His Word what He has
Himself written on the human heart." These
are samples which might be paralleled a hundred
times. Perhaps, if we care to mark a difference,
as well as a similarity, between Channing and
the British teachers, we may do so by saying—

with a reversion to the sentence set down just now—that it was the *possibility* rather than the *necessity* of a response from man's nature to God's on which Channing laid stress; a placing of emphasis, by the way, to which Erskine himself ultimately turned, as we shall see. What it means is that man's moral and spiritual greatness bulked largest in Channing's eyes. " It was," we are told, " while reading one day in the former (Hutcheson) some of the various passages in which he asserts man's capacity for disinterested affection and considers virtue as the sacrifice of private interests and the bearing of private evils for the public good, or as self-devotion to absolute universal good, that there suddenly burst upon his mind that view of the dignity of human nature which was ever after to ' uphold and cherish ' him, and thenceforth to be the ' fountain light of all his day, the master light of all his seeing.' " [1]   But in the main, he stood where Coleridge and Erskine stood—not that he possessed the philosophic reach and insight of the first or used the exact words of either, but that for him, as for them, the sure testimony of a divine revelation was the recognition by man, when God spoke, of an appeal coming " from like to like."   And remembering all these things—remembering above all how Channing's Christ, if not the Christ of the orthodox Trinity, was nevertheless a Christ supernatural and saving, and how in the admission

[1] *Memoir of William Ellery Channing*, by W. H. Channing, i. 62.

of this lies orthodoxy's final test—we must surely find that Channing has made out his title to be placed first in order of time, and not last in order of merit, on America's Liberal Orthodox roll.

CHAPTER VI

DEVELOPMENT : GERMANY AND OTHER EUROPEAN COUNTRIES

WE take up now the consideration of Liberal Orthodoxy's progress and change, in Germany and to some extent in other European lands, after its journey, from Schleiermacher's system as its starting-point, began. It will be remembered that the period immediately following upon Schleiermacher—the first of those two Liberal Orthodox periods at which we have to look— was described as presenting in Germany a succession of systems, each one, after the fashion of the German mind, complete in itself, though raised upon a foundation similar to that of the one before, and each one becoming somewhat more restrained in the surrenders it was ready to make. We shall discover, in other words, a growing conviction that in Schleiermacher's theological construction too much had been conceded—this conviction being to a great extent forced upon Liberal Orthodoxy's champions by attacks against which Schleiermacher's system provided no adequate defence; and we shall see, therefore, men who were in the main Schleiermacher's disciples building for themselves theological edifices strengthened, as they hoped and believed, at the weak spots, tightened up at the places where the winds and rains of attack were found to be beating in. To this section of the history we have now to turn.

It was from the Hegelian base—Hegel (1770–1831) was Schleiermacher's contemporary—that the new attacks just spoken of were made. And yet it had not been at attacking Christianity, but rather at establishing it, that the Hegelian philosophy had at the outset, and under the handling of its author, aimed : at any rate, it was an establishment of Christianity that Hegel supposed himself, even if only incidentally and as part of his general scheme, to have achieved. The wonderful system which this wonderful thinker built up is far too complicated for close description here.[1] All that need be said is that for Hegel the entire universe is the progressive unfolding of the Absolute Reason, which is the one reality; or, to put it another way, the universe is the Absolute Reason on its way to complete self-consciousness : all is thought : also, as the Infinite Mind comes to at least partial (in religion to complete) self-consciousness in the mind of man, the mind of man, in an apprehension of its own dialectical processes, comes into touch with the Absolute; or rather, such an apprehension actually *is* only the Absolute coming into touch

---

[1] See *The Secret of Hegel*, by J. Hutchison Stirling, for the profoundest study in English; or, if a briefer exposition be desired, the volume by Edward Caird in Blackwood's *Philosophical Classics*. The chapters on Hegel in Matheson's *Aids to the Study of German Theology* are worth careful reading, though Matheson interprets Hegel much more evangelically than the system warrants.

with, and returning upon, itself. Now all progress of thought is on this wise. The mind puts
forth, discovers, a truth; and for a time this
newly-born truth holds the field as it were by
its own right. Presently, however, the opposite
of this truth is in its turn discovered or put
forth; so that there is a clash of contending
" rights." Finally, the opposition is lost in a
higher truth reconciling the two erstwhile foes,
and combining them in a unity once more. This,
because it is the " dialectic " of the finite mind,
is the " dialectic " of the Infinite Mind as well;
and it is along this line that the eternal and
original Idea thinks itself toward perfect self-
consciousness. Moreover, while the finite mind
mirrors the Infinite, it is itself, in all its " dialectic," an actual part of that " dialectic " which is
the Infinite Mind's own; from which it follows
that every concept emerging in the process of
human thinking is an item in the process of the
eternal thought as well. It follows also from this,
so far as religion is concerned, that on the one
hand every religion which has appeared in the
history of mankind has been, at the time of
its appearance, a self-unfolding of the Absolute
and Infinite Reason *so far ;* while on the other
hand a claim on Christianity's behalf to be the
perfect religion can be easily enough made out.
For in the Christian conception of the Trinity
we find the religious formulation of the *eternal*
dialectical process above described—the Father
as God the self-contained *initial* unity; the Son
as God the self-differentiating; the Spirit as the
final unity wherein Father and Son recognise

themselves to be one once more. That is, you
have in the formulation of the doctrine the
Infinite Idea coming to an apprehension of itself
as it eternally *is*. And further, we have in the
Christian doctrine of redemption through Christ
these same three " moments " reappearing once
again. The " otherness," the " self-differentia-
tion," of God is, in time, constituted by the world
of nature and of man : that this " otherness "
should know itself as not really separate from,
but as one with, the Infinite Mind, is what must
take place in order that the " self-differentiated "
Infinite Mind may return upon itself again; and
in Christ this idea of oneness leaped upon the
temporal stage, to become, after Christ's death,
progressively operative and realised in the consciousness of the race. That is, we have, in the
formulation of the doctrine of redemption through
Christ, the Infinite Mind " looking before and
after " from the stage of self-consciousness it has
attained in man, realising the extent to which
its self-consciousness in respect of its eternal
process is matched by its self-consciousness in
respect of its objectified process in time, and
bending itself to make the correspondence complete. Of the many problems all this inevitably
raises—particularly the problem whether, on this
reading of things, we can really go on to say that
we have in the historic Christ the actual fact, or
must content ourselves with asserting that we
have the idea, of " oneness "; whether, in short,
Hegel really overthrew essential Christianity
instead of defending it as he undoubtedly supposed himself to be doing—we need not speak.

Interpretations have varied from top to bottom of the possible scale; and as to what Hegel really meant to say, whether he meant what he said and said what he meant, the contending voices have been and still are loud. For that matter, one ventures with great diffidence on even so brief a statement of Hegelianism as the one which has just been made; for almost everything that can be said upon the basis of Hegel's own writing can be met by a contradiction similarly based. However, it is of Hegel's disciples rather than of Hegel himself that we are to speak; and in view of what has to be said in connection with Hegel's disciples, the principal thing to be borne in mind is that for Hegel and in Hegel's system the universe is the self-unfolding of the eternal Thought or Idea, and that it is this unfolding of the eternal Reason which is reproduced in the thought of man.

For a brief space of time it seemed as though Hegel's attempted establishment of Christianity on the philosophical basis was to be pressed; as if a new form of Liberal Orthodoxy on the Hegelian foundation were going to be built up. One or two theologians—Marheineke (1780–1846) and Daub (1765–1836), professors at Berlin and Heidelberg respectively—accepting Hegel's conception of the final movement in the self-evolution of the eternal Idea as the reconciliation of the Infinite and the finite, or rather the re-assuming of the second back into the first, and accepting also Hegel's view that in Christ this " Idea " was given—thought themselves warranted in springing from this platform to an assertion that in

the historic Christ the union of the divine and
human had actually taken place. They made their
problematical inference, spoken of just now, the
inference from the appearance of the *idea* to
the appearance of the *fact*, apparently without
any consciousness of the chasm across which
they thus gaily leaped, and apparently without
realising that for the process of self-unfolding
under which Hegel summed up all things they
were substituting a real intrusion of the Infinite
into the self-unfolding process, thus viewing
religion as fastened into the eternal background,
not by one nail, but by two. But this mood
could not endure. It soon became clear that
there was no bridge from Hegelianism to the
Christ in whom the Church of the ages had
believed. Biedermann (1819–1885), a somewhat
later theologian who worked from the Hegelian
standpoint with constructive intention so far
as it could be entertained, could get no further
than this—that in the historic Christ the union
of the divine and human had indeed occurred,
but only in the sense that the *idea* of that union
had been the constitutive element in His consciousness, and thus through Him become an
inspiration to the race. In fact, Biedermann
becomes negative in spite of himself, thereby
showing clearly enough the direction in which
the Hegelian force must necessarily rush when
it is allowed to have its will. He only gave
another proof (his *Christliche Dogmatik* appeared
in 1868) of what had been evident from the
beginning. The main Hegelian conception of
evolving *Thought* speedily disentangled itself from

all else as the thing which dominated and gave character to the system; and so soon as the strict application of this conception to Christianity began, its destructive consequences were seen. Idea, the evolution of idea, was everything : the business of the investigator, when he turned himself to religion, was therefore to trace the evolution of religious ideas. Such an evolution there must be, since human ideas simply emerge in the self-development of the eternal Idea, and since it is really by a sort of eternal intellectual fatalism that they are what they are.   But when you have traced the evolution of some one religious idea, and have accounted for it as coming out of antecedent ideas or half-ideas, you have not done anything towards proving the reality of the alleged facts connected with or embodying the idea : in fact, you have done a good deal towards getting rid of the alleged facts, inasmuch as you have shown how, without their actual existence or occurrence, belief in them may have arisen.   On the other hand, if you approach the alleged facts *wanting* to get rid of them, you can easily do so by showing that they are the vehicles in which men would naturally have sent the just-evolved idea on its journey round the world. This is certainly one special application of a principle, or rather one special usage of a method, taken over from Hegelianism rather than the full and pure Hegelian gospel itself; and in point of fact, some of the destructive critics who more or less derived from Hegel can be called Hegelians only in a somewhat loose sense.   Still, we may be tolerably certain that without the preparation

of the way which Hegel performed, the work of
Strauss, for instance (1808–1874), would not
have been done—at least, by him and when he
did it. The line sketched in a few words just now
is the line which Strauss pursued. The religious
idea—the idea of a Saviour, of a Saviour who
performs mighty works, of a Saviour who is an
express revelation and incarnation of God—
makes its appearance upon the field of human
thought : if now some small foundation in actual
fact can be found, legend, working *from* the fact,
will exaggerate the fact itself, the mythical
tendency (the tendency to clothe ideas with a
factual dress) will work *towards* the exaggerated
fact as legend has left it ; and thus the total result
is sufficiently explained.[1] On this wise Strauss,
working upon the contents of historic Revelation,
and specially upon the Gospel narratives of
Christ's words and works, satisfactorily engineered
everything supernatural away.[2] Nor did the
thing stop there. For some minds, the charm of
Strauss' theory lay in the opportunity it afforded
of proceeding to something more radical still ;
and while Bruno Bauer (1809–1882) substituted
deliberate invention by the individual for the
action of " myth," Feuerbach (1804–1872) advanced to the conclusion that in all the activity
of religious faith man was the victim of a sort of

[1] Legend starts from a basis of fact, and develops the
fact into an idea. Myth starts from an idea, and develops
it into an alleged fact. Strauss' theory requires the working
of both, though myth is the more important.

[2] The *Leben Jesu* appeared in 1834 and 1835, the *Christliche Glaubenslehre* in 1840, the second *Leben Jesu* not till
long afterwards, in 1864.

lunacy, and that all religious beliefs were merely
inventions wherewith man sought to satisfy his
own wishes for what he imagined ought to be.
Feuerbach, indeed, sank the whole thing into an
absolute materialism, denied reality to anything
save what could be seen and tasted and touched
—how far from the doctrine, with which the
philosophy leading to all this had begun, that
the only reality is Thought !—and in his famous
sentence to the effect that " man is what he eats "[1]
expressed his conviction that even in our supposedly spiritual yearnings and aspirations we
are but material forces' sport.   So had the river
of Hegelianism, after starting in the highlands of
speculation and flowing with many turns and
windings between banks from which strange
things were thrown into it, become a muddy
stream.

From another quarter, though still a quarter
illuminated by the Hegelian rays, direct attack
upon the historicity of the New Testament
narratives was made.   It is at this point that
the famous " Tübingen school "—so famous that
it is not necessary or customary even to call it the
" later Tübingen school," in distinction from the
" early Tübingen school " we met with before—
comes into sight.   Ferdinand Christian Baur
(1792–1860), finding Strauss' theory of " myth "
too vague and general to account for the New
Testament as it lies before us, fell back upon the
conception of " thesis, antithesis, and synthesis "

---

[1] The phrase loses in English the effect of the play on
words, as given in the German " Der Mensch ist was er
isst."

as Hegel had set it out, and applied it to the New Testament records with startling results. Up to this time New Testament criticism had not progressed very far, although the genuineness of certain Epistles had been questioned, and the problem of "oral tradition" *versus* "written documents" as embodying the original sources of the four Gospels had to some extent come into debate. Among the men whose names have been mentioned in our earlier pages were some whose work in this field gave to New Testament criticism in the modern sense— that of a detailed examination of documents, with a view to discovering the mental atmosphere wherein they originated, the various strands of thought they embody, and their value as dependent upon these things—an impetus from which students of to-day draw benefit still, even though many of the older conclusions no longer stand. Eichhorn, De Wette, and Semler had dug in this mine; and Schleiermacher, following Griesbach (1745–1812) on this point, had elaborated a theory according to which John's was the only Gospel coming straight from the hand of its reputed author, Mark being compiled by an alternative use of Matthew and Luke, Matthew being based upon a collection of " logia," and an " oral tradition " finally, or rather originally, lying behind them all.[1] But Baur worked much more thoroughly than any of his predecessors had

---

[1] The topic of Biblical criticism can be only cursorily alluded to in this chapter or elsewhere. Special works must be consulted, such as H. S. Nash's *History of Higher Criticism*, or Bible Dictionaries and Encyclopædias for the individual Biblical books.

done; and he worked, as has been said, from the standpoint of the Hegelian idea. Beginning with a conflict between Jewish and Gentile Christianity—between the universal Christianity of Paul and the restricted Christianity of Peter, the view which looked upon the new religion as designed to compass the whole world and the view which regarded it as merely a fresh version of Judaism, to be combined with Jewish ceremonies and leaving these obligatory upon its converts still—beginning thus, Baur found in each of the New Testament writings either the representative of one of these " tendencies " or the reconciliation of the two. Matthew, for instance, stands among the Gospels as the strongest presentation of the Jewish side, while Luke is charged with the spirit of Paul : the Book of Revelation, again, is Jewish; while in the Pastoral Epistles we have the Pauline party making concessions to the Jewish, in the Epistle of James the Jewish party making concessions to the Pauline, and in the Acts of the Apostles a picture of Christianity's earliest years (of course not in accordance with fact) drawn after compromise had been perfected, and accordingly designed to show that there had never been any difference or friction at all. " Thesis " and " antithesis " had met together; and in the final " synthesis " two opposites had exchanged the reconciling kiss. Of course the New Testament books, at any rate those which belonged to the " reconciliation " stage, had to be brought down to dates much later than those usually accepted, in order that time might be allowed for the reconciling process to bear its fruit; and in the end only four of Paul's Epistles (to take the treatment of these as typical)—those to the Corinthians, Galatians, and Romans—were permitted to go forth under Paul's name. Upon the conception of Christ, and upon the story of His life, all this necessarily had a bearing most momentous. For the two "tendencies" spoken of had been at work practically from Christ's own days. Jesus had Himself, in His emphasis upon rightness of character and heart, given its first start to the "universal" conception of His religion; for this was directly opposed to the Jewish view of religion as constituted by a legal and ceremonial system whose benefits were the privilege of the few. But some of His disciples still clung to their faith in Him as Messiah in the narrower sense; and in belief in His resurrection (whatever in actual fact the event so called may have been) they found their justification, their consolation, and their joy. Jesus had risen to vindicate the Jewish national consciousness, and prove Himself to be in *their* reading of the term " the Messiah " for whom the nation looked. On the other hand, those who had imbibed the larger spirit which had been Jesus' own found in the idea of His resurrection (the *idea* of it, let it be noted once again, whether the *fact* of it existed or not) a justification for *their* point of view; and Paul, more especially, putting together the death and resurrection of Jesus, found in the first a direct contradiction of the narrower Messianic opinions —since if they had been true the Messiah would never have died at all—and in the second a

M

vindication of that universal view of Jesus'
work which he wanted to put in its place. To
the idea of Christ's resurrection, therefore, both
" tendencies " run back. But the important
thing to notice is that to set the long process of
" thesis, antithesis, and synthesis " into ordered
working, all that is required is the *idea* (not the
fact) that Jesus had risen from the dead. The
whole history of doctrine's development is, Hegelian-wise, an interplay of *ideas ;* and it is upon an
idea that we may be content to hang it when we
are tracing it back to its earliest support. Nay,
it is upon an idea that we *must* hang it; for
an alleged history, written under the influence
of " tendencies " and preconceptions, cannot be
taken as history at all. So the historic Christ
disappears, leaving only a haze wherein men
take for realities the shadowy images of Him
which their own minds project. The Hegelianism which had unwittingly sent forth Strauss and
his " mythical theory " as an enemy against the
historic faith, threw forward in Baur and his
" tendency-theory " a yet more threatening foe.

Whether, in face of these pressing dangers, the
Christian faith, and the historic Christ hitherto
deemed essential to it, were sufficiently safe-
guarded in the theology of Schleiermacher,
was a question which naturally thrust itself upon
those who dwelt in Schleiermacher's camp.
Was it enough to say that, if you started from
that developed feeling of dependence which
Christ produced in you—and that indirectly—you
came ultimately to a historic figure which was

in its main outlines like the one of which the
Gospels spoke? If you found, when you reached
your goal, that criticism, working from the
Hegelian direction, had swept the historic Christ
away, and you were confronted by an assertion
that the *idea* of Christ was all you needed, what
was the reply to be? If you accepted the
assertion, the new route to the historic Christ
and the historic Christian faith which Schleiermacher had constructed with such toil was
condemned as leading merely to the edge of a
cliff whence you tumbled out into the abyss.
If you refused to assent, were you to abandon
" feeling," the Christian consciousness, as your
theological starting-point, and devote yourself
to a strictly logical, doctrinaire defence of the
New Testament, its contents, its Christ, its
avowed or implied faith? To do this was again
to confess defeat. It was to the sound of the
throbbing drums of questions like these that
Liberal Orthodoxy had to re-dress its ranks and
change its step. And what we actually find, in
the thinkers who may rank as Schleiermacher's
disciples in greater or less degree, is the making
of an attempt to preserve Schleiermacher's essential basis while at the same time giving fresh
security to the historic Christ and to the doctrines
gathered round His name.

By some (if indeed these can be rightly called
Schleiermacher's disciples at all) this attempt
was carried so far that in the end we find them
working, not *forward* from the basis of feeling to
Christian doctrine, but *backward* from Christian
doctrine to feeling; that is, they are so deter-

mined to discover Christian doctrine as given in Christian feeling that they carry it thither with them, and put it in, by way of making sure. Of Twesten (1789–1876) [1] and Nitzsch (1787–1868) something like this may quite fairly be said. The former unmistakably reversed, while professing to follow, Schleiermacher's method of interrogating the Christian consciousness to learn what it would say; and his treatment really turned to something in the nature of a cross-examination in which the Christian consciousness (his starting-point, however, being the Christian consciousness of the " new birth " rather than the Christian consciousness in the more general sense) was ruthlessly compelled to say what the examiner desired. Nitzsch was not so arbitrary, but was not a whit less resolved upon demonstrating that all the orthodox articles of belief whereto Schleiermacher had built no crossing-bridge from the side of feeling could be quite easily so connected after all. In fact, so keenly bent were these theologians upon a defence of the orthodox positions that, notwithstanding the tincture of Schleiermacher's spirit with which their work was coloured, they stood in the end practically alongside the men who, stirred by the new Hegelian dangers to the faith, at this time put up a vigorous fight on behalf of Lutheranism without looking in Schleiermacher's direction at all—of whom Hengstenberg (1802–1869) bears the best known name. Similarly actuated by an overmastering desire to save the old formulas,

---

[1] It should be said that Twesten's system was not completely worked out at his death.

while availing themselves so far as possible of
Schleiermacher's help, were the " confessional "
theologians, or the writers of the " Erlangen "
school, so called from the University to which
its leaders belonged. These, however, were
themselves possessed to some extent by the
spirit of that Hegelianism to whose anti-Christian
developments they were so strongly opposed :
the conception of " development " gripped them
hard ; and what they sought to do was to demonstrate that the Christian consciousness, if you
interrogated it in Schleiermacher's manner, drove
you at last, not only to the historic Christ, but
to a developing revelation (the particulars of
which are supplied in the Bible *as it stands*)
whereby the Trinity—as a fact, not an idea—
passed, Hegelian-wise, into perfect self-realisation
and self-reconciliation through the union of God
and man, this revelation proceeding onward
from the creation of the world and being at last
consummated in Christ, although it is of course
only through man's self-identification with the
perfect humanity in Christ that the revelation's
purpose is finally achieved. The conception of
a developing revelation is of course a rich and
fruitful one ; and, in other settings and rightly
applied, it produces most valuable results. But
in the Erlangen scheme the idea is put forth only
to be lost again. There is here no suggestion
of a slow unfolding of God to meet the slow
unfolding of human apprehensive powers ; no
suggestion that the ideas of God entertained by
men of ancient days were enriched or corrected
by later teachings. Every incident recorded in

the Scriptures is to be taken at its face value; and all that is meant by a " developing revelation " is that from the standpoint of present Christian experience we can see *why* each incident had its place in the causal sequence whereby present Christian experience has been made possible. What we have, therefore, is not a *developing* revelation at all, but (a very different matter) something which *develops into* a revelation; and it is a revelation, not at each stage of its progress, but only at the end; and the ultimate aim of the revelation is to prove that each item of the foregoing history led on by inevitable sequence to the next. It is a little difficult to make the matter clear, but an illustration may help. Hofmann seriously affirms that from the soul's experience of the new birth you can get back, among other things, to a necessity for the separation of the human race into many distinct nations—which is surely a *reductio ad absurdum* of the whole thing. It enables us at least to see what a " developing revelation," on this system, really is. It is, in short, on the parenthesis inserted a few lines above—the parenthesis referring to the particulars of the revelation as given in the Bible *as it stands*—that emphasis has to fall. The Old Testament, taken *as it stands*, is a detailed prophecy of all that was to be; and the New Testament fulfils the Old—not in the general sense in which all would say so, but in a sense which covers the smallest details too. It is with Hofmann (1810–1877), perhaps the outstanding man of the Erlangen school, in view that these points have been set down; but in the main they hold good of the other members too. It should be added that in elaborating their conception of a self-developing Trinity Hofmann and his fellow-thinkers were led into unorthodox views of the Person of Christ and of His atoning work; so that their purpose of defending the established Lutheranism defeated itself after all. The strict Lutherans, as a matter of fact, charged heresy against Hofmann and his friends. But that was an accident of the situation, and need not detain us here. What, once again, the Erlangen school endeavoured to accomplish was to show that Schleiermacher's method brought you to the Bible *as it stood.* They did not, any more than did Nitzsch or Twesten, really plant themselves at Schleiermacher's starting-point and go out not knowing whither they went. They had their own promised, or desired, land full in view; and there needed no wandering in any deserts before they entered in. It was a case, to change the figure, of knowing the answer to the sum before the working was begun. The Erlangen men gathered from the Bible and the creeds what, because it *was* in the Bible, the Christian consciousness *ought* to give, and then descended upon the Christian consciousness to ask for it. Assuredly the doubt recurs, and persists, whether in any real sense thinking such as this can be said to follow Schleiermacher's lead. And certainly it was not through this curious blend of Hegel, Schleiermacher, and Biblical literalism that Liberal Orthodoxy—which, whatever else it may or may not do, cannot take every Scripture word

and every formulated doctrinal article as of
equal worth—could be saved.

It was by other men than those we have named
that the defensive movement of true Liberal
Orthodoxy was carried on; and Dorner (1809–
1884) and Rothe (1799–1867) may be cited as the
two most prominent workers along this line.
In the main they may be described—although
Hegelian influences touched them, this being
practically inevitable at the time [1]—as followers
of Schleiermacher who extended in a *speculative*
direction that *rational* process which Schleiermacher, as we saw, pursued when once his firm
position upon " feeling " had been taken up.
Giving a rational account of what the Christian
consciousness involved, Schleiermacher had been
borne on to a Christ who corresponded in the
main to the historic Christ of the Scriptures and
the Church; but he had *not* been borne on, we
found, to the specific formularies wherein the
doctrine of Christ's Person, of the Trinity, and
of other mysteries, had been enshrined—nor, for

---

[1] Classification is somewhat difficult in the case of thinkers
who so to say stand at the focus of converging lines of
influence. Dorner is usually classed as an " eclectic," into
whose system various elements from various systems are
gathered. (So by Pfleiderer in *The Development of Theology*.)
On the other hand, Frank (in *Geschichte und Kritik der
neueren Theologie*) puts him among those who sought to
carry theology back towards the faith of the Church, while
Adams Brown (in *The Essence of Christianity*) makes him
a Hegelian. Rothe is classed among the " speculative
theologians," as a disciple of Hegel but with leanings toward
Schleiermacher, by Pfleiderer, and as a disciple of Schleiermacher, with leanings toward Hegel, by Frank. One can
make out a case for all these methods of placing the men.
But on the whole, it seems to me that it is behind Schleiermacher they fall in.

that matter, to any other formularies in substitution for these. Dorner and Rothe could not
rest while empty places thus stared at them from
the walls whereon the results of thought were
hung : their minds could not be content to let
the darkness suddenly close down against them
just when they were crossing the border into the
land whence the subtlest problems of all were
calling; and they were all the less ready to leave
things so because the new negative and dissolvent criticism was making it doubtful whether
even Schleiermacher's abridged creed could stand
unless fresh supports were put beneath. But if
it were possible to show that, after the *immediate*
implications of the Christian consciousness had
been drawn out and their limit reached, thought
—making what was in a manner a new start,
and yet not working altogether independently,
inasmuch as the Christian consciousness and
its implications are assumed as precedent—
could produce a case for such an Incarnation
as the orthodox faith proclaimed, then the fresh
supports would be found, and the Christian would
be able to keep all that Schleiermacher had
given him just because he had, from a source
which Schleiermacher did not tap, received what
Schleiermacher professed himself unable to give.
By meeting the pronouncements of the Christian
consciousness with the pronouncements of speculative thought in the stricter sense, and through
the reciprocal imparting of strength which each
would perform as they touched, *both* would be
secured. If the hostile critics countered the
demand of the Christian consciousness for the

historic Christ by saying, " All that your inner
voices really call for, certainly all that they
guarantee, is no more than the *idea* of the historic
Christ, and this is all we can let you have," the
Christian consciousness would be able to call in
the aid of its ally and to declare that thought—
once the Christian consciousness had taught it
what to look for—had found, not merely the
idea of the historic Christ, but justification for
faith in the historic Christ as a *fact*. " Once
the Christian consciousness had taught it what
to look for " is, however, a necessary phrase;
for the programme was that speculation should
begin *after* the Christian consciousness had been
interrogated and had given its reply, and carrying with it clear recollection of what the Christian
consciousness had said. Dorner—to speak of
him first—describes his method by saying, " When
the enlightened Christian mind is in harmony
by its faith and experience with objective
Christianity, which faith knows to be its origin,
and which is also attested by the Scriptures and
the scriptural faith of the Church, then such a
mind has to justify and develop its religious
knowledge in a systematic form." [1] It is not,
let it be noted, a method which reconciles philosophy and theology, or which evolves the second
from the first : it is a method which turns to
philosophy, *after* the primary theology offered
by the Christian consciousness has uttered its

[1] Quoted by Pfleiderer (*Development of Theology in Germany since Kant*, p. 157) as from Dorner's *Christliche
Glaubenslehre*. I have not been able to identify the precise
sentence, but in the *Glaubenslehre* Dorner often expresses
the idea in one or another way.

last word, in order to ascertain what more there may be to say; while at the same time there *is* more to say, for the mind has not only to " justify," but to " develop," its knowledge " in a systematic form." And this is what Dorner endeavoured to do. He sought—given the Christ whom the Christian consciousness demanded—to show, not only what can, but what must, be said of Him from the speculative side. This, of course, meant grounding Him in the eternal nature of things, so that the moment Dorner began his speculative construction it was back upon the most fundamental problems that he found himself thrown; but the Christological question shone steadfastly in Dorner's sky as the star under which, let him begin his journey where he might, he must by-and-by come to stand; and all the countries of thought through which he moved, their measurement and exploration and character, interested him chiefly as his eye could pick up sign after sign that he was getting near the home boundary-line and would soon reach his goal. It was natural, this being so, that Dorner should feel a kindling interest in the history of Christological doctrine; and his *History of the Doctrine of the Person of Christ* (*Entwicklungsgeschichte der Lehre von der Person Christi*, 1856) is in fact undoubtedly his greatest work. Still, through his study of the history he was laying his road to his own developed system—his own Christology and the speculative process which involved it—as he was at last to give it to the world in the *Glaubenslehre* of 1879–1881. In his actual speculative processes an

unmistakable Hegelian influence appears; not
that Dorner's God is, like Hegel's, the Absolute
Idea, but that Dorner adopts something like
the " thesis, antithesis, and synthesis " conception which is the very pivot of Hegel's scheme.
With Dorner it is not, however, the coming of
an Absolute to self-realisation that is in question,
but the coming of a *Revelation* to its *fulness*.
God is at the same time a self-maintained or
self-sufficient Personality and a Personality which
must impart itself to others—wherein we have the
basis for the doctrine of the Trinity with its
Father and its Son and its Love uniting both.
In the nature of God Himself, therefore, " thesis,
antithesis, and synthesis " are duly given. But
God as self-imparting necessarily reveals Himself
as He is—that is, both as self-maintaining or
self-sufficient *and* as self-imparting; and Revelation is the action of this double process upon
the world. In the world's concrete history the
ethnic religions have too closely identified God
with the world, thus failing to do justice to His
self-maintenance and self-sufficiency: the Jewish
religion, on the other hand, has put God too
far away, thus failing to do justice to His
self-impartation; while in Christianity the two
elements are properly linked together, each in
its due proportion, so that " thesis " and " antithesis " have given place to " synthesis " once
more. But Dorner's Hegelianism need not be
further laboured. The important matter is
that, according to Dorner, this final " synthesis,"
so to call it, revealing at the same time what God
is in Himself, what He is towards man, and what

man should be towards Him, could only occur through a real incarnation of God in Christ; for the gradual self-impartation of God to man—to which Dorner's speculation has led him—must end, if mankind *as a whole* is to experience and benefit by it, in an *individual* in whom God and man are one. At this point then, Dorner, having travelled along the speculative road after taking temporary leave of the Christian consciousness, comes within hail of that Christian consciousness again : the Christ whom, according to Schleiermacher, Christian consciousness demands is met by a Christ emerging at the close of the speculative process; and the two are discovered to be one. In the details of Dorner's system—in what he has to say of the " mode " of the Incarnation, of the significance of atonement, of inspiration, and the rest, all these things being linked up with his conception of revelation as God's self-communication in His double aspect to the world—there is much suggestiveness. Dorner's work is indeed a mine of richest yield; and he deserves, as much as any and perhaps more than most, a thorough study by all who would probe theological problems to their depths. But for our present purpose, in order to show his place in Liberal Orthodoxy's history, his likeness to and his difference from his master Schleiermacher, whose peculiar greatness he declared himself ever more and more fully to perceive— for this what has been set down will suffice. As to Rothe, fewer words will be enough. His chief work, the *Theologische Ethik* (1845–1848), came earlier than Dorner's *Christliche Glaubens-*

lehre ; but, though Rothe is a good deal more
Hegelian than Dorner, there is much general
similarity between the coin produced in the two
speculative mints. Rothe certainly runs *two*
lines of speculation, a philosophical and a theological, the former starting from the individual's
thinking act (this being the manner in which
his more emphatic Hegelianism is displayed),
and the latter from the religious consciousness;
but once he begins his progress along the second,
the track is laid and the wayside stations are
built much upon Dorner's plan. The division
between speculation of the philosophical and
that of the theological order gave Rothe an
opportunity of incorporating in the first a good
many elements which from various quarters his
own thinking had picked up; for pietism,
mysticism, theosophy, the cosmogony of Baader,
and various other things had gone to his moral
and intellectual making. It was, in fact, as
a theosophist (though the word in his usage
did not mean what it means upon the general
tongue to-day) that he classed himself, declaring
in 1847 that if he should come to be thought
worthy of a place near the theosophist Oetinger,
he would be well content.[1] Still, his distinctly
theological thinking works down from a starting-
point similar to Dorner's to an end like that which

---

[1] " Das kann ich voraussehen, dasz, wenn mir überhaupt
ein bescheidener Platz in dem groszen Hause der Theologie
zugewiesen werden sollte, ich in das Kämmerchen der
Theosophen zu stehen kommen werde, in die Nähe Oetingers.
Ich gehöre auch wirklich nirgends sonst hin and wünsche
mir keine bessere Stelle. Mir soll innig wohl sein zu den
Füszen des lieben Mannes."—Preface to Auberlen's work on
Oetinger's theosophical system.

Dorner reached. The self-maintaining God of Dorner is in Rothe the God who " affirms Himself as ego." But this very affirmation of Himself as "ego" carries with it an affirmation of Himself as "non-ego" too, at first in thought, subsequently (this, however, being by a free act of will, whereas the affirmation in *thought* was bound up in and simultaneous with the affirmation of Himself as " non-ego ") in the material world. Then comes the progressive re-spiritualisation of God's " other ego " through the moral and spiritual development of man, the failure of this re-spiritualising process through man's sin, the restoring of it by means of a new miraculous act (the sending of the supernatural Christ) wherein God resumes from a fresh point the reconciliation of his " other self " with His " self," and finally the blending (through man's relationship with Christ) of this second reconciling process with the broken and interrupted first. It will be seen that, while somewhat more Hegelian in its framing, at any rate in its expression, the whole construction is in its broad outlines much like Dorner's own, giving us a progressive revelation of God to the world both in His essential self and in His " otherness," a progressive union of man with the God so revealed, and a linking up of the progressive revelation and the progressive uniting process in an Incarnation which consummates the one and potentially at any rate completes the other. Which is to say that Rothe, like Dorner, shows us a speculative process superadded to the process of direct inference from the Christian

consciousness, and leading in the end to the
Christ for whom the Christian consciousness calls.

If we go no further than these two names, or
at least give other names no more than bare
mention, it is not because there are no other
names worthy to be dwelt upon, but because
limits of space restrict us, so far as any detailed
treatment is concerned, to a selection of men
who may be looked upon as types. But the
reader must take it that all through this period
the influence of Schleiermacher was strong upon
not a few, and that in all the theological fields
there were workers who took up much of what
he offered them, subtracted from it whatever
carried for them little or no appeal, added to
what was left whatever material of their own
they had at hand, and so pieced their own com-
pleted mosaic together. In fact, practically all
the theology of this period which counts for
the student—of course outside that of strictly
Hegelian descent—is, at one or two or more
removes of relationship, connected with Schleiermacher's own. If a theologian who desired to
secure Christianity by other than purely conservative ways—if he made a point *against*
Schleiermacher, he did it, and knew that he
could do it, only because Schleiermacher himself
had taught him how : if he differed from certain
of Schleiermacher's own applications of Schleiermacher's own central idea, it was only because
that central idea itself appeared, when the
question was referred back to it, to compel the
difference now : if he worked in some department (ecclesiastical history, for example) not

lying so close up against that central idea as
some others, he set it at such an angle that some
of that central idea's illuminating brilliance
might be caught as it slid down : let his own
special contribution be what it might, it was in
relation to Schleiermacher that he conceived it,
as an embroidery upon Schleiermacher's ground-
work that he traced it out. To set out but the
smallest list, one sees in Tholuck (1799–1877)—
greater as a preacher than as a theological
thinker, but not by any means negligible as this
last—how a man of evangelistic (not merely
evangelical) temperament could slake his soul's
thirst by drinking at Schleiermacher's springs;
in Neander (1789–1850) and Hagenbach (1801–
1874) [1] how the writing of Church history could
be made the record of a vital spiritual process
when baptised in Schleiermacher's spirit, just
as it had been rendered a mere record of growing
folly and error when written from the rationalistic side by Spittler and Planck; [2] in Bleek (1793–
1859) how Biblical criticism could, under the
same inspiration, be both thorough and spiritually
fertilising; in Julius Müller and Ullmann [3] how
special doctrines, treated with Schleiermacher's
fundamental position in view, might be made
tenfold significant, even though on the special
doctrines themselves Schleiermacher's own pronouncements might be varied to greater or less

[1] Hagenbach really belongs to German Switzerland, but
may be conveniently mentioned alongside of his fellow-
historian.

[2] Neander, rather curiously, had been a pupil of Planck's.

[3] Müller (1801–1878), *The Christian Doctrine of Sin;*
Ullmann (1796–1865), *The Sinlessness of Jesus.*

N

extent; while Lange (1802–1884) deserves to be
mentioned beside Rothe and Dorner as a systematic theologian who, having learned Schleiermacher's primary lesson that it is in the Christian
consciousness a Christian theology must begin,
reinforced what he found in that primary source
by what he found in a vigorous pursuit of the
speculative line. But a mere list of this kind is
of small value except as indicating how much
there is for an enquirer to search out. The sum
of the matter is that, following upon Schleiermacher himself, there came a sequence of
Christian thought, a series of Christian systems,
in which it was sought, with all faithfulness to
the master mind, to fill what gaps he had left,
and to forge such stronger bond as the newest
criticism made necessary between the Christian
consciousness and the historic Christ as He was
portrayed in the historic Christian faith.

It is worth while to take a look beyond the
borders of Germany upon countries directly or
indirectly affected by Germany's thought. It
can be no more than a look; but a look may
bring out the fact that in all the major lands of
Europe the same spirit was at work. Purely
destructive or negative criticism was of course
in evidence elsewhere as well as in Germany;
and if theological thought in general were our
theme, we should have to take some account of
Renan, Reville, and others. But our limits
being what they are, we may pass them by. In
connection with our special topic one of the outstanding names is that of Martensen (1808–1884),

who in Denmark taught a system much like
that of Dorner, his close and life-long friend.
Martensen, however, instead of leaping over from
the Christian consciousness and its immediate
suggestions to an entirely detached new starting-
point in the speculative realm, made a shorter
stride from the Christian consciousness of
redemption to the Christian consciousness of
revelation, and held it for the business of theology
to ascertain the contents of the second, to
harmonise them with the first, and to make out
of the offerings of the two a synthetic whole.
It was thus really from two adjacent pieces of
ground upon the same territory or—since the
Christian consciousness of revelation must itself
be a part of the Christian consciousness of
redemption—from a piece of ground marked off
by a circular line within a larger one, instead of
from two territories quite alien in manners and
speech, that Martensen began or professed to
begin; and the closer relation between the two
subsequent processes enabled each to afford the
other more support. Necessarily, the drawing out
of what was contained in the presumed Christian
consciousness of revelation became a matter of
pure speculation after all; for while it might
be plausibly contended that the Christian consciousness testified to the *fact* of a revelation,
it could hardly be held, in view of the robe of
many colours which theology was wearing, that
the Christian consciousness gave any direct
account of how the revelation had been given or
of the eternal processes behind it. Nevertheless, if you could say that in adopting a certain

speculative idea you were filling up an outline
which the Christian consciousness had sketched,
pouring in a draught for which the Christian
consciousness was already holding the prepared
vessel forth, something was gained, and you
obviated that sense of jerk, of flight through the
void, which—if you attempted from two *distant*
and quite *unrelated* points to bring speculation
and the Christian consciousness together—you
had to endure even before you could begin; and
it was this advantage that Martensen sought to
secure. In some sense, Dorner had sought to
secure a similar advantage by his careful planting
of his feet upon the history of doctrine in the
Church : as he spread his wings for the flight to
the speculative starting-point, he could to some
extent take his bearings and shape his course by
noting the tracks, as that history showed them,
along which other soaring minds had come down
again to earth. Martensen's method led him
to attach much less value to history, or at any
rate to make much smaller use of it, than Dorner
did; and for him the Christian consciousness
of revelation—though surely a much more pre-
carious footing, and one which it would not
need a very strong wave of criticism to wash
away—took the place of the historic evolution
of thought. But notwithstanding these differences in method, the final theological construction of the two men was much the same; and
their systems, if not precisely twin, are at any
rate clearly of one family group. Passing from
Denmark to Holland, the " Groningen school "
demands a word, although it soon had its little

day and ceased to be. Almost simultaneously, though Utrecht was slightly in advance, the Universities of Utrecht and Groningen originated a movement of theological enquiry inspired partly by a study of Plato, partly by Schleiermacher, partly by the men (some of whom we have named) who touched Schleiermacher's system with modifications and additions of their own. At Utrecht the Platonist P. H. van Heusde (1778–1839) was the leader, at Groningen P. H. de Groot; but the two circles speedily coalesced, establishing a society in 1835 and a magazine of their own in 1837. Of the school's special doctrines not much need be said here. They followed Schleiermacher in starting from " feeling "; but while one has to say of Schleiermacher that with him Christology was central, one has to say of the Groningen men that it was practically the only matter with which they dealt. Also, and more unfortunately, their special treatment was largely of a negative kind. They held, as Schleiermacher held, to the possibility of Christ's miracles, and explained by a special act of God the coming of Christ to the world; but while Schleiermacher had contented himself with sitting loosely to the customary credal formulas wherein the doctrine of the Incarnation and its related doctrines had been embodied, merely saying that the witness of the Christian consciousness did not carry him so far, the Groningen school repudiated these same formulas with warmth. Of a Trinity or an Atonement they would hear nothing; nor did they attempt to take the current doctrines as symbolic, or as expressions " thrown out at " an only partially expressible truth, expressions for which other expressions more approximately true might be substituted as insight quickened. They simply swept them all away. In respect of Christ Himself they spoke in the Arian fashion; and it is only their manifest spirituality which entitles them to be put on the " Liberal Orthodox " list. In German Switzerland Schweizer (1771–1843) followed perhaps more closely in Schleiermacher's steps than any other theologian even in Germany itself; his chief addition to his master's method lying in his greater emphasis on the Christian consciousness of the Church as manifested in history in contrast with the Christian consciousness of the individual man. Of course, Schleiermacher had made the development of Christian feeling in the individual to be mediated *through* the Church; but that is not quite the same thing; and when it came to doctrinal construction, to exposition of what in the way of articulated belief the Christian consciousness warranted, Schleiermacher had—so Schweizer thought—too closely identified his individual " feeling " with the Church's own. Working from his broader ground, Schweizer found the test of individual feeling to be transcended by the test of the Christian "ideal" of the spiritual perfection of man—this ideal being reached in, and its apprehension being part of, the collective feeling of the Church as a whole. In the end, however, valuable as this conception is in itself, it became destructive rather than constructive in Schweizer's use of it; for the apprehension of an " ideal " is necessarily a gradual process; and to make a developing ideal the source or the test of doctrine is to say that certainty cannot at any time be more than relative; and from this it is only a step—indeed hardly a step—to say that what is now held for true may to-morrow be found untrue after all. Schweizer, in fact, tended markedly to the negative side so far as the great Christian doctrines are concerned. In French Switzerland Vinet (1797–1847) showed some far-off touch, no more, of Schleiermacher's influence, though he had little or no constructive theological ability, and did not get much further than a general adoption of the " Christian consciousness " idea in opposition to Biblical literalism : indeed, " individualism " is Vinet's own word. It was on the liberty of the individual conscience, and on the test of doctrine by conscience when freed, that he planted himself when his thinking began. In France itself the elder de Pressensé (1824–1891), a far greater man, put to usury the talent he had first received from Vinet, and by his work both in general theology and (more particularly) in ecclesiastical history laid future students heavily under his debt. But for details of these movements and these men the reader must look elsewhere. This bare mention of them will at least suffice to show that over a good many of the European tracts the lamps of Liberal Orthodoxy—and chiefly the lamp of Schleiermacher's kindling—were stretching their shafts of light.

In Germany itself, then, we have noted,

together with a general maintenance of Schleiermacher's method, a growing feeling that in
Schleiermacher's system and by Schleiermacher's
method the historic Christ and the historic faith
were not sufficiently secured; and we have noted
the new securities which Schleiermacher's successors and disciples sought to provide. But
were the new securities enough? One cannot
wonder that Liberal Orthodoxy should, in some
at least of its representatives, feel the touch of
misgiving as the question probed and pricked.
For even against that speculative process wherewith Dorner, among others, endeavoured to
supplement and confirm the witness of the
Christian consciousness it might be urged, from,
say, the Hegelian side, " Your speculative process
only gives you the gift you ask for because you
have given it to the process first. You fling your
thought out in such a direction that its further
end *must* fall where you want it to. You say
that your speculative process brings you to the
same historic Christ for whom Christian feeling
calls; but it only does this because you had that
historic Christ in view from the first as demanded
by Christian feeling; and a man always walks
straight towards any object on which his eyes
are fixed. Suppose we do not grant your initial
statement, and insist that the *idea* of the historic
Christ is all that Christian feeling asks for—what
then? Just as *your* speculative process meets
the Christian feeling in *your* reading of it, so *our*
speculative process meets the Christian feeling
on *our* reading of it; and our circle is as complete
as yours. Why prefer yours, when ours thus

gives all that yours can give, and at the same time preserves, as yours does not, the absolute unity of the world-process from start to finish?" Such questions would serve to bring out the weakness inherent in making—as we saw that Schleiermacher's system after all had made—acceptance of an idea *about* Christ the fundamental and constitutive thing for Christian experience and Christian life. It is no wonder that, when such searching questions were possible, Liberal Orthodoxy should by some of its representatives ask itself whether the entire method of beginning from the pure Christian consciousness were not suspect, and should look round for another base. At any rate, the quest was made. And indeed, the mention of some of the names in this chapter has already brought us into the Ritschlian years.

CHAPTER VII

DEVELOPMENT : GREAT BRITAIN AND AMERICA

OUR next task is to turn to Great Britain (taking also such a look upon America as may be necessary) and to enquire how there Liberal Orthodoxy fared after the revival spoken of in our fifth chapter had set in—in other words, to complete our survey of Liberal Orthodoxy's first period up to and including the appearance of *Essays and Reviews*. We briefly characterised the period, it will be remembered, as one in which Liberal Orthodoxy, having dealt with and compromised upon one doctrine in chief—the doctrine of the Bible's verbal inspiration and inerrancy— and not having systematically thought out the consequences of this for theology as a whole, had these consequences thrust upon it to its own surprise; " realising, dimly at first, more vividly later, what had been involved in its own initial act; and awaking in the end to find that inasmuch as it had kept no watch and ward upon the stream of unfolding change, it had been carried into strange realms upon the rapid tide." [1] This hastily-sketched outline has now to be filled up. Treatment of the period, it may be said

[1] *Supra*, p. 100.

in anticipation, can be more swift and brief in the case of Britain than in the case of Germany, and the touch upon each incident can be lighter, since it is not by complete theological systems calling for description that we are faced; but certain names demand their rights.

Something about the background against which Liberal Orthodoxy unfolded itself must needs be said at the start. One learns with no surprise that Conservative Orthodoxy stirred uneasily as it saw progressive religious thought setting its face steadfastly for what was taken to be a long march to an unknown, or rather a too well known, goal; and one has to picture, side by side with the growing feeling in the minds of some that theology must move forward from the positions it occupied, a parallel growth of conviction in the minds of others that it must rather move backward to the standing-ground of ancient authority if any theology at all were to be left. Some might hold that both wine and bottles must be new : there were others—intellectual and spiritual giants, too, whom, though one may think them mistaken, one dare not despise—who held that the old wine was better, and that, if the bottles were to be changed, it must be for still older ones than those in use at the time. John Henry Newman has told us how he, the greatest figure of the " later Oriel school," watched the on-coming of that " liberalism " which he hated with perfect hatred, and how in his own mind and in that of many others at Oxford there went on that movement of thought and feeling—of feeling perhaps rather than of thought—which at last,

when it had reached its climax of power, swept
him and so many more up to the safe rock of
Rome.[1] The story is not here our concern;
but the student of Liberal Orthodoxy must
discern, behind the ranks of those who welcomed
doctrinal change with a smile or helped it on
thinking to do Christ service, the set and sad
faces of not a few, thinkers and saints, to whom
the growth of change meant at least a temporary
victory for anti-Christ rather than the spread
of Christ's name. And he may spare them an
interested glance the more readily because, while
they sought to stay " liberalism's " career and
succeeded so far as the personal adherence to
" liberalism " of not a few was concerned, they
really, as the final issue from the interplaying
forces they set in motion, helped on " liberalism's "
cause after all; for to press the dilemma between
" liberalism or Rome," and to give what seemed
so signal an illustration of its inevitableness,
could have but one result in the process of the
years. But the Oxford Movement can here be
no more than named. More immediately ger-
mane to our purpose is something else that
catches our eye as the " background " is scanned
—the presence of influences which, after the period
now under consideration was over, were to push
Liberal Orthodoxy further, to shape its contentions, to set the key for much of its speech.
At this time, as has been said, Liberal Orthodoxy
was mainly concerned in discovering the consequences and implications of the one theological

[1] See Newman's *Apologia pro Vita Sua*, chap. i, also
note A.

surrender to which it had already committed itself; but new problems were rearing their heads and preparing themselves to put tests which by-and-by Liberal Orthodoxy would have to confront; and perhaps even Liberal Orthodoxy's process of self-discovery, as we have described it, was quickened by their dim prophetic movements, and carried on with an underlying consciousness of the tests to come in the period beyond. Changes in the current geological views, such as those brought about by the publication of Lyell's *Principles of Geology* in 1830–1833—the new views, with their insistence on the earth's antiquity and their denial that a series of " catastrophes " and " special creations " was necessary to account for the various strata and the fossils they contained, involving the surrender of the early chapters of Genesis in their literal reading— suggested that science and religion might soon have to re-adjust their boundaries either in friendly conference or upon the stricken field after war. Indeed, attempts were made, by Dr. Pye-Smith in the *Congregational Lecture* of 1839, and by Hugh Miller in *The Testimony of the Rocks* (1852–1855) to overcome the difficulty, not by taking up the later Liberal Orthodox position that it was not the business of the Bible to teach science, but by maintaining that Genesis, if you understood it aright, really taught, or was at least in harmony with, the new geology rather than the old. The general conception of evolution was shaping itself in Herbert Spencer's brain; and besides publishing *Social Statics* in 1850, *The Principles of Psychology* in 1855, and

contributing to the *Westminster Review* various
articles in which his "Synthetic Philosophy"
was adumbrated, he issued a complete syllabus
of his system in 1860, the year with which this
chapter's survey is to close. Darwin was hard
at work on the investigations which were to lead
to the theory of *The Origin of Species* in 1859,
and to place upon a more truly scientific basis
the ideas of development put forth anonymously
by Robert Chambers in his *Vestiges of the Natural
History of Creation* so long ago as 1844. And
besides all this, certain direct assaults upon
orthodox doctrine should be named as apper-
taining to the "background" we are sketching
out. Charles Hennell in *An Inquiry Concerning
the Origin of Christianity* (1838)—a book which
powerfully influenced George Eliot away from
the Christian religion wherein she had been
trained—Francis Newman in *Phases of Faith*
(1850), and William Rathbone Greg in *The Creed
of Christendom* (1851) blew from their hostile
trumpets against the walls of the Christian
citadel blasts which might well summon the
defenders armed and alert to their posts. Hennell
was a disciple of Strauss : Greg may be described
as rationalist in the older German sense, negativ-
ing revelation and miracle and everything that
involved any supernatural intervention of God in
the history of the world; while Newman's book
came in the end to be a vehement repudiation
of religion altogether in the sense of anything
more than morality, at least a reduction of all
religion to a sort of vague emotion which would
not accept Christ Himself, even when criticism

passed His alleged utterances as genuine, for an authoritative guide. Such attacks as these would naturally help to make Liberal Orthodoxy realise more keenly than before that religion could not meet them with mere negligence or haughty disdain, and that only because religion had formerly claimed too much could these formidable counter-claims now be launched against it : they would make it the more anxious (particularly as it was against the traditional theory of inspiration that all the writers just named delivered thrust upon thrust, evidently assuming that if this were overthrown their complete victory at all points would follow as a matter of course) to distinguish itself from that Conservative Orthodoxy out of whose exaggerated conservatism the attacks derived whatever legitimacy they possessed; and so the process of drawing out the consequences and implications of Liberal Orthodoxy's first theological surrender would be helped on. But all these things—the protests of Conservative Orthodoxy, the threatening mien of science, the direct assaults of scepticism—belong to the " background "; and it is the process itself we must now turn ourselves to watch. It is well, nevertheless, to be conscious of the " background " and of what it contains, since these things, besides being not quite without influence on the then present, assuredly pointed to the future and to the necessities which Liberal Orthodoxy would in the future have to meet. And it is for this reason that the " background " has been thus drawn.

The early theological liberalism of Britain, we

saw, took its stand above all things (and this, though that early liberalism may be divided into two sections, holds good of both) on the principle that treatment and interpretation of the Bible should be free. That was really its one contention, and it came to other contentions only as they seemed to be implied in this. Actual criticism of the Scriptures, in the customary modern sense—and such criticism would both be fostered by the surrender of the older belief as to the Bible's verbal inspiration and inerrancy, and would tend to further weakening of that belief in its turn—was gathering power in these years. The work which had been commenced in tentative fashion by Bishop Marsh [1] as early as 1801, in his book on *The Origin and Composition of the Three First Canonical Gospels*, was being continued and enlarged by investigators more competent and better equipped; and Stanley's *Commentary on Paul's Epistles to the Corinthians*, Benjamin Jowett's *Commentary on Paul's Epistles to the Romans, Galatians, and Thessalonians* (both in 1855), and Davidson's edition of Horne's *Introduction to the Critical Study of the Holy*

---

[1] Marsh was Bishop of Peterborough from 1819 to 1835, and previously Bishop of Llandaff from 1816 to 1819. He had published in 1793, when Lady Margaret Professor of Divinity at Cambridge, a translation of Michaelis' *Introduction to the New Testament*, with annotations of his own. His theory as to the three Synoptists, which has now only a historical interest, was that all the writers had a common original Hebrew document, Mark and Luke possessing a Greek translation as well. Matthew retained the Hebrew, but some one else translated his work into Greek, being helped by the Greek translation which Mark and Luke had already made.

Scriptures (1856),[1] in which work Davidson gave
up the Mosaic authorship of the Pentateuch as
untenable, may be taken as marking the beginning
of that long line of British critical work which
has never since died out. Of course the appearance of Coleridge's *Confessions of an Inquiring
Spirit* in 1840 had fanned the critical flame.
But, as has been previously said, Biblical
criticism can be only cursorily referred to in these
pages. It can only be mentioned as acting on,
and in turn acted on by, the spirit of freer
Biblical treatment which was abroad. It is the
thread of strictly theological development that
we have to find.

Picking up this thread, it is with the men of
the Coleridgean section, so to call it—the men who
added to the negation of verbal inspiration the
positive idea that a revelation's test lay in its
correspondence with the moral constitution of
mankind—that we may begin; and among the
disciples of Coleridge, Julius Charles Hare (1795–
1855) must first be named. The mention of him
carries us to the University which, much more
than Oxford, was to be the home of theological
liberalism in the near future, and certainly the
University wherein the special type of liberal
thought derived from Coleridge was to exercise
its strongest spells. As we have seen, Thirlwall,
of the other British school, was a Cambridge man;

[1] Horne's book had appeared in 1818, but Davidson
practically re-wrote it. Davidson was a professor at Lan-
cashire Independent College, and lost his Chair on account
of his views. It should be understood that Davidson's
espousal of the extreme views of the Tübingen school in
regard to the New Testament belongs to a later date.

o

but speaking generally, the theological liberalism
of Oxford was then, and for a good while to come,
of the "Oriel" or "Noetic" order, while the
warmer type affiliated with Coleridge had its
home at the sister seat. For Hare's direct
indebtedness and discipleship to Coleridge we
have his own emphatic testimony when he tells
us, in the preface to *The Mission of the Comforter*,
that to found himself upon "the great religious
philosopher to whom the mind of our generation
in England owes more than to any other man"
has been his aim in all he has written. He was
not a great religious thinker, and to eyes which
glance back only casually his light is lost by
reason of the greater lights which dazzle us against
the smaller ones while they attract us to themselves; but his strenuous assertions in the volume
just named, that the Holy Spirit is not an influence magically and once for all communicated
in baptism, and that the Spirit's gifts do not
consist in the miraculous powers which have at
various times appeared in the Church's history,
nor even in any sudden moral effect wrought as
by an "electric transmuting flash" upon the
individual soul, but that the Spirit and His gifts
are to be identified with the abiding presence
and influence of God Himself in the human heart
—his other equally strenuous assertion, in *The
Victory of Faith*, that faith was not intellectual
assent, but the response of the human soul to
the Spirit's call—these things at the same time
indicate where he stood, and give him a claim
to the gratitude of those who realise that not
without greater recompense of reproach than

they would now incur could such assertions then be made.

But both these assertions were merely fresh statements, rather than fresh applications, of Coleridge's chief idea; and for that matter, Hare was probably well content just to echo his master thus. More was soon to come. From Hare we may pass to the later books of Erskine, mentioned on a previous page as having given fuller application to Erskine's initial idea. "Truth must commend itself to the moral constitution of mankind"—so, more than once, have we summed up the fundamental principle of those who thought as Erskine thought. How, then, if we read the Scriptures in the light of that principle, are we to construe the idea of salvation? It was not by chance that this question came to be the one pressing most closely upon Erskine's mind, and that the interest which Coleridge (and at first Erskine himself) had diffused over various "illustrations" of the fundamental principle came to be concentrated on this; for the position stood thus—that the very formulation of the principle by which Scripture was henceforth to be read contradicted the doctrine of salvation which the leading passages of Scripture, read on the older principle, had been supposed to support. That doctrine proclaimed man as utterly severed from God and God's grace, with a great gulf fixed between himself and all divineness, without any operative share in God's pardoning love until, by identifying himself with an atonement which *offered* grace and love, man drew grace and love out of their potentiality

and made them effectual for his own individual
life and fate. And even so, what was accomplished was only a sort of external application
of grace and love—an application of them to
man's *position* rather than to man *himself*. But
if this represented the facts, what room could
there be for speaking about a recognition of
truth by the moral nature of man? Moral
nature, in any real sense, he had none—certainly
no moral nature capable of answering to the
approach of any heavenly revealing ministry.
There was no guarantee that even *after* the
moment of salvation such a moral nature would
be born within. And while such conceptions
of man, forgiveness, God, and grace might be
entirely consistent with a scheme founded upon
acceptance of a verbally-inspired Book, they
were utterly inconsistent with the foundation
which Erskine desired to substitute for this.
The new method of reading the Scripture necessarily involved a new doctrine on this, the most
vital doctrinal point of all. In his later books,
therefore, Erskine contended for the larger and
richer view of man's nature, of God's grace, of
salvation, which was so necessary, if his great idea
—the idea of response out of man's moral constitution to the revelations of God—was to stand.
In reality, it came to this—that emphasis passed
from the *necessity* to the *possibility* of such a
response from man's nature to God's: the
essential moral worth and spiritual greatness of
man came to be stressed; and Erskine really
found himself, by this shifting of the accent,
standing where we saw that Channing stood.

In *The Unconditional Freeness of the Gospel* (1828), and in *The Brazen Serpent* (1831), he maintained that because Christ is the Head of the race—not merely in the sense that the earthly Christ was the representative of what man ought to be and of what man might become, but in the sense that *in* Him and *through* Him, not otherwise, all humanity had as a literal fact had its life since human history began—Christ's life and death had necessarily reconciled *all* men to God : in the perfect obedience Christ had rendered to God's will by His sinless life and the sacrifice whereto it had led, He had carried all the members of the human family with Him, *if they would have it so ;* from which it followed that not a new issue of pardon, a new patent of reconciliation, from God's chancellery, but a *consciousness* of the pardon and reconciliation they already possessed, was what men really required. The life of Christ which was already in them must wake to a consciousness of itself, its position, its possibilities, its hopes and powers; and that consciousness must rule. It was, in short, the first outstanding declaration, in anything like the key which has become so familiar of recent years, of the immanence of the divine life in man. And once Erskine had given the note, others took it up, to sound it from varied instruments of their own. Since we are at the moment in Scotland and with Erskine, we may speak next of McLeod Campbell (1800–1872) Erskine's friend, and of his book on *The Nature of the Atonement*, though this did not appear until 1856. Long before, Campbell, as minister of the parish of Row in Dumbarton-

shire, had been charged with faithlessness to
the standards of the Scottish Church because,
in opposition to the stringent doctrine of " election " which limited the benefits of Christ's
redeeming work to a chosen few, he taught that
Christ had died for all; and the arraignment had
ended in his deposition in 1831. The precise
steps by which he had reached to his belief in a
universal Atonement have an interest of their
own. The low spiritual standard with which
the bulk of his hearers were content distressed
his soul : searching for its cause, he came to the
conclusion that men and women lacked the
impulse to moral and spiritual striving which a
perfect assurance of God's love would have given :
this lack, in its turn, arose from uncertainty as
to whether or no they were counted among those
whom Christ's saving work embraced; and it
could only be removed, therefore, by lifting on
high before them the glorious truth that the
embrace of Christ's saving work went round, not
a limited number, but *all* the families of men and
all the individuals these comprised. After his
deprivation, Campbell sought through prolonged
meditation for a more complete and systematic
grounding of this faith, which had rather sprung
upon him as an inspiration under the necessities
of his ministry than been reached as a logically-
attained conclusion; and the book on the Atonement was the result. In effect, the book re-
states Erskine's thought in Campbell's own words
and from Campbell's special point of view.
Once again we come upon the conception that
Christ is the race's Head. In Christ's sufferings

and death He accepted God's point of view,
identified Himself with God's hatred and condemnation of sin : as man in his turn identifies
himself with Christ, Christ's attitude towards sin
is reproduced in man; and thus man is, not so
much reconciled to God, as brought to a realisation and consciousness of the reconciliation which
Christ has already made. It was Erskine's note
struck with a touch only slightly different from
Erskine's own. But before Campbell's book
appeared, an English teacher whose name and
work have become far more widely known than
Campbell's had been insisting on very similar
fundamental ideas. Maurice (1805–1872)—himself, as he confesses, largely influenced by
Erskine's writings—had found in the conception
of Christ as the Head of the race the central
conception of Christian truth, and had made it
the touchstone for the rest. In various books—
of which perhaps *The Kingdom of Christ* (1842),
Theological Essays (1853), and *The Doctrine of
Sacrifice* (1854) may be singled out as specially
significant—he had maintained that Christ was
in every man and consequently every man in
Christ, that every man (it is in reality only
putting the same thing in other words) was already a child of God and needed not to become
one, that sin lay in refusing to recognise this fact
and salvation in awaking to its glory and its
truth. It is perhaps somewhat unfortunate that
the controversy to which the last of the *Theological Essays*, that on " eternal life and eternal
death," gave rise, and which lost Maurice his
Chair at King's College, as also Maurice's so-

called " Broad Churchism," with the peculiarities
which hung upon it, should have tended with
many to the obscuration of Maurice's principal
line of thought.   There are, in fact, many things
about Maurice which lend themselves to the
production of a similar effect.   One remembers
his curious mixture of charity and bigotry—the
charity which would have gathered all schools of
Christian thought within the doors of one Church,
the bigotry which would not base such inclusion
on general " toleration " grounds, but only on
Maurice's own conviction (repudiated by many
who were to be invited in its name) that every
one was God's child.   One remembers the social
enthusiasm which drew Kingsley to his feet and
inaugurated the " Christian Socialism " of which
so much has since been heard.   And remembering
these and other things, one forgets, or loses grasp
upon, the one basal thing.   One has to say, also,
that Maurice's literary style produces in the
reader, unless he knits his brows and draws in
all the outposts of his thought to reinforce the
main attack, a quite painful sense of bewilder-
ment, and raises the question, not only whether
the reader is understanding Maurice, but whether
Maurice understood himself.   Yet there can be
no doubt—and a closer scrutiny always ends on
this assurance—that through everything Maurice
sets down a straight uniting thread is run.   And
the thread is this—God, through Christ, is in
every man.   Man's nature is essentially divine,
and it is the call of his own nature that man must
hear if he would have all things well with him.
If he really believes that Christ is in him and

that he is himself in Christ, the belief will have such constraining power that all his life will be morally transformed. So from Maurice's voice in England did the note which in Scotland Erskine had sounded go clearly forth. And it is still the note—perhaps one might say with some supplemental notes added to make a richer chord —which Coleridge had raised when the century was young.

Coming down the line of development from the other starting-point of Liberal Orthodoxy at home—that lying in the " early Oriel school "— and enquiring how fuller application was given to first principles as time passed on, we meet with one great name, that of Frederick William Robertson (1816–1853), which claims our homage and arrests our steps. Perhaps, however, it would be unjust to omit at least a bare pre- liminary mention of two names which have almost passed into oblivion now. Of A. J. Scott (1805–1866) comparatively few people have ever heard; and not many who possess some acquaint- ance with the works of Erskine and McLeod Campbell know that Scott was the friend of both. As a matter of fact, Scott was deposed from the ministry of the Scottish Church at the same time as Campbell, afterwards becoming Principal of Owens College, Manchester. He has left only a small volume of *Discourses*—or rather, he left nothing at all, for friends gathered these few fragments up after he had passed away; but to read them is to feel the touch of no common mind. Scott can hardly, upon the evidence of the book, be ranked as strictly of the Coleridgean

school, for which reason he is mentioned here
rather than among the Coleridgean names. Nor
indeed is the volume, in its actual substance as
distinct from its atmosphere and spirit, of great
account. But when one finds that George Macdonald revered him (it is to Scott that *Robert
Falconer* is dedicated, and there is a sonnet to his
memory besides), and that Baldwin Brown ac-
knowledged a debt, one discerns him as a figure
standing behind more famous men for their
inspiration and their strengthening, and feels
that one must beckon the shadowy form out of
its retirement and look for an instant upon its
face. The other name is that of Frederic Myers,
who died in 1856, and whose *Catholic Thoughts
on the Bible and Theology*, though not published
until 1874, was printed for private circulation in
1848. The book is, in short summary, a plea
for larger ideas of revelation than those ordinarily
entertained, a protest against mechanical views
of inspiration, and a declaration that you cannot
form a theological system by mere juxtaposition
of Biblical texts. The contentions which we
noted as characterising the Oriel men—the contention that time, place, and spirit must be taken
into our reckoning when we are dealing with the
Bible's contents, that different portions of the
Scriptures appertain to different stages of development in the world's history and are therefore
not all of equal worth—reappear in Myers' work;
and he goes further than did his predecessors in
affirming that as there has been progress behind
the Bible's production, so there must be progress
in the Bible's interpretation too. If Myers made

no special contribution to theology—or if, which possibly better represents the case, what he contributed has been with us so long that we have forgotten it ever needed to be given at all and have also forgotten what uglier things his gift displaced—he merits at least a line in a record of the pioneers. But Robertson of Brighton—one bows one's head at his name. The man who wrestled his way to spiritual and intellectual peace through deserts, dangers, and fiend-beset paths as numerous and terrible as any whereof the *Pilgrim's Progress* tells—who spent days and nights in anxious watching and prayer over the fate of his own soul and of the souls committed to his charge—whose heart was almost broken by the thought that the religion whose minister he was had sullied its own beauty so sadly—and who died at thirty-seven under the burden of it all—he was truly one of the saints of the earth. And though it is with the thinker rather than with the saint that we are here concerned, it would not be meet that the saint should be quite forgotten nor that recognition of his saintliness should be quite withheld. But to turn to the thinker—it is, as has been said, to the line dropping down from the " Oriel " beginning that Robertson belongs. He developed and applied that general principle of freer Bible treatment for which the Oriel men had fought. Yet this must not be misunderstood. If in any of the Oriel men something of coldness is discernible—if the impression made by some of them is that of intellectuality in the main—what has already been said of Robertson will have shown that to

him these things do not apply. Arnold with
his spiritual passion is the man to whom, among
those of the Oriel school, Robertson is most
closely akin. Against the traditional theories
of inspiration, and against the cold dogmatism
to which those theories led, he revolted with all
the passion of his nature—and then, the moment
he looked beyond the mere words of the Book to
the realities behind them, he saw a new Christ,
a new God, and new operations of both upon man.
In fact, it was Robertson's own hungry heart—
his heart so hungry for a living communion with
God—and his recognition of a similar hunger in
the hearts of men, that made him break with the
Bibliolatry of the older evangelicalism, and that
gave form to the positive teaching which the
Sermons, his gift of undying value to the world,
contain. What we find in him is the freer treatment of the Bible brought specifically into the
service of such a hunger, and turned to its satisfying. Hence Robertson's insistence on the
humanity of Christ, and his constant declaration
that by an apprehension of Christ's true humanity
you must come to the conclusion that He is more
than human after all : hence his ceaseless efforts
to turn every religious belief into a practical one
—one which suggested a programme of spiritual
culture and a method of carrying the programme
out : hence his dread of anything stereotyped
in religious speech, since the repetition of set
forms and phrases might come to be the giving
of stones for bread, and the souls which received
it might not know how they were being betrayed.
Robertson the thinker is in fact one with Robert-

son the saint in the end; and it was his spiritual passion which determined the lines on which his thinking ran. Because he was spiritually passionate and aspiring, the older dogmatism, based on the older idea of what the Bible was and of how the Bible had come, repelled him. His starved soul could not feed on husks such as these. And once he read the Bible, not in slavish pupilage to its mere words, but in order to drink in its large spiritual ideas, that inward passion and hunger showed him how to read and how to understand and how to apply, and every religious truth leaped into immediate contact with his inner nature and its needs. It was by the saint that the thinker, and by the saintliness that the conditions of the thinking, were made. In the result we get, not a systematic treatment of theology—for Robertson was a preacher above all things, and touched theology only so far as pulpit uses required—but a fresh and unconventional turning of each truth into such a position and to such an angle that souls which shared Robertson's passion would find in it a help, an inspiration, and a joy. Nor did this involve anything in the nature of " heresy "—though of course it did involve the *not* saying of many things which conventional religion said, but which from Robertson's standpoint were useless or worse, and though, equally of course, the omission of these things was quite sufficient to set the heresy-hunters off in full cry. There was really nothing negative in Robertson's preaching—save for that one negation of " mechanical religion " which was at the foundation of it all. He simply accepted the deliverance of mind which the possibility of a freer Bible treatment offered him, and showed how, in contact with this religious truth and that, deliverance of the mind might be made to assist the deliverance of the soul. It is in this that his liberalism—and his greatness—lie.

Our stay with each of these men has been but short—shorter than it would be if their intrinsic merits, the amount of attention which in himself each one deserves, were the deciding factor in the case. For our present purpose, however, no longer stay is needed, however attractive, or however well-deserved, a longer stay might be. For we want to obtain not so much a detailed knowledge of what each successive thinker held, as a general view which will enable us to see each thinker's place in Liberal Orthodoxy's development, so that in the end it shall be the line of that development, not the ideas of individuals, that is impressed most strongly upon our minds. And for this, what has been said will serve. And to sum up, we have seen all these teachers putting to larger application that principle of freer treatment of the Bible upon which at the beginning of its career Liberal Orthodoxy had thrown itself with such ready abandon, finding out some of the consequences which that principle entailed. To Robertson, in the emancipation of soul which descended upon him together with the first emancipation of the mind, in that passionate spiritual aspiration of his which had as it were flung itself helplessly against a steadfast wall so long as mechanical readings of the Bible and its doctrines had been his programme, and which, now that the wall was beaten down, went roaming through all the fields of religious thought to find its response—to Robertson every Christian doctrine spoke with new voice to confirm the soul-emancipation he had won, and to whisper a secret whereby it might be turned into a means of satisfying the aspiration unsatisfied until now. To Erskine, Campbell, and Maurice the truth that divine revelation must find a response in the moral constitution of man, and must prove itself by so doing, became a finger pointing to the further truth—really the same truth looked at from another quarter and along another line— that man possessed a divine quality in that human nature which had hitherto been condemned as wholly un-divine. For all of them, it was the drawing out of what had been, unknown to them, involved in the acceptance of an initial idea. Over and above that, one can see, perhaps, how close to the idea of a veritable life-dynamic in Christ all these thinkers came— how those of the Coleridgean order overshot it, how Robertson just stopped short. Declaring that man's great need was not to *receive* the divine life, but to waken to the *consciousness* of it, the Coleridgean school passed to the other extreme from the idea that in man there was nothing divine at all, incurred the danger which more recent resurrections of the same extreme position have revealed, the danger of making Christ's redeeming work one of moral influence alone, and missed the middle line of teaching— the position surely nearer to the truth than

either of the other two !—that man needs a new
baptism of God's life to save him, that this
baptism is offered him moment by moment in a
living Christ, and that man can receive it precisely *because* the measure of divineness he already
possesses constitutes in itself a capacity for
more.   And Robertson, passing through the bar-
riers which snapped and fell as the old theory of
a mechanically-inspired Bible disappeared, went
out far enough into the broad lands before him
to find the Christ of wonderful humanity, who,
because so wonderful in His humanity, must be
in the fullest significance of the term divine, and
who by the glory and wonder of what He once
was becomes a present inspiration to all who put
themselves beneath the story's spell, but not far
enough to find the Christ who, by virtue of what
He *is*, can ceaselessly put Himself into His own
so that it shall be not they that live but Christ
that lives in them.   In both cases, so near and
yet so far !   And in both cases, it meant that
the constitutive act of Christian discipleship remained at a right *understanding* of things, when
all was done.   It was one of the lost opportunities
from which Liberal Orthodoxy has too often
turned its face away.

When in 1860 *Essays and Reviews* appeared, the
timid souls who had listened with growing apprehension to such voices as those of Maurice,
Robertson, and the rest, thought that full justification of their fears had arrived.[1]   The book,

---

[1] On *Essays and Reviews*, see Hunt, *Religious Thought in
England in the Nineteenth Century ;* V. F. Storr, *Development*

of which a very brief account will suffice, contained seven papers on various theological themes, though at the basis of all the essays lay the idea which had inspired the liberal movement hitherto—the idea that interpretation of Scripture should be free, and that the mere letter of it must not be taken as a binding force. In fact, it was various applications of that idea that the book set forth. Of the seven essayists five were Oxford men; but the two Cambridge writers, Williams and Goodwin, really belonged, by their manner of thinking, to the Oxford line of liberalism, and did not echo the accents of Maurice. Stanley, it is worth while to add, was asked to contribute, but declined. The moving mind—although each essayist was responsible for his own statements, and it was not claimed that any one essay necessarily represented all the essayists' opinions, the book being a collection of separate stones put into one containing receptacle rather than a planned building—was that of Henry Bristow Wilson, vicar of Great Staughton in Huntingdonshire; and his own contribution to the volume consisted of a paper on " The National Church." The contention of the paper was that in the Church of the nation all theological statements should be accepted as merely provisional, that subscription should accordingly be abolished, that a national Church ought to be a moral agency rather than a distinctively religious one (it need not even be Christian, Wilson does not

---

of English Theology in the Nineteenth Century 1800–1860; Cornish, History of the English Church in the Nineteenth Century, ii. 215 ff.

P

hesitate to say), and that all varieties of religious
thought, together with men of no specifically
religious thought, should find room within it.
Temple, then headmaster of Rugby, subsequently Bishop of London and Archbishop of
Canterbury, wrote the first essay in the book
under the title " The Education of the Human
Race "—Lessing's title covering much of Lessing's
thought. The paper merely asked for recognition of the facts that there were " stages " in the
spiritual development of the race, that the eras
of Law, of the Son of Man (who entered the world
just when the world was at a point of growth
fitted to receive Him), and of the Spirit followed
in due succession, and that in the era of the Spirit
" principles," not fixed formulas, were to be the
guide. Baden Powell wrote on " The Study of
the Evidences of Christianity," seeking quite
legitimately to substitute stress on " internal "
for stress on " external " evidences, but carrying
the matter so far as to make it clear that for him,
as for Matthew Arnold later on, the question of
miracles could be satisfactorily disposed of by
airily remarking that " miracles do not happen."
Mark Pattison, in the essay on " Tendencies of
Religious Thought in England 1688–1750," exposed the failure of the merely rationalistic
eighteenth century apologetic, thus doing what
would have been most valuable service if he had
only gone on to indicate what the new apologetic
ought to be. Rowland Williams wrote on
" Bunsen's Biblical Researches," setting out
some of the conclusions to which German
criticism had come in respect of various Bible

books, and drawing the inevitable inference that in view of these established conclusions the conventional conception of revelation must be revised.[1] Jowett, taking for his theme "The Interpretation of Scripture," reiterated with resounding emphasis what had been uttered in many tones, though some of them had been less arresting and more tentative than his, since the century's beginning—"Interpret the Bible as you interpret any other book." Which meant, "Make allowance for the personal idiosyncrasies of each writer; remember the local conditions; plant yourself in imagination at the historic point each writer occupied; and then test each writer's meaning, as thus ascertained, by the knowledge of your own time." Goodwin, a layman and one of the Cambridge authors (Williams was the other) wrote on "The Mosaic Cosmogony," maintaining that revelation did not profess to offer instruction on subjects for whose investigation man's ordinary faculties were fitted, and that consequently all the "harmonisings" of science with Genesis were so much labour lost. And now the reader, if this brief description has left such a track upon his mind that he can with one of memory's glances see from its beginning to its end, will be able to understand what was

---

[1] Bunsen's life and labours (1791–1860) are worthy of the reader's separate research. He was a man of profound learning and profounder piety, politician, reformer, historian, student, and much else. He was Prussian ambassador in London from 1841 to 1854, and married an English wife. His *Memoirs* were published in 1868, and there is an article in the *Encyclopædia Britannica* which deals with him at some length.

meant by saying that the book embodies various applications of the one idea that reading and interpretation of the Scriptures should be untrammelled and free.

We need not, even in fancy, go out into the storm which the book's publication brought pelting down. Nor need we notice at any length how Frederic Harrison, in the *Westminster Review*, made merry over that suicide of Christianity which he took the book to signalise, since it left (according to him) nothing but " a revised Atonement, a transcendental Fall, a practical Salvation, and an idealised Damnation "; how some of the writers were cited before the ecclesiastical Courts; how the final acquittal moved Dr. Pusey to wrath, to such wrath that he engineered a petition to the Archbishops for a formal condemnation of the book, the said petition bearing eleven thousand signatures, most of them, as Hunt rather unkindly has it, those of " the lower orders of the clergy "; how various writers refuted, or tried to refute, one or other of the essayists; how the redoubtable Burgon, fearing nothing, rode full tilt at all the seven. What concerns us most is to mark the significance of the volume in Liberal Orthodoxy's history, to note how and why the volume ended, as we have before stated that it did end, that first period of Liberal Orthodoxy's development in which Liberal Orthodoxy made without any hesitation, and without much thought of consequences, the surrender which it could not avoid. It is not without significance, in this connection, that Thirlwall, one of the first pioneers of theo-

logical liberalism, was among those who attacked
Essays and Reviews. And we shall see presently
how, at any rate for a time after 1860, the spirit
of Liberal Orthodoxy became somewhat chast-
ened, its steps more cautious, its readiness to
make offers more restrained. The hatred—it is
not too strong a word—of the extreme orthodox
party towards the book and its writers is easily
understood. But was there anything in the book
that justified the fears which it aroused even in
many of the liberal school?

It was certainly not, in its actual contents,
destructive of any of the Christian essentials as
Liberal Orthodoxy would reckon these, if Baden
Powell's negation of miracles be left out of the
account. Looking through the papers to-day,
one is at first surprised that men of liberal
tendencies, at any rate, should have taken alarm.
And yet one presently perceives why alarm was
taken. The outstanding fact about *Essays and
Reviews* is that the entire book is negative,
dealing in the last analysis with beliefs which are
not to be received, and that no indication is given
as to where the process of stripping off true faith's
excrescences is to stop. And indeed, this being
so, the very fact that one of the essayists ran far
ahead of the rest, at the end of his course laying
destroying hands upon matters which belonged
to the central truth of all, would appear to have
a sinister significance. Must the journey end
for all where it ended for him, if they followed the
straight road? The question might well arise.
But whether it arose or not as out of Baden
Powell's essay, the bringing together of so many

" applications " of the initial idea, the succession
of " nay, nay " with scarce ever a " yea " inter-
spersed, the rush and roar made when so many
little rivulets of negation coalesced, as they had
not coalesced before, to make a broad and swiftly-
running stream—all this could not but give pause
to some. Amid the crash of walls and the
splintering glass the haunting query would in-
trude, " How much of the building will be left,
since no limit to the destructive process has been
fixed ? Soon there will be nothing but a vacant
space to gaze at. How is a new building to be
raised ? " And the final issue of it all with regard
to the supreme interest of Christianity, the Person
of Christ Himself, there were no safeguards in
respect of that !—so the sudden realisation would
heave up in their breasts. There, in fact, lay
the weakness, and the danger, of the thinking—
the thinking which simply took one negative idea
and applied it—whose climax was reached in
Essays and Reviews. Mr. Storr quite rightly
points out, as one of the most striking things
about the book, that it contains no article on the
Person of Christ.[1] The travellers on this road
had not been sufficiently careful to see the end
from the beginning, to decide the point beyond
which they would *not* go, and to avoid gathering
such momentum as would carry them past the
point assigned. It is no wonder that some of
them began to wonder whether already the
final catastrophe had not been incurred. In
fact, with the publication of *Essays and Reviews*

[1] *The Development of English Theology in the Nineteenth
Century 1800–1860,* pp. 446, 447.

Liberal Orthodoxy in Britain began to realise
that its first initial act of surrender—inasmuch
as in making it Liberal Orthodoxy had possessed
no clear outlook beyond the act *itself*, and because
the implications and applications of the act had
not been related to one another and to the central
Christian reality, so becoming an act positive
and constructive instead of a mere denial—that
its first initial act of surrender had been too
heedlessly and too blindly made. The supposedly
untouchable *minimum*, in order to preserve
which Liberal Orthodoxy had made its concessions so freely, was being found not untouchable
after all; and the conditions of the bargain which
Liberal Orthodoxy fondly imagined itself to
have made, but in respect of which it had taken
no security, were already being infringed. The
effect of this realisation upon Liberal Orthodoxy's
future we shall see a little further on.

As once before, we have to pass for a moment
from Britain to America, since Bushnell (1802–
1876), surely one of America's greatest names,
must not be passed unnoticed by. Bushnell's
work belongs in part to a time beyond the strict
limits of our chapter, for *The Vicarious Sacrifice*
was published in 1865, and *Forgiveness and Law*
not till 1874. But *Christian Nurture*, the work
in which Bushnell first made his general position
clear, appeared so early as 1846; and all the
subsequent books rested upon the same fundamental principle as did this. If we want a brief
characterisation of Bushnell, we may with justice
term him the American Vinet, since Vinet's

leading idea—that doctrine must commend itself to conscience—was most emphatically Bushnell's too. It was from the standpoint of this idea that Bushnell worked over some of the orthodox doctrines—those of original sin, of atonement, and others—leaving them considerably modified when he had done. In many ways he recalls Channing, although he had been opposed to Channing in those earlier controversies of the century which had led to the Unitarian secessions from the Congregational ranks. In spirit, at any rate, the two men were very near akin; but while Channing proclaimed that doctrine must commend itself to the reason, Bushnell made conscience rather than reason the warder, so ranging himself, as has been said, at Vinet's side. So far as one particular doctrine is concerned, the application of Bushnell's test brought him to an assertion similar to the great assertion of Erskine and Maurice; and, for that matter, the principle that doctrine must commend itself to conscience is only the same principle, less philosophically grounded and formulated, as that from which the Coleridgean school worked—the principle that revelation must be in consonance with the moral constitution of mankind. From the doctrine that God was the Father of only a few and of none till they were called, that all men were by nature hopelessly degraded and vile, with no single spark of the divine among the dust and ashes within, Bushnell violently recoiled as conscience raised its protest against the consequences which that doctrine involved, taking the opposite view with an earnestness as warm as that which the English thinkers showed. Similarly the old forensic theory of the Atonement, with its conception of a God who could not be appeased unless sin's due punishment were endured, but who *could* be appeased if that due punishment were laid on one by whom no punishment had been incurred, had to go. Further, since erroneous conceptions of the Trinity— conceptions which took the word " person " in the common literal sense—were, in Bushnell's eyes, largely responsible for erroneous views of the Atonement, and were in turn supported by the erroneous views to which in the first instance they had given birth, Bushnell so modified the Trinitarian doctrine as to bring upon himself a charge of heresy in this regard, though there was nothing Arian in his estimate of Jesus Christ. And finally—since the mere text of the Bible appeared to buttress many of the ideas he challenged—Bushnell came to advocate the reading of the Scriptures in the spirit rather than according to the letter, thus ending where we saw the English thinkers begin. One may believe that Bushnell often fought against popular misconceptions of orthodoxy rather than against orthodoxy itself, though, if one makes the criticism, one must go on to admit that many pulpits and much theological writing gave him abundant excuse, as many pulpits and much theological writing give abundant excuse for a similar procedure now; and one may acknowledge the danger, in matters of faith, of making individual conscience the ultimate judge. But one cannot do otherwise than admire the man who, shutting

himself away from all voices save that in which
God spoke to his conscience and that in which
his conscience answered back to God, built up
his temple of truth as the awe-inspiring echoes
rang round his retreat. Bushnell's crown will
not quickly fade, nor the memory of him, as one
of Liberal Orthodoxy's champions—a champion
as pure of spirit as he was keen of brain—die soon
away.

And with this said of Bushnell, we may come
back to nearer regions once again.

CHAPTER VIII

WE left Liberal Orthodoxy in Germany in doubt whether, even with " speculation " added to the testimony of the " Christian consciousness," adequate safeguards for the historical Christ had really been found. The general method of men like Dorner and Rothe, while it did indeed reinforce faith in the historical Christ for those who held that some sort of passage from the Christian consciousness to the historical Christ already existed, offered no final reply to the obvious criticism from the Hegelian side—the criticism that it was only to ideas *about* the historical Christ that the passage really led. And in saying, as we said, that our survey of the men who followed that general method brought us " into the Ritschlian years," we touched upon the name of the theologian who sought a fresh means of overcoming the difficulty, and whose influence in Germany was during the closing decades of the nineteenth century at its height. It is at Ritschl (1822–1889) and his system that we have accordingly now to look.[1]

[1] A volume on Ritschl and his school is in preparation for this series. The student should consult chiefly *The Ritschlian Theology*, by Principal Garvie, D.D.; Mozley, *Ritschlianism ;* Ecke, *Die Theologische Schule Albrecht*

Description had best begin by stating that Ritschl is at one with Schleiermacher in starting theological construction from the experience of the Christian, but that he differs from Schleiermacher in declining to start it from Christian experience alone. So far as a comparison of the two men is concerned, that is the essential point, though of course minor differences exist, and though apart from these, the major divergence just indicated brings certain consequential divergences in its train. For instance, while Schleiermacher—beginning with Christian experience *per se*, and declaring that when you passed from Christian experience as it were out into the dark of unnamed possibilities, you found yourself brought up against a Christ in the main like the Christ of the New Testament, because the experience of men required the previous appearance in history of an archetypal Christ in whom that experience was perfect and out of whom it was born for the race—while Schleiermacher, in following this line, necessarily came into contact with that very " speculative thought " from whose thraldom he had sought to escape, Ritschl was able, by his particular method, to thrust " speculative thought " more effectually behind his back and to keep it there. But this will be clearer presently. To return

---

Ritschls. But the relevant literature is immense. Ritschl's chief work, *Die Christliche Lehre von der Rechtfertigung und Versöhnung*, appeared from 1870 to 1874. Ritsch was professor of theology successively at Bonn and Göttingen. For a little while he was an adherent of the Tübingen school, but this phase speedily passed.

to the principal statement. Schleiermacher began with Christian experience—so did Ritschl, but not from Christian experience *alone*. And because Ritschl began from Christian experience *plus* something else, the question which Schleiermacher had to face, " How travel from Christian experience to the historic Christ ? "—had no existence for him at all. For the " something else " *was* the historic Christ. That this phrase does not, in Ritschl's system, after all mean precisely what at a first reading it would be taken to mean, we shall presently see; but for the moment it must stand. " How travel from Christian experience to the historic Christ ? " Ritschl's reply is, " There is no travelling to be done. If you are at the point of Christian experience, you are already at the point of the historic Christ as well; for Christian experience and the historic Christ are given you *together ;* and in knowing anything of the first you must and do know the second as its source." In other words, Ritschl reads off the contents of the Christian consciousness in a fashion different from Schleiermacher's. The primary fact of which we are conscious is not a feeling whose cause, because it is not immediately proclaimed, must, if we wish to know what it is, be sought and found by an independent process : it is the correspondence of something within ourselves with something in Christ as He stands in history; and an experience which announces itself as " a correspondence " necessarily gives us in itself the *two* elements which " correspond." Were we drawing up an exhaustive account of

the Ritschlian system, and exploring it in all
its rooms and corners, there would be many
other things to dwell upon—that according to
Ritschl Christian experience does not consist,
as with Schleiermacher, in a simple feeling of
dependence, but in a consciousness of freedom
and victory over the world, of deliverance and
uplift into a spiritual realm, similar to Christ's
own; that it was for the establishment of the
"kingdom," a community of men and women
thus morally victorious and free, the revelation
in Christ was given; that through self-identification with the society which Christ set up does
the individual fulfil his destiny and obtain the
full "freedom and victory" which are the
Christian's signs and rights, though he may
obtain them in part by a study of the written
New Testament word. But in view of our
present purposes, the mere statement of these
points will suffice, though the statement, while
it need not be enlarged upon, is necessary for
a complete understanding of Ritschl's main
position. Weaving these points, now, into
what has already been said, the matter stands
thus. When we are investigating religion and
man's knowledge of God, we are really investigating religion and man's knowledge of God as
these are brought upon man in the historic
Christ : we need not enquire whether there *was*
any such historic Christ as the Church has
believed in; for, if we recognise facts as they
are, the question answers itself; and we are
put beyond the question in the very act of asking
it. The man of to-day—however the conflict of

voices may have confused the matter for him—
reads the New Testament books which tell of
Christ's words and works, and in the reading
of them the historic Christ, or rather the *record*
of the historic Christ, touches him; or he reads
those other New Testament books which tell
of the effect wrought upon men, for example
upon Paul, by a similar contact with Christ's
words and works, and in that reading the historic
Christ, or rather the *record* of the historic Christ,
touches him as it were at second hand; or he
studies the history of the Church, its saints, its
heroes, its martyrs, and as he does so the historic
Christ, or rather the *record* of the historic Christ,
touches him across the centuries again, and in
this case with accumulated power. This is
what is happening wherever there is any true
religion, any true knowledge of God, whether
the process is recognised or not. And since
religious experience, the knowledge of God, is
thus found to be in the final analysis a moral
impression and up-lift produced by recorded *fact*,
the movement of man's inner life into correspondence with Christ's inner life as history
portrays it (not that religious experience and
the knowledge of God, being found mysteriously
present, are subsequently *inferred* to have been
thus brought about, but that they are *seen*
actually *being* thus created, and are *not* seen to
be created in any other way), the *original* source
of religious experience and of the knowledge of
God lay in the *actual happening* of the facts
which do their work through the record now.
Yet one other thing must be emphasised. " The

record of the historic Christ," is a phrase which
has just now been interpolated more than once.
For Ritschl does not mean that the Christ who
once, by the happenings of His life, wrought a
moral and spiritual transformation upon man
exercises a *direct* transforming ministry now : to
say this would land him in that "speculation"
which he is so desperately anxious at all costs
to avoid and, worse still, in that mysticism
which he so bitterly detests : in this system no
place is found for a Christ who to-day lays His
heart close against the beating heart of man
and meets man in a living embrace. It is the
record of what Christ *was*, either as we read it
from the written page or as it comes to us on
the voices of those who have themselves read
and been spiritually recreated by the reading—
Christ's portrait as it hangs upon the wall and
enables us in imagination and memory to vision
the activities which the portrayed Figure long
ago performed—it is these things through which
Christ's grace is offered and received. Christ's
actual personal working is shut up within those
earthly years of His, and does not overflow
(except in such wise as the perpetuated story
of it can make a continuation of it and for it)
into our modern time. In fine, it is in the
strictest and most limited sense of the term the
"historic Christ" who, according to Ritschl,
redeems man. There is no religion, no revelation, save that which comes that way. Consistently with this, Ritschl will hear nothing of
any value in "natural religion," in those groping
thoughts and feeble guesses and fevered efforts

to penetrate the clouds and darkness gathered round the utmost hiding-place of God which, grotesque as many of them have been, most other thinkers hold to have been not quite in vain, and to have been in some sense preparations of man and of man's mind and of man's soul for the full light of the knowledge of the glory of God in the face of Jesus Christ. There is always a haunting fear lest by allowing any worth, however small, to these things you should admit the possibility that, apart from the " historic Christ," something of God can be known and something of fellowship with God attained. Nor, on the other hand, will Ritschl say anything but words of reproach—often indeed he will say words of utter scorn—to the " mystics " who claim that here and now God visits them in strange and incalculable ways, that for them God keeps a special language which only they and He can understand, and that secret ways to His presence, closed against most others, are known to them. For this, again, involves the unspeakable heresy that apart from the " historic Christ " something of divine revelation can enter the world. The plain fact of the situation, if you will open your eyes, is, Ritschl insists, that all the knowledge of God there is in the world, all the experience of redemption, of soul-freedom, of victory over the world, is actually being given to men through the knowledge of the Christ as He lived and moved and spoke and worked all those centuries ago. It is not that men, possessing these things, ought in all reasonableness to *infer* that it is

Q

thus they are becoming their own. It is the patent *reality* of the thing—you can see it going on before you—that these gifts are given to men through the " historic Christ," and that they are given in no other way. True spiritual experience and the historic Christ alight *together*, an inseparable two in one, upon the platform of the world.

But how does this get us out of our difficulties on the critical side? How does it come to be, or how does it make an opening for, an adequate apologetic as against the hostility with which Christianity is faced? For what defensive operations does it prepare the ground and train the guns? The short reply is that it makes possible, not so much a direct defence against assault, as retreat to a shelter which no assaulting force can reach. The Christian disappears into a region far from the battle-field, with a deep ravine, so to say, between his new situation and the old battle-field which the enemy has no means of traversing, and a region which is beyond the enemy's furthest fire. Ritschl's instruction is in effect this : " Fasten yourselves down upon the concrete, positive fact of the situation—the fact that the ' historic Christ,' in the sense previously explained, produces in you a sense of victory and up-lift over the world and of membership in the spiritual kingdom : then claim your right to say *all* that this fact enables you to say, and admit your obligation to say *no more*, and all trouble with criticism is at an end. Never travel outside the four corners of the concrete, positive fact itself. Let all

your credal declarations be simply *translations* of
the fact, not such metaphysical *explanations* of
the fact as you could only offer by going, or
claiming to have gone, behind the fact and
scrutinising the processes whereby it came to
be a fact. So long as you do this, you are
issuing no challenge which scientific enquiry can
take up : what you state to have happened in
your world has no point of contact, whether
friendly or unfriendly, with what scientific enquiry states to have happened in *its* world; and
to talk of conflict between science or philosophy
and Christian faith becomes, under these conditions, like talking of a conflict between mathe-
matics and love."

So much for the general procedure. But we
must pursue the matter further before it is
perfectly clear. What, if we thus fasten ourselves down to the one positive, concrete fact,
confine ourselves rigidly within its boundaries—
what, more particularly, can we say and what
can we not ? And here we touch upon Ritschl's
famous theory of " value-judgments," the theory
which has excited so much discussion, not to
say so much misunderstanding, among both
foes and friends, and of which something must
be said before we can answer the question just
asked.[1] It is not to be denied that, in respect
of some of its ultimate implications, a good many
clouds hang about the theory, or that some of

---

[1] For a brief account of " value-judgments," and of the
varying views of them held within the Ritschlian school,
see a paper in Garvie's *The Christian Certainty and the Modern
Perplexity*, pp. 230–278.

Ritschl's followers, while starting from it, have developed it in ways different from Ritschl's own. The differences, however, really turn, in the last analysis, upon the question whether the final act by which we give shape to a Christian faith, is simple or complex, whether the term "value-judgment" covers the *whole* act or whether (as Julius Kaftan [1] holds) the primary "value-judgment" leads on to a "theoretical judgment" based upon the "value-judgment" itself, the actual act of formulation embodying the two. But the question thus suggested, though of interest from the purely epistemological point of view, is irrelevant otherwise. Even if the second alternative be chosen, the "theoretical judgment" based upon the "value-judgment" does not carry us into a field beyond that of the "value-judgment" itself—that is, it does not bring the total process, resulting from the combination of the two "judgments," or the superimposition of the second upon the first, to the speculative level. Kaftan, it is true, declares that religious judgments—the "theoretical judgments" added to the "value-judgments"—give us knowledge of things as they are. (Not that Ritschl denies this, but Kaftan is anxious to set the point beyond dispute.) We may go on, for instance, to affirm that God is Absolute. Still, we make the affirmation on the basis and under the guarantee of our religious consciousness; and what Kaftan permits us to do is simply to take a term from

[1] To be distinguished from the Theodore Kaftan mentioned later on.

theoretical judgment—a quite empty and negative
term, he says, as theoretical judgment employs
it—and fill it out with a content which our
religious consciousness provides. Leaving this
point as relatively unimportant, let us see what
a " value-judgment " is. It is, in brief, the
appreciation and appraisement of any reality
in its *relation* to us and in its *effect* upon—otherwise, its " value " for—ourselves. In forming
our appreciation and appraisement of the reality
concerned, we do not approach it with the
mind's eye turned upon an already-possessed
system of realities and of truths about them with
the intention of discovering what the new reality
is relatively to the already-possessed realities, or
how into this already-possessed system of realities
and truths the new reality and truths about it
may be fitted; but we approach it as it were
holding for a lamp in our hands the effect
which the new reality has produced upon us
and with the intention of reading back into
the reality *what the effect finds within itself,* no
more and no less. The reality has been " worth "
this and this to us—we judge it therefore to *be*
this and this. The value-judgment formulates,
for description of the reality, the effect it has
produced within us : the reality is the exact
effect before it entered through our personality's
gates; or, to express it another way, in our
judgment we put back into the reality precisely
what the reality has put into us. Nor—it is
necessary to say—does this mean that in framing
our value-judgments we are only framing a
hypothesis which may or may not be true, and

whose actual validity we have no means of
bringing to the test, or that we are evading the
true issue by flinging over it a veil of words
whose mere sound drowns the difficulty's call.
Some such charge has repeatedly been thrown
against Ritschl's theory; and Ritschl has been
accused of being content if he can say that the
reality with which he is in contact *seems like*
this or that—that he is affected *as if* the reality
were this or that.   It was to meet such suspicions
that some of Ritschl's disciples modified their
master's epistemological doctrine on the lines
indicated above; for if the doctrine were that
in the final process of estimate a " theoretical
judgment " was superadded to the " value-
judgment " with which the process began, the
whole thing appeared to be brought into closer
relationship with the common mental operations
of every day.   But, apart from any such modification, the accusation has no ground.   Ritschl
never hinted that a value-judgment has smaller
validity than any other, or that it arrives at
anything other than the absolute and objective
truth.   Perhaps the term " value-judgment,"
or " judgment of worth," has about it a ring
which may to some extent account for the
misunderstanding; [1] and the fall of it upon the
casual ear may recall cases in which, for senti-
mental or similar reasons, we credit certain
possessions of our own with a value which they

[1] So far as the " man in the street " is concerned.   But
not in the case of those who know Ritschl at first hand.
And it is remarkable how certain scholars, who must be
presumed to have read him, reiterate the charge.

do not intrinsically possess, cases in which something *in us,* something purely subjective, is worked into, and consequently heightens, the effect which on its bare merits and by virtue of its inherent qualities the possession would produce. A paltry trinket, for instance, may for association's and memory's sake come to have for its owner the " worth " of gold. And the critics referred to take it that in his value-judgment Ritschl is crediting with the " value " or " worth " of gold something which, if truth were uttered, is of far baser metal after all. Nothing could be more out of correspondence with the facts; and perhaps if we were to sub-stitute " equivalent-judgment " or " equivalence-judgment " for " value-judgment," there would be less danger of falling into the mistake.[1] There must be *equivalence*—and the judgment asserts the equivalence—between what we find in ourselves and the reality out of which it has emerged : what *is* here *was* there. If one may fall back on a homely illustration once more, we may put it thus : the matter runs parallel with a " judgment " that if we suddenly find, after a hand-clasp, twenty shillings in our palm, we know that there was at least a pound in the hand that was laid in ours. In fact, what the theory really comes to is neither more nor less than that we can infer a cause exactly corresponding to the effect. We are obliged to credit the opera-tive reality with what will account for the effect : we are debarred from crediting it with more. " Equivalence " is the word. In value-

[1] *Werturtheil* is the German word.

judgments a cause, unknown otherwise, becomes *so far* known by the work it accomplishes. And into this class religious judgments, Ritschl holds, because they are judgments of realities unknowable except by such an accomplished work, will always fall.

We can come back, now, to the question propounded a little while ago. In our religious experience we are conscious of a moral and spiritual effect wrought upon us by the historic Christ. That is the primary fact of the situation, if we look close. Remembering that all formulation, detailed exposition, further expansion, of this primary fact must be in the nature of such a "value-judgment" as has just been described, what can we say and what can we not? We *can* say, as to God, that He is love; since in His working upon us for our moral and spiritual up-lifting through the only revelation of Him we possess—the revelation in the historic Christ— He is given to us so, is shown to us as drawing us into His kingdom and making us one with Himself. To say that He is love is but to turn the experienced fact over upon its obverse side : it is but stating the experienced fact from behind instead of from the immediate front. But that God is love is about the only thing we can say. We can *not* say that He is three in one, that He is absolute, that He is infinite, or any of the other things which "metaphysic" ascribes to Him; for none of these things is given to us in the effect wrought upon us by the historic Christ. If we assert them, we have surrendered the one sound method of judging by "values," of

" equivalent-judgments " : we are no longer carrying back into God what we find within ourselves after the historic Christ has touched us, but are passing into the unsound method of declaring what, on a process of inference, it seems that God ought to be. Along the same line, Ritschl rejects the conventional " proofs " of the being of God, because they do not start from " effects " whereof we are conscious : they are not the converted " values " of anything that the historic Christ has wrought. And of Christ Himself? We *can* say of Him that He is God to us, for the effect of the historic Christ, as that effect spreads through us—that moral and spiritual victory over the world which He transfers from Himself to us—*is* God revealed and energising; so that in affirming Christ's divineness we do but ascribe to Him the " value " of what through Him we possess. We can *not* say of Him that He is " two natures in one Person," or that He was pre-existent, nor can we use about Him any of the metaphysical phrases of the creeds; for He achieves nothing in us that can be called the " equivalent " of such things; and to affirm them is accordingly to relinquish the one sound method again. And what of miracle? Here, too, the question is one of " value." You *can* say, if any recorded miraculous act of Christ's helps you, by its moral and spiritual impression, to membership in the " kingdom " of the spiritually victorious ones, that *something* of an altogether divine quality confronts you; but you can *not* talk, by way of explanation, of " interference with

natural laws " or similar things; for in talking
thus you are going beyond the limits which the
method of " value-judgment " sets. It is fair
to say, however, that Ritschl himself is chiefly
concerned with the *total* moral impression worked
by the historic Christ and His character and His
words, and gives no sign that *individual* miracles,
for him, do yield any such spiritual " up-lift "
as would make an opportunity for value-judgment to come into play. And, of course, criticism in the strict sense is at liberty to do its work
upon the record—Ritschl being personally quite
indifferent to its results so far as isolated events
are concerned, because the fact remains that the
total " historic Christ " *does,* here and now and
in him, bring about redemptive effects. This is
what was meant by saying a little while ago that
the " historic Christ " of Ritschl is not necessarily the " historic Christ " as commonly understood. Also, it is this personal indifference to
particular miracles which has led the critics
previously spoken of to make against Ritschl—
in addition to the charge that in calling religious
verdicts value-judgments he does not mean to
assert that they are objectively true—the further
charge of denying miracle altogether. Yet here
again, the charge rests upon an entire misunderstanding of Ritschl's meaning. He *does* say—
thus showing that personal indifference mentioned
just now—that the religious man will be so
conscious of miracle within himself that he will
not trouble about miracles which others have
experienced.[1] But he has said immediately

[1] It is not even " miracles which others *say* they have
experienced." The quotation is thus led up to. " Die

before that extraordinary events through which
special impressions of God's grace are received
do possess the " value " of miracle—that is,
have in them a divine something of a special
kind; this interpretation of Ritschl's meaning
not being in any degree contradicted by the
caution which, quite consistently with his entire
method, Ritschl goes on to give against calling
the extraordinary event an interference on God's
part with natural law. We are back, then, on
what was said before as to Ritschl's view of

---

religiöse Betrachtung der Welt ist darauf gestellt, dass alle
Naturereignisse zur Verfügung Gottes stehen, wenn Er den
Menschen helfen will. Demgemäss gelten als Wunder solche
auffallende Naturerscheinungen mit welchen die Erfahrung
besonderer Gnadenhilfe Gottes verbunden ist, welche also
als besondere Zeichen seiner Gnadenbereitschaft für die
Gläubigen zu betrachten sind." Then come some significant
sentences, to be referred to again presently. " Man begeht
eine vollständige Verschiebung der religiösen Vorstellung vom
Wunder, wenn man sie von vornherein an der wissenschaft-
lichen Annahme von dem gesetzlichen Zusammenhang aller
Naturvorgänge misst. Wenn jedoch gewisse Erzählungen
von Wundern in den biblischen Büchern gegen diese Regel
zu verstossen scheinen, so ist es weder eine wissenschaft-
liche Aufgabe, diesen Schein zu lösen oder ihn als Thatsache
festzustellen, noch ist es eine religiöse Aufgabe, jene erzählte
Ereignisse als göttliche Wirkungen gegen die naturgesetze
anzuerkennen. Man soll auch nicht seinen religiösen Glauben
an Gott und Christus aus einem vorausgehenden Urtheil der
Art schöpfen." And then the sentence quoted : " Aus dem
religiösen Glauben aber wird jeder an sich selbst Wunder
erleben, und im Vergleich damit ist nichts weniger noth-
wendig, als dass man über die Wunder grübele, welche
Andere erfahren haben." Most remarkably, Dr. Denney
(*Studies in Theology*, Lecture I, note C) quotes these sentences
as illustrating Ritschl's "surrender of the Biblical facts."
Surely they are a definite assertion at least of the *possibility*
of the " Biblical facts." They are from Ritschl's *Unterricht*,
§ 17. The fact is that Dr. Denney does not sufficiently
distinguish Ritschl's own position from that of some of his
followers—of which more presently.

particular miracles—if any recorded miraculous
act of Christ's helps you, by its moral and spiritual
impression, to membership in the " kingdom "
of the spiritually victorious ones, you are entitled
to declare it a special divinely-energising act,
though you are *not* entitled to say any more.
And we may go on in this connection—partly to
illustrate the method by a concrete case, and
partly to show further how baseless is the charge
of denying miracle under which Ritschl is sometimes made to lie—to notice Ritschl's attitude
to the miracle of the Resurrection, the supreme
miracle of all.   Here is a " miracle " which,
on the " value-judgment " basis, is accepted by
Ritschl himself as it has been accepted by the
Church down the years.   In this record, at any
rate, is something which inner experience accepts
as the " equivalent " of something contained
within inner experience itself—the inner experience, at any rate, of the Christian community
taken as a whole, with whatever voice individuals
may speak.   The continued life of the Church—
the " full birth of the Christian community," to
use Ritschl's own wording—balances the manifestation of Christ to His disciples after the Cross
had done its worst.   The two things match—the
growing and continued " victory over the world "
of the Church is the correlate of that victory
over the world which in His rising Christ Himself
won. Ritschl's statements are categorical enough,
to the effect that our view of a true view of
Christianity as a whole must include a recognition
of the resurrection of Jesus as a fact.[1]   Certainly

[1] " In dieser Hinsicht nämlich ist zu beachten, das
unsere Gesamtanschauung vom Christentum die Anner

he goes on (and this will bring us back again to our main line) to caution us against metaphysical explanations of the fact, and against making statements about it which involve entrance into the speculative realm. We are not to trouble ourselves about deciding whether Christ's resurrection was purely " spiritual " or whether it was " bodily " as well, are in fact to pronounce no opinion on the point. There is no material —if we restrict ourselves to the " equivalence " or " value " method—on which a decision can be reached. We know that Jesus manifested Himself to His disciples as victorious—just that, no more, no less. And here we may make the last point which, before the final summing-up, requires to be made. This refusal to adopt the philosophical or metaphysical explanations does not mean—whether in respect of Christ's resurrection, Christ's pre-existence, God's trinity in unity, or anything else—that the philosophical or metaphysical explanations and statements are *denied*, or are handed over to science and criticism to be treated as these may choose. It certainly does not mean that, when for a few moments we step off the " value-judgment " platform and practise " theoretical judgment " for a while, we fall in with the denials of them so

kennung der Auferweckung Christi voraussetzt, als einer Thatsache, an der das Privilegium Gottes, zu schaffen und aus dem Tod Leben zu schaffen, auf das direkteste bezeugt wird. Wir würden die christliche Gesamtanschauung preisgeben, wenn wir diesen Schlüssel für unsere religiöse Gesamtansicht mit dem Argument preisgäben, dasz die Herstellung eines Toten in das Leben dem Naturgesetz widersprache." Ecke has brought together some other passages with this in *Die theologische Schule Albrecht Ritschls*, pp. 198, 199.

loudly given from the philosophical and scientific side. A significant sentence in the quotation previously given [1] explicitly affirms that while it is not the business of religion to say that a miracle is an interference by God with nature's order, neither is it the business of science to insist that, if it happened at all, it would be this, and on that account to turn it out of doors with contumely. And in respect of the resurrection, while we must not say that it was a " bodily " happening, we must not say, either, that it was a " spiritual " happening alone.[2] According to Ritschl, science and philosophy (if indeed, which is a doubtful point, anything worth calling philosophy is at all possible on Ritschl's reading of things) cannot go beyond what is actually present to observation : to form a unified conception of the " whole," otherwise than in the sense of numbering, arranging, classifying, and so forth—let us say in the sense of determining the original source of all things, tracing the road by which they have travelled, prophesying their goal—is beyond their powers; and indeed, when the scientific man or the philosopher endeavours to do these things and to form opinions upon anything not strictly within observation's limits, he is really feeling

----

[1] See *Supra*, footnote on p. 235.

[2] " Mann hat sich nicht darauf einzulassen, wenn die liberalen Theologen eine ' geistige ' Auferstehung Christi, aber nicht leibliche annehmen. . . . Mann hat sich aber auch nicht darauf einzulassen, was demnächst die ängstlichen Apologeten vorschreiben, dasz Christus nicht blosz geistig, sondern auch leiblich auferstanden sei."—Quoted by Ecke, as previously cited, p. 199.

an unidentified *religious* impulse rather than a
philosophic pull and push, is really becoming
religious as it were without knowing it and in
despite of himself, and ought therefore to adopt
the method of value-judgments on the spot.
He has unconsciously begun to work in another
medium, and is foolishly trying to do so with
his former tools.   So that—it may be incidentally
remarked—when as religious men we abstain
from the metaphysical and philosophical explanations before spoken of, it is not because,
if we accepted and proclaimed them, we should
be trenching upon ground properly reserved to
ordinary thought.   It belongs no more to ordinary
thought than it does to religion.   Any judgment
in this sphere must be a " value-judgment ";
and while the religious man does not find within
himself enough to justify the ascription, to the
realities with which he is in contact, of such
" values " as the adoption of metaphysical explanations concerning them would imply, the
scientific man, as such, has no material for a
" value-judgment " at all.   In the one case,
testimony does not go far enough : in the other,
the witness has no competence whatever.   In
fine, then—coming back again to the main
question—we *can* say, in respect of God and
Christ, such things as that God is love and that
Christ is God for us, because the saying merely
reads back into the confronting realities the
equivalent of what they have put into us; but
we can *not* adopt any of the metaphysical
explanations into which these things have been
stretched (though on the other hand philosophy

and science cannot deny them, and the said metaphysical explanations are thus sent out into the void and left shivering there, out of all relation, positive or negative, to human thought and human feeling alike) since to adopt them would be to assert as contained in our own inward experience what our inward experience does not really yield.

In what fashion the Ritschlian system becomes an apologetic will now be clear. It becomes an apologetic by shutting its eyes to the existence of the very questions with which apologetics as generally understood attempts to deal. Religious declarations and declarations of philosophical kind, each class being instructed to remain strictly " positivist " and to keep itself strictly within the limits of what is immediately " given "—not being permitted to become anything more than a transcription, so to call it, of what is perceived at first-hand—cannot come into contact or conflict, because each stops short of that ultimate region wherein, if anywhere, the meeting would occur. Religion is as it were at one end, and philosophy at the other, of a line drawn within the experience of man; but the line must not be taken as a base-line for further construction, nor must any sloping line of inference be flung upward from either point with the idea of making the triangle complete; so that no convergence, friendly or hostile, can ever take place. Or, to change the figure, both theology and philosophy—not only one, but both—are forbidden to emerge from their own separate chambers, so that there can be no untoward *rencontres* with frowns and challenges for their end. Theology is safe from the attacks of general thought because it utters no provocative word in respect of matters which, if any thought at all has the right to touch them, general thought might declare to be peculiarly its own; while by putting general thought also under restraint, and declaring that it cannot *deny* those things which theology, if it did illegitimately travel beyond its province, would be likely to *affirm*, assurance is made doubly sure. There would have to be *two* transgressors before any conflict between theology and philosophy could take place. Of course this safety for theology is purchased at a price. The whole procedure ends in barring us away from any knowledge of ultimates. Our knowledge of God, for example, remains partial, not simply in the sense in which it is universally confessed to be so—in the sense that we can say many things about God which we know to be true in outline though we cannot tell exhaustively what, as said of Him, they contain—but in the sense that when we speak His name we are really looking into the void, except as by flinging " equivalences " into the void's blackness we cause something of form to appear. And of course our view of things remains dualistic when all is done—not, it is true, dualistic in any fashion which involves contradiction, but dualistic none the less. It is in two separate compartments that our knowledge is kept. The two kinds of knowledge have not even such an amount of common speech or common subject-matter as

R

would enable them to hold a dispute : far less, then, is there any prospect that they will ever consent to publication of the marriage-banns. There is no possibility that we shall ever see our general knowledge and our theology " fitly framed together," one complete whole being made by the union of that which each constituent supplies, our philosophy and our theology alike running back to one eternal ground whence the material of both—the experience with which both deal—has proceeded. We shall never have present to our mental sight any " background-process " wherein both the philosophical and theological movements of thought are held and wherein, because they are both held in it, they find and hold one another in mutual support; or if we imagine that such a " background-process " is discerned, it will only be because the imagination is born out of the wish. And the fair vision of a single unified system, gathering up into itself all the elements of reality which human apprehension has painstakingly collected one by one, justifying and beautifying and fulfil-ling every one by showing it to its place alongside the rest, thus constructing a fabric without rents or straggling ends or material left outside unused—the fair vision which has hung upon the philosopher's horizon since philosophy began—vanishes at Ritschl's touch. Theology is safe; but the thinker—and not the thinker as theologian alone—must pay the price.

But is the position which Ritschl instructs us to take up a possible one ? Can men thus clamp themselves down to the immediately

" given," refuse to step over the border into the land of " ultimates," keep theological and other knowledge in entire separateness, surrender the desire to know " the causes of things," hold down their heads groundward instead of lifting them to the far horizons? Antecedently one would give a negative reply, and from the after-development of the Ritschlian school the echo of the negative floats down. One might indeed ask other questions as to the real practicability of the method we are told to adopt. One might enquire whether it is really possible to disentangle the purely " historic Christ " from " metaphysical " statements about Him; to declare that it is to *this* and not to *that*, our Christ-produced spiritual consciousness is to be referred; to say with complete confidence that no contribution to the total spiritual impression is made by the association of this or the other " fact " with the " explanations " of it which the thought of the Church has framed; and one might ask, further, whether, if one attempts the disentangling, it can be accomplished by any other means than that of judging the " explanations " as philosophically valid or invalid, the main position being thus given up in the very effort to maintain it. One might suggest that in ascribing to Christ the " value of God," we are already calling in an idea which we have plucked elsewhere than out of the effect of the " historic Christ " Himself—the idea of God; and that the process of " value-judgment " in this instance really involves, not *two* " quantities," if the term may pass—our own spiritual consciousness and the historic Christ who has created it—but *three,* both the two first being judged as " equivalent " to the third.   But for our purpose here all that we need to do is to enquire whether that dualism, and that surrender of enquiry into "ultimates," which Ritschlianism would impose, is permanently possible to the mind of man.   And the reply, as given by the school which amid all its many divergences owns Ritschl himself more or less as master, is " no."

What took place was that the Ritschlians, under the imperative necessity (inherent, after all, in human nature, however Ritschl himself and some of his first followers may have succeeded in suppressing the sense of it) of holding some definite view as to those ultimates at which Ritschl refused to look, proceeded some on one and some on the other of two alternative roads. To two of the principal points in the Ritschlian procedure, indeed, they held themselves firmly fixed—all theological judgments were to start from the " value " basis; and what is a consequence of this, and what is besides more important in this connection, anything that was said as to the ultimates, as to a final explanation of things, was not to imply any " arrangement," any actual partnership, between philosophy and religious thought.   The disability as to final verdicts, under which Ritschl left *both* philosophy *and* theology, was to be removed in respect of *one* alone.   This, as has just been said, was a necessary consequence of the determination to preserve the value-judgment method; for had any other course been taken—had it been admitted that,

while the process based on value-judgments had
power and right to stretch itself into the region
of final explanation, it must or might be met
there by, and be united with, a process coming
up from the philosophical quarter—it would
have been tantamount to an admission that
value-judgments, having undertaken the work
of theological construction, found themselves
incompetent for the task after all. In respect
of final explanatory verdicts, the method of
value-judgments must do nothing or all. If
therefore the ultimates were to be probed,
explored, and proclaimed, *either* theology or
philosophy, but not *both*, must perform the
search. And according to the choice made
between them, Ritschl's disciples travelled along
two radically divergent paths to diametrically
opposite goals. If theology claimed the right of
pushing upward and onward into the further
realms, then the results of what theology had
already done along that line regained their title
to acceptance; only, since philosophy was not
to be called upon for help, those results could
only be put forward upon the authority of Bible
or creed or Church; so that *this* choice brought
the Ritschlian who made it back upon, at any
rate back toward, the older conservative position
once more. If, on the other hand, philosophy
obtained the vote, then philosophy's current
negations of the older theological formularies
held the field : theology, now, could not interfere
when philosophy made them, for this would
have been to introduce the " partnership " conception again : the method of value-judgment

could not, just because things turned out displeasingly, re-claim the field of ultimates which it had but a little while ago surrendered; and thus *this* choice set the Ritschlian at a point where he found actual opponents of Christianity, or at least of fundamental Christian doctrines, fairly close to his side. If these things be grasped, it will be understood why the school of Ritschl has shown so many varieties of theological shape and colour; why some of Ritschl's followers, in their anxiety to be faithful to one of Ritschl's first positions, have finished by occupying positions which Ritschl himself would have disowned; and why certain thinkers are reckoned by some expositors among Ritschl's friends and by others among his foes.[1] (For, as to this last point, it is indeed quite possible for a thinker to be both.) The sum of the matter, then, is that the Ritschlian ground—that is, the Ritschlian ground precisely as Ritschl himself measured and laid it—hardly affords a *permanent* position for many, and that members of the Ritschlian school pass, or tend to pass, from Liberal Orthodoxy, some by the gate leading back to the conservative territory, and some by the gate opening out upon rationalism's fields.

We need not dwell long upon individual names; but some few may be cited as examples of what has been said; and it is with the names of those who illustrate the return to conservatism

---

[1] Ecke puts it that " innerhalb der Ritschlschen Schule eine Fortbildung und zugleich eine Umgestaltung der Theologie Ritschls stattgefanden hat." (*Die theologische Schule Albrecht Ritschls*, p. 308.)

that we may begin. We noted how Julius
Kaftan held that in religious verdicts a " theoretical judgment " was superadded to the
" value-judgment " with which the religious man
starts off. This involved comparatively little
in the way of change, though it prophesied more
than it actually involved; but, as the impulse
toward extending the power of theological formulation into the further fields waxed stronger,
his suggestion was adopted and its scope and
application enlarged.[1] Häring, for instance,
allows the superadded theoretical judgment to
do a larger work than Kaftan allotted to it,
a work which goes beyond the certifying as
objectively real of what the previous value-
judgment has given, and permits it to operate
as it were on its own account. It can, of course
after experience has caused the value-judgment
to arise, carry us so far as the declaration of an
antecedent necessity that God's approach to man
should become manifest and real in a historical
Person, in whom God's inmost life and working
should be revealed; and still further, to the
declaration that Christ as the bearer to us of
God's eternal love, must Himself have had a
real pre-existence in God's love and have been

[1] Of course no attempt is here made to trace in detail
the development of the early Ritschlian school or the
modifications which Ritschl's first followers introduced.
Else—to say nothing of others—Herrmann, and his partial
recall into the system of the mystical element which Ritschl
sternly banished would have to be named. Our special
purpose and its limitations must be borne in mind. A list
of the chief Ritschlian writers and their works may be found
in Adams Brown's *Essence of Christianity*, pp. 264–266. See
also the works mentioned earlier in this chapter.

God's ever-loved Son. Our inner experience, and the value-judgment founded upon it, creates what may be termed an expectation whereto these faiths respond. This is not yet to give to these formulations an independent authority of their own, though it has a look that way; but it is certainly to bring back what, on Ritschl's original rendering of things, was to be kept excluded to the end. In the " positive theology " of the early twentieth century the matter goes further. Its exponents are indeed so far from Ritschl's position that it may reasonably be asked whether they ought to be labelled with the Ritschlian name; and yet it is fairly certain that, unless Ritschl had gone before them, their line of work would not have been run precisely as it has been. They are, as a matter of fact, like Schleiermacher rather than Ritschl in that they start from experience *as such* instead of from " experience mediated through the record of the historic Christ "; and moreover the specific Ritschlian phraseology, as to " value-judgments " and the rest, has disappeared. But they are distinctly Ritschlian in refusing to permit any association of philosophy with theology in the effort to reach religious verdicts; and they are as distinctly sub-Ritschlian—of Häring's order intensified—in that they are determined upon reaching ultimates by means of one or other, and bid theology, not philosophy, be the one. Even if their final position be far more rigidly conservative than Häring's, so that it is as a modification of a modification they at last appear, still the genealogical line from Ritschl to them, bent between Ritschl and Häring and bent again between Häring and the " positive " school as it may be, can be clearly traced. So, then, the " positive " theologians, starting from experience or from some particular aspect of it—the experience of justification or of God's love—work their way onwards, coming at last to ascribe definite authority, competent for an original formulation and imposition of belief to-day, to Scripture or to the dogmas of the Church. The process of " theoretical judgment " founded upon " value-judgment " (for we may employ the terms although they be not the set language of the school), as carried through out of the experience of the past and of the Church as a whole, has resulted in *these*—in the formation of the sacred Canon, in the shaping of the creeds : these are accordingly in themselves a mediated revelation which will descend with power upon him who already possesses an experience of his own. *Only* upon him, of course, because embodied experience can appeal only to those in whom at least a rudimentary experience along the same line has found a home; but to him most surely. Because these things have come out of the large experience of the Church, they will be as the goal, given beforehand, to which he knows the process of theological construction, carried out with his own individual experience as foundation, ought to reach : what was *subjective* in its origin, although none the less valid when it emerged, will present itself as *objectively* authoritative to him; and what was a mediated revelation will become in effect a revelation direct. So, to

take two examples, does Seeberg look upon the
up-rising of the " Logos-doctrine," and of other
formulated articles of belief, as absolutely necessary because the experience of the Church was
what it was, and therefore as having a right to
the assent of Christian men to-day : so does
Kähler hold that, the Bible as a whole and as it
stands having been born out of that same
Christian experience, it can claim acceptance of
its records and of practically its entire content.
This last position does not—at any rate for Kähler
—shut out a certain working of criticism; but it
does restrict criticism's legitimate working to
very narrow limits indeed.   And in the case of
Theodore Kaftan an extension of the method
sets us standing face to face with " the Word,"
and forbids us to do anything else than unquestioningly accept.   But it is not necessary
to tarry longer upon the " positive " school.
In some respects it is still in the act of " becoming," [1] and its final theological systematisa-
tion is not yet reached.   But what has been said
will be enough to show how those who diverge
from the strictly Ritschlian method in the direction of making theology the searcher for ultimate
verdicts tend more and more to drop back upon
the ultra-conservative base.

But the other road diverging from original
Ritschlianism, the road taken by those who
handed over the attainment of ultimate verdicts

---

[1] " Im Werden und Wachsen," as Grützmacher put it in
1908.   See his account of the school in his edition, brought
up to the date named, of Frank's *Geschichte und Kritik der
neueren Theologie*, pp. 484–532.

to philosophy rather than to theology, was the one more in consonance with the original Ritschlian idea; and one finds without surprise that it was the road chosen by not a few. For if, after making in the Ritschlian position the first breach implied in admitting that *either* by philosophy or theology, though not by *both*, the task of reaching the final word upon ultimate problems was to be performed—if after that, you elected theology to the vacant post, you found that you had committed a further breach by bringing about that very conflict between theology and philosophy which Ritschlianism had been bent on stilling for ever. For theology's election was one which philosophy, in the persons of many of its representatives, would refuse to recognise : the theologian might bid philosophy be silent, saying that theology's " positives " were to be accepted as decisive on these themes; but in the last resort philosophy would *not* be silent; so that the theologian could only take as settled the question which he himself had raised —the question as to the respective competence of theology and philosophy for the attainment of a satisfactory world-view—by refusing to admit into court what claimed to be an essential witness in the case if the case were going to be tried at all. And since philosophy would not submit to its exclusion without making very voluble protest in the world outside, there must come heated strife of tongues, things being thus flung back into the very chaos and welter of contention out of which Ritschl had sought to draw them. If, on the other hand, the theologian

took the other way, and consented that the
making of final readings and explanations should
be put upon philosophy's programme—if theology
agreed that its assertions should continue to
be pulled up short before the border into those
further regions was crossed—the case would be
different : theology's voluntary surrender of
these things to philosophy would preserve that
harmony which, if theology claimed them as
against philosophy, would inevitably have been
broken up; and the first breach in the original
Ritschlian position would be also the last. It
was the method least out of relation with Ritschl's
own. But then, if it were adopted, philosophy's
negations of, at any rate philosophy's agnosticism
towards, many of the historic doctrines of the
Christian Church, incarnation, miracle, and others,
held the field; and the theologian who took the
method up tended more and more to join in
philosophy's denial of these, at best to rank
himself with philosophy in ignoring them, and
thus to drop them, as irrelevant to real Christianity, out of his scheme—in other words, to cut
down more and more, as if in fear of trespassing
upon philosophy's reserved territories, what along
the line of value-judgments he found himself able
to say. He edged, in fact, in the direction
leading to pure rationalism at last. And the
Ritschlian or sub-Ritschlian thinkers who admit,
or who will not deny, philosophy's title to make
pronouncement, unquestioned from any quarter,
in the ultimate realms do tend towards an avowed
or unavowed surrender of so many things that
what is left constitutes in some instances a very

abridged Christianity indeed. In some cases, the "metaphysical" doctrines are denied, as when Lipsius,[1] after admitting that out of our religious experience (if from *that* basis the search for ultimates were carried on) we should naturally go on to speak of the God given in that experience as *both* absolute *and* personal, proceeds to declare that the "Absolute" as reached by philosophy *cannot be* personal because for philosophy absoluteness and personality are irreconcilable, and that consequently—since religion must not encroach upon philosophy's rights—our idea of God as infinite consciousness and will remains a mere "symbol," affording us no real knowledge of what the God of our religious experience actually is. Philosophy with its denial, in short, remains master of the field. In other cases, philosophy's demand that the Christian religion shall, for the sake of unity, be set in its due relations with the other religions of the world and with the entire process of moral development which preceded it, coupled with naturalistic philosophy's reluctance to admit the introduction of wholly new factors at any point of the evolving history, leads to a declaration like that of Tröltsch —that while Christianity carries off the palm as the highest religion hitherto, we must not take it as proved that no loftier religious development can or will ever take place; which of course

[1] Lipsius has in his general theological system many points of dissimilarity from Ritschl which cannot be gone into here. He is one of those who is sometimes reckoned as Ritschl's follower, sometimes as his opponent. But he may be characterised, I think, as a Ritschlian who returned to philosophy the rights which Ritschl withdrew.

means that God did *not* make in Christ a new supernatural advent into the life of the world. In other cases yet again, the picture of the " historic Christ " with whom, so far as the religious side of things is concerned, we find ourselves in contact, shrinks to smaller dimensions because with some of the factors which enter into the picture as it stands a strictly scientific philosophy is at war; and in the end of the day it is in Christ the teacher, or in Christ the example, or in the great ideas which Christ proclaimed, that the centre of the Christian faith is found. So Wendt would lock us up within Christ's words of instruction and encouragement : so Weiss bids us " imitate " the Christ who is left after removing " from the picture of the Christ to be imitated whatever elements are out of keeping with the spirit of our modern life " : [1] so Harnack finds the " essence of Christianity " in the fact that Jesus proclaimed the great inspiring conceptions of the Fatherhood of God, of immortality, and the commandment of love, but will say no word of frank faith in Christ's recorded " mighty acts." [2] It need not be said that this reference to Harnack, as also the former one to Tröltsch, is made with full

[1] An aptly descriptive sentence quoted from Adams Brown, *The Essence of Christianity*, p. 279. Apparently it is not meant to be satirical.

[2] See *Das Wesen des Christentums*, translated under the title *What is Christianity?* in the " Crown Theological Library." Harnack is said by some to be returning towards the evangelical platform. He is of course known to have been moving in a conservative direction in regard to certain critical questions, dates of New Testament books, etc. But that is another matter.

recognition of the priceless services rendered by each in his special division of the historical field. But it is the theological tendency that is in question here. And that a " minimising " tendency is at work through all this cannot be disputed, even if in some cases there may be doubt as to how far it has been allowed to go. The guiding principle, more or less fully invested with regulative authority, is that we must not, in the process of expressing our " value-judgment " of what Christ has wrought in us, carry back into the " historic Christ " anything that philosophy, to which we have now returned the rights and powers which original Ritschlianism withdrew, may challenge or deny. Which means, of course, that the Christ of the Church's faith is pushed aside on philosophic grounds. And how far things may extend along this " minimising " line, this line of substituting ideas for the Christ whom the Church has known and loved, may be gathered from the fact that Drews, at the far end of this development of the Ritschlian left, finds the presence of the " ideas " in itself sufficient, feels it unnecessary to account for them by assuming for them any such author as the Jesus whom the Gospels portray, and, resolving Him into a sun-myth, denies that Ritschl's " historic Christ " ever lived at all. If the movement to which the Ritschlian right commits itself quits Liberal Orthodoxy by becoming ultra-orthodox, the movement whereon the Ritschlian left embarks takes an equally emphatic farewell at last by becoming rationalistic through and through.

A few sentences will suffice for what more
requires to be said as to the place of Ritschl
and Ritschlianism in Liberal Orthodoxy's tale.
It is but recapitulating what has already been
said or implied. The system of Ritschl clearly
marks the setting in of what was termed Liberal
Orthodoxy's greater caution, the up-rising within
Liberal Orthodoxy of a consciousness that no
sufficiently strong grasp had been kept upon
the fact of Christ. Successful though Schleiermacher's theological construction had been as
a retort against the strictly rationalist onset, it
had become clear under the succeeding Hegelian
attack, and through the only partially victorious
endeavours to meet it, that too much had been
given up. The road along which Schleiermacher
invited his followers to walk from the Christian
consciousness across to the actual " archetypal
Christ " was not laid with such security as to
make the journey safe and its triumphant close
secure : it did but lean out from the starting-
side over an abyss, and whether it reached and
was fastened to *any* other side no man could say.
In starting from the " historic Christ," and
calling upon men to recognise that in religious
experience this Christ was given as the primary
fact of all and that thus the very question as
to His existence answered itself, Ritschl endeavoured to bring back what had been lost.
Nor is this reading of the matter discounted by
the fact, which must of course be admitted, that
on certain themes—such as that of Christ's
death and the atoning efficacy ascribed to it in
the historic creeds—Ritschl refused to move

backwards, rejecting the ordinary formularies upon them because those formularies lay quite beyond " value-judgment's " reach. The new insistence on the " historic Christ " indisputably manifested the conservative touch. Over and above that, Ritschl's work as clearly continued the protest of Schleiermacher's against taking Christianity simply as a system of ideas; here Ritschl followed Schleiermacher's lead instead of halting and turning back. With him, as emphatically as with his predecessor, experience— none the less that it was experience together with the historic Christ—was the platform on which theological thought must make its preparations for whatever it essayed to do. Ritschl was above all things anxious that the theologian's reading of Christianity should find in Christianity not merely truth accepted by the mind, but a power penetrating into human nature's deeps. One may surely say that this, in conjunction with the conservative element in Ritschl, brought the system close up against the " life-dynamic " idea—yet once again the idea was missed; in part perhaps (if one may surmise as to instinctive psychological workings) because the presence of the Hegelian philosophy upon the field seemed to suggest that the launching of any such conception might only add another weapon to its armoury, but in part also by reason of that hatred of mysticism which filled Ritschl's soul. Down upon the actual, concrete, objective history, therefore, Ritschl settled himself, accepting the limitations which this involved both for philosophical and for religious thinking, and with

s

everything else rigidly shut away. How, thereafter, matters worked out, we have seen—how for Ritschl's successors, the agnostic position on which he himself appeared so easily able to maintain his footing became impossible, how consequently those successors had to make choice between going back and going forward, how those who went back found their path sloping down to the ultra-conservative plains, how for those who went forward the pilgrimage resulted in making Christianity a system of ideas, and of ideas reduced to a *minimum*, once again. And the sad sum of it all is that, as we quit Germany, Liberal Orthodoxy's complete and permanent theological building has after all failed to appear.

[*Addendum.*—It is not necessary at the close of this chapter to take any long look beyond Germany to other European lands. If we mention for Switzerland the name of Frommel, who continued Vinet's work, but modified Vinet's insistence on conscience as the test of truth by emphasising the thought that conscience could only use its freedom rightly if it had first recognised its obligation and bondage to something higher than itself—and if we add that of L. G. Sabatier for France—as being both worthy of the student's further enquiry, we need do no more. For the most part, Liberal Orthodoxy, as indeed theology in other than Liberal Orthodox departments, produced elsewhere than in Germany no " native " school, scarcely even any noteworthy modification of the German school, and did little more than echo the German voice.]

CHAPTER IX

LATER YEARS (*continued*) : BRITAIN

To come upon a statement that in respect of the later years running from the publication of *Essays and Reviews* to the present time there is comparatively little to say concerning our topic, and that the period may be dealt with in somewhat brief space, may touch the reader with a sense of surprise. Surely theological controversies were throughout the period numerous and hot : surely it was a time of very pronounced theological advance ! And truly, if we endeavour to recall the names of those who during those years fought and suffered in the cause of larger and progressive religious thinking, or the topics round which successive controversies raged, the lists grow long. Those of us who are at middle life can well recall how in the two closing decades of the nineteenth century, more particularly, the thermometer registering theological interest went rapidly upwards, how the man in the street turned upon religious matters that kindled, if not very penetrating, eye which he has never since turned away from them; how on all hands it was felt that a new era of religious construction was about to rise. Yet, as we look back, disentangling the essential from the accidental,

unifying things which seemed under the immediate
thronging and sound of them to have little inter-
connection, we can see that the various cross-
currents and the many attracting or repellent
rivulets of thought were really comprised within
one stream of tendency, flowing in a set direction
apparent now, though then undiscerned.   It is
as if out of the confused evolutions, wheelings,
and inter-threadings of many units in a demonstrating crowd, a straightly-advancing procession
at last breaks away—even though while the head
of it moves towards the goal the preparatory
movements of those who have not started yet are
still going on further behind.   And as it is the
final movement, the ultimate line of march—
and the place of last arrival, so far as the present
development of movement and march enables
us to speak of it—as it is these things with which
we are concerned, not all the previous evolutions,
not all the names of those who made them, need
be noted.   It is, in brief, the underlying tendency
of the period that we are seeking to trace, the
general trend of the road which, often unknown
to itself, Liberal Orthodoxy trod; and only over
some of the most prominent of those who laid
the road—as these come into view at successive
curves and corners—need we pause.   Thinkers
who are left unnamed the reader, as the various
ranks and classes grow clear, will be able to
place for himself.

We are now, as was said earlier, at the period
when Liberal Orthodoxy's first readiness in con-
cession, the first largeness of the offers it made
in its unshaken confidence that the indispensable

minimum would be left after all was done—when these things gave place to greater caution as the sense of danger grew. Undoubtedly the doctrines on which Liberal Orthodoxy was compelled to surrender or to make terms became, as the period went on, doctrines nearer to the heart and essence of the Christian faith : as the foe drew his lines closer, the forts round which the battle raged came more and more to be those bearing upon the inmost citadel's defence; and when Liberal Orthodoxy's greater caution is spoken of, it is not meant that the process of change was stopped. It is the mood and manner of Liberal Orthodoxy that are in view. What is meant is that though it had to go onward along the road of change, its pace was slower; or that, if its step was quickened, it was not quickened from its own choice. It was throughout under compulsion that it moved. It was as a prisoner whose guards set the speed and forced it to keep in step. (That it had flung away arms which would have enabled it to make effective resistance has been suggested before and will be suggested again; but that is not relevant just now.) We do not in this period find Liberal Orthodoxy flinging itself almost gaily upon one new belief, or upon some drastic modification of an old belief, and then going forth as it were on its own account to apply its new principle here and there and everywhere round the doctrinal circle— which is what we found Liberal Orthodoxy doing through the " development " period we looked at a little while ago. At the consequences of this procedure, as manifested in *Essays and*

Reviews, Liberal Orthodoxy had taken alarm; and we find it now, in this subsequent stretch of time, changing only what it *must.* And the point is worth noting for another reason than that of its own intrinsic interest; for it may serve to explain why out of all the theological unrest of the recently by-gone years so little in the way of positive result has issued. In the cautiousness which has beset it Liberal Orthodoxy has been afraid to let the constructive impulse come into play; and so for the things that have been removed no adequate substitutes have been found or made. Of course the process of change has not been wholly negative, for this would have meant the entire disappearance of the Christian faith; but what of positive construction there has been has been little more than the offering of a less objectionable alternative, in face of attack upon attack, pushed resolutely home, when all is said. What really took place—and though there is an element of paradox in the statement, the thing is natural enough after all—was that the lack of constructiveness in the movement of the earlier period, as this was suddenly thrown into illuminated relief by the book wherein that movement came to a head, produced in the later period a cautiousness which resulted in a lack of constructiveness in its turn. Had the earlier movement struck a more positive note, had it forced its lightly used strength into the service of a constructive impulse, matters would have been otherwise. But that is one of history's many " might-have-beens." The facts are as given. In the first case the absence of positive results (for so far

as the line of development traced down from the
" early Oriel " school is concerned, such positive
results as Robertson had reached were swamped
and forgotten under the negations of *Essays
and Reviews ;* and those other positive results
which along the Coleridgean line had been
achieved, or were supposed to have been achieved,
fell into discredit in the general alarm)—in the
first case the absence of positive results had been
due to carelessness, in the second to over-much
care. Certainly that theological reconstruction
so much hoped for in the nineteenth century's
twilight has, by common consent, failed to
appear; and the sense of a new era at hand has
turned out so far to point only to a " false dawn."
In Liberal Orthodoxy's consciousness that it had
moved too readily before, and in its fear lest it
should move too readily again, the reasons lie.
It had been so sure of its irreducible *minimum*
in the earlier time, and had suddenly discovered
that much of this had been filched away ! Now
it felt only the lowlier hope that, whatever
surrenders it might be compelled to make,
something worthy of the name of revelation and
of Christian faith might still be left.

This does not mean that there was on the part
of Liberal Orthodoxy any return upon that older
inspiration theory against which the first revolt
had been directed : to have made such a return
would have been for Liberal Orthodoxy nothing
less than *felo de se.* The principle that interpretation of Scripture was to be a larger and
freer matter than under the old theological conservatism it had been—a larger and freer matter

than the old theological conservatism still declared it must be—was established. It had passed, so to say, into the common stock for those who admitted the reasonableness and inevitableness of any change at all. Of course (and here we pass from introductory remarks into the actual story) the protest of theological conservatism went on; so that besides making whatever adjustments were found necessary in order to meet assaults from the critical side, Liberal Orthodoxy had to justify itself as against the reproaches of those who held that by the adjustments already made it had betrayed the faith. It was, in fact, just as the *Essays and Reviews* controversy had spent its first force that the famous Colenso quarrel sprung up. Bishop Colenso of Natal (1814–1883) had received a certain bent in the liberal direction through the reading of Maurice; but it was not until he commenced his translation of the Bible into the Zulu tongue that his movement along the liberal line grew swift. Arrested by an intelligent native's question as to whether it was really possible for all kinds of animals to have been with Noah in the ark, Colenso made a close examination of the Pentateuch from what might almost be called a mathematical point of view (he was a skilled mathematician himself), with the result that he came, as he supposed, upon many statements which must on simply mathematical grounds be set aside. Calculations as to the number of tents and kneading-troughs which two million people would require—estimates as to the space of ground such a massed crowd would cover and as to the possibility of their leader's voice being heard by them all as many narratives in the " books of Moses " state that it was— proofs that according to the story as it stands Judah must have been a great-grandfather at forty-two—these and similar matters arrested and offended the Bishop's mathematical soul. But these were only preliminary; and Colenso, passing on from these points to notice diversities and contradictions in different accounts of the same event—for instance, the Flood—and other signs that various hands had held the recording pen, arrived at a composite theory of the Penta-teuchal authorship similar in general outline, although not of course in detail, to that which is a commonplace for all competent Biblical scholarship to-day. We need not pause over the clash and clang of harsh tongues which followed upon the publication of his book, nor tell how a movement for Colenso's condemnation was made and how on a technicality it failed.[1] The incident is of interest here simply as showing that if Liberal Orthodoxy had itself become possessed by some sense of alarm as *Essays and Reviews* revealed it to itself, Conservative Ortho-doxy too had felt the sense of crisis, and the necessity of beginning—or rather of strengthen-ing, for it had begun before—that long course of ardent and often angry controversy which it has ever since maintained. For Colenso and David-son (whom we named a little while ago) [2] were

[1] For a short account, see Cornish, *The English Church in the Nineteenth Century*, ii. chap. xii.
[2] *Supra*, pp. 192, 193.

but the forerunners of many, not all so prominent
as they, who have had to submit to arraignment
for treachery to Christianity on similar grounds.
One at least of the most famous deserves to be
named in the briefest *résumé*. Twenty years
after Colenso's first book, *The Pentateuch and the
Book of Joshua critically examined*, saw the light,
Professor William Robertson Smith (1846–1894)
one of the finest scholars of the nineteenth century,
lost the chair of Oriental languages and Old
Testament exegesis at the Free Church College
in Aberdeen because he dared to hold and teach
that questions of authorship, date, and integrity,
in connection with the Old Testament books,
must not be looked upon as fore-closed, and to
proclaim on these problems conclusions which
the critical method—deemed sacrilegious and
profane by his adversaries—had enabled him to
reach. And this, be it noted, brings us down to
1881. Many others, besides, there have been—
and in even later years than this—whom Conservative Orthodoxy has, for the same hated
heresy, ostracised so far as its power has allowed,
and whose names, if it were the history of the
conflict between old and new we were telling,
would have to be recalled. But the two instances
given will suffice to show on the one hand that
Liberal Orthodoxy stood fast to the principle
which had caught its eye in the hour of its first
stirring from the centuries' theological sleep, and
on the other hand that it has been compelled to
hear evil spoken of its good. Biblical criticism
in the strict sense and freer interpretation of the
Bible's contents—these disciplines, acting and

reacting upon one another, have moved on with the years. It is worth noting that even if Liberal Orthodoxy, in the mood of caution which came upon it after *Essays and Reviews*, had felt inclined to step backward from the position which on these matters it had taken up, it would have found itself unable to do so by reason of the stronger attack upon the old " inerrancy " and " verbal inspiration " theories directed from the scientific side. To the changes in geology, and their effect upon religious thought, allusion has already been made.[1] But with the publication of Darwin's *Origin of Species* in 1859, and the springing of the evolution doctrine fully armed upon the scene, it became more than ever impossible to maintain that those chapters of the Old Testament which had been supposed by the older school to afford scientific information could stand the scientific test. Between the " verbal inspiration " doctrine and science the choice had to be made. Of course many preferred to say that the new science was but pseudo-science after all; as when Bishop Wilberforce, mingling misrepresentation with anger, congratulated himself publicly on not being descended from a monkey, or as when Manning described the new philosophy as " a brutal philosophy—to wit, there is no God, and the ape is our Adam." But by degrees more moderate voices were heard; and when *The Descent of Man* appeared in 1871, the tide of vituperation swept far less violently in and rose far less high.[2]

[1] *Supra*, p. 189.

[2] On the reception of Darwin's books, see Andrew D. White, *A History of the Warfare of Science with Theology*, ii. 70–84.

Perhaps, indeed, it may be taken as a happy coincidence that *The Origin of Species* was given to the world just when *Essays and Reviews* had begun to make some of even the freer spirits fear lest unshackled enquiry might prove a steed which would not bear either bridle or bit; for the new scientific conclusions showed once again that religious thought, if it were to have any claim upon the acceptance of educated men, must not proceed to balance whatever heedlessness it had hitherto shown by an utterly retrograde movement now. Those conclusions were in some sense a fresh confirmation for the mission of orthodoxy of the newer type, by reason of the fresh attack they directed against orthodoxy of the old. Whatever Liberal Orthodoxy might do in the future, it must at any rate hold fast—and did hold fast—what it had.

But while the general principle of Biblical usage and interpretation kept its largeness and freedom, applications of the principle were much less large and free. Of theological constructiveness on any marked scale there was for years comparatively little. The line of Liberal Orthodoxy which traced its descent from Coleridge through Maurice practically died out, unless indeed we reckon Westcott (1825–1901) as continuing it; and even Westcott's principal work was done in the department of Biblical exegesis and criticism rather than in that of theology properly so termed. And if we turn to the other line, we find no one who did as Robertson had done, and who, with a survey which, if it was not systematic, at any rate ranged far and wide, endeavoured to show what the liberalised method of reading the Scriptures could achieve. It has been already mentioned that the influence of such a positive use of the " freer interpretation " idea as Robertson had made was drowned under the influence of the negative use to which the authors of *Essays and Reviews* had put the same idea, and of the results whereto that negative use had led. What we do find, in the way of positive theologising, is really no more than this —that every now and again a certain doctrine, one or two doctrines more particularly, came into debate for a palpitating hour; and this, not so much under the pressure of a purely theological interest as because the increasingly humanitarian spirit of the age (if humanitarian be the right word), which could assert itself with less reproach now that the mere quoting of a text was not held sufficient to prove its requirements wrong, moved some preacher or writer to challenge the sterner views of the past. Naturally enough, the doctrine of retribution was one of those thus singled out for revision and re-statement; and while Canon, afterwards Dean, Farrar (1831–1903)—in a series of sermons preached in Westminster Abbey (1877) and subsequently published under the title *Eternal Hope*—denounced the " material hell " of conventional red-hot evangelicalism with its literal fires, and contended that some at least of the human race would have an opportunity of repentance behind the closed doors of death, others, like Samuel Cox and Baldwin Brown, went further, proclaiming universal restoration as a certainty rather than as a hope. Another escape from the horror of the traditional doctrine was found in the idea of " conditional immortality," or the annihilation of the obstinately wicked, Edward White being the chief champion of this view.[1] The doctrine of the Atonement was also, though less frequently, brought out for review, as here and there a sense of revolt against the cruder presentations of it stirred some protesting mind to speak. Of course the doctrine of the Atonement was taken—and quite naturally and properly—to be nearer the heart of Christianity than any doctrine of retribution could be, since if it were whittled down so far as to mean nothing very special and to be without significance in respect of a real effect on the relations between God and humanity, the question must naturally arise whether Christ had really done for man anything that man could not do for himself. It is not surprising, therefore, that some religious thinkers who must on general grounds be classed as among the Liberal Orthodox of the period should have sought to administer a tonic to the generally flaccid and indeterminate—one might almost say uninterested—mood into which on this, as on other topics, so many were falling, and should have attempted something like a positive reconstruction of a doctrine in some respects the most difficult and the most important of all. Perhaps the name of Dale (1829–1895) is the outstanding one in this connection, though others could be given. Using once again Maurice's

---

[1] John Foster (1754–1844), the famous essayist, had long ago emphatically declared his refusal to believe in the traditional hell.

idea of Christ as the Head of the race, though using it with much more caution than Maurice himself had shown, Dale endeavoured in the final chapter of his book *The Atonement* (1875) to mediate between the older view and the uprising of that modern instinct which roughly termed such a view untenable because it was unjust. The measure of his success need not here be gauged : his endeavour is mentioned only to show that now and again Liberal Orthodoxy felt the need of doing something else than slide into a purely non-theological religiousness, and that the very caution which led Liberal Orthodoxy thus to slide because it was afraid to make definite theological affirmations sometimes turned round and worked the other way. And there were other writers who worked over single doctrines, or over one or two doctrines, which for one reason or another caught their thought. But there was no great attempt at furnishing the theological house from bottom to top; and the writers alluded to, though outside the tendency before us, were not strong enough to create a tendency of their own. On the whole, notwithstanding the occasional coming of special questions to the front, Liberal Orthodoxy took the path to which some previously-employed expressions point. Towards positive doctrine it fell into what may be termed an indeterminate and almost uninterested mood. It slid, or began to slide, into a purely non-theological religiousness. Being afraid to launch out upon the theological waters and let down its nets for a draught, it could show no harvest from the deep it dreaded so. And then, the natural thing was for it to persuade itself that theological formularies really mattered little—this by way of self-consolation for its theological poverty, or (shall we say?) by way of disguising from itself the fact that it was afraid to take risks. The principle of " freer interpretation " came to mean simply that the older formularies were impossible, not that satisfactory substitutes for them could and must be found : it came to stand for mere theological emptiness, for a reduction in the quantity of the things which the religious thinker need believe. Of course it was held that there *was* an absolute theological truth somewhere behind; but an agnostic attitude was adopted towards it without regret or shame. In respect of the Atonement, for instance, the statement was glibly passed round that men are saved by the *fact* of the Atonement and not by any *theory* of it—this obviously true statement being made to carry the as obviously false implication that one's rightness or wrongness of theory, or one's utter lack of theory, makes no difference to one's use of the fact. What the whole thing came to was a process of reduction, the rendering of religion non-theological, the pushing of " dogma " and " doctrine " behind the curtain on the tacit assumption that they were neither beautiful nor necessary, that they could neither be used as they were nor re-shaped by any available tools. In fact, the mood which would neither use the old theological formulations nor construct new ones came to mean the virtual abolition of theology at last. All this from that caution,

that dread of a pronounced theological movement, which Liberal Orthodoxy had learned too
well, and (for one has to come back upon the
old story once again) from persistence of the
error that acceptance of Christianity must mean
primarily the acceptance of a system of ideas.
What was left, for those who yielded to the
" reducing " and " minimising " spirit, was a
few general religious conceptions, such as the
Fatherhood of God, the brotherhood of man or
the law of love, sin as selfishness, the idea of
immortality, together with an acknowledgment
that in Christ these great conceptions had broken
out upon the world with the authority and power
of a supernaturally-given message, and that the
spirit of Christ showed the pattern for our own.
These were the remaining " positives." By some,
indeed, they were accepted and proclaimed as
constituting, not all that was *left*, but rather all
that was *needed ;* and the abolition of the rest
was looked on, not in any wise as a deprivation,
not as leaving empty places whose emptiness
must be borne with for a while, but as a riddance
from so much superfluous lumber which had been
piled upon the real treasure and hidden it too
long. It was to minds whose revolt against the
harsher features of the traditional theology grew
specially hot that the matter presented itself
thus, of which minds that of George Macdonald
(1824–1905) may perhaps be taken as the type.
To the fineness of his spirit and the purity of
his moral passion full recognition must be given.
But the Calvinism of his native Scotland so grated
on his sensitive soul that it came to be the

T

standard—the negative standard, as it were—
whereto religious faith must *not* conform : to
the exact opposites of its leading ideas Macdonald
swung over as to the positives which it was his
chief business to assert; and his main doctrinal
affirmations were really indignant denials of
ideas which appeared to him to do dishonour
to God, God's justice, and God's love. Of the
old doctrine of the Atonement he says, in a phrase
which may fairly be taken as an index to his
constant mood, " For the love of God my heart
rose early against the low invention." For
Macdonald the Fatherhood of God was the one
regulative conception, indeed practically the one
truth that Christ came to teach. In book after
book—whether the book's immediate gift were
poetry, fiction, or more directly religious teaching
—he drove the conception home, employing it as
a means to kindle hope, to rouse conscience, to
stir those noble activities which must follow upon
a conviction that because every man is God's
child every man must be his brother's keeper
too. As against the crudeness and cruelty inherent in many presentations of Calvinistic
doctrine, Macdonald's protests were both necessary and successful; and for his work in that
regard the world will always owe him thanks.
But when—from that standpoint, commanding a
historical survey, which we are seeking to occupy
—we enquire whether Macdonald gave to Liberal
Orthodoxy as a whole the gift needed to confirm
its good and to prevent its good from turning to
weakness or even to harm, we have to admit
that this gift was not in Macdonald's hand. He

looked too exclusively one way : he sought to
bestow on religious thought the boon of liberty
from a bondage it ought never to have borne,
but without conferring upon it the discipline
which would have enabled it to use its liberty
aright; and it was the ugliness of obtrusive error
rather than the large architecture of truth as a
whole that he had constantly in view. And the
sum of it is that he, passionately and of set
purpose, did what Liberal Orthodoxy—occasion-
ally with a passion like his own, but oftener in
listlessness or in dread of daring anything great
—was doing through all these years. For the
entire tendency was in the direction of reducing
the content of the Christian system to two or
three leading religious ideas, selected from (and
thereafter put forward not as a selection, but as
practically exhaustive) those which were supernaturally revealed, either by proclamation from
Christ's lips or by exemplification in Christ's life,
as the four Gospels enable men to reconstruct
His words and works for the mental sight and
hearing of their day.

We can see now, though it was scarcely anticipated then except by a few, that from such a
position as this theology must either advance or
recede. Through the later years of the nineteenth century, and in the first years of the
twentieth, unlooked-for consequences from this
" minimising " or " reducing " process—consequences in the way of causing Liberal Orthodoxy
to loosen its hold upon what was supposed to
be safe for ever—made themselves felt. And in
order to appreciate these, it is necessary to speak

of the influence which all this time the idea of
evolution—not in the restricted Darwinian sense,
but in the larger sense associated with Herbert
Spencer's name—was exercising upon religious
thought, the questions which the evolutionary
idea was putting, the answers which under cross-
examination theology gave. For the point to
be made is that, precisely because the ideas which
theology held to be revealed and guaranteed by
the supernatural Christ had, under the " minimising " or " reducing " process, become so few,
theology was tempted, when faced by the objections which the evolutionary theory made against
such an intrusion into the general order of things
as a supernatural Christ implied, to " minimise "
the supernatural Christ Himself. And the pity
of it was that certain re-statements of Christian
truth which were made in the light of the evolutionary idea and which were in themselves wholly
valuable were, under the actually existing conditions, forced to do a destructive rather than a
helpful work. There was not, one may venture
to put it, enough demand for the supernatural
Christ, in those ideas which were now taken as
summing His revelation, to make Liberal Orthodoxy invincibly strong against what wanted to
take the supernatural Christ away : in brief,
though of course no one would have put it so,
and the statement is a translation into brutal
frankness of what was no more than an instinctive
feeling then, the supernatural Christ was not so
much worth while as He had been. So one by
one the insignia of His supernatural royalty were
surrendered (always with the excuse and con-

solation that so many still were left !) : so ray by ray shrank the supernatural halo upon His brow; till at last His kingliness came to be, at least for those who remembered the former glory, only the shadow of a shade. But this was at the end of the process which carried Liberal Orthodoxy over the line where it lost right and title to its name. At the process itself we must glance, though our glance may be swift.

The evolutionary philosophy, as Spencer conceived and taught it, was of course a challenge which Christianity had somehow to face. According to the theory, the whole world, including that inner world of man and man's nature and man's character which crowned the world below, was brought under one law of development : and everything that existed had become what it was through a series of successive conditions, each one of these having been contained *in posse* in the one preceding, having been pushed up out of the enfolding sheath in the fulness of the time, and, when it emerged, having contained within itself *in posse* the one next to come. And so far as change in man's character was going on, the law still held good. But Christianity—even in the non-theological form it had now assumed— spoke of moral and spiritual processes in man which were not natural, but supernatural, produced not by the thrust of forces from behind and below, but by the introduction of forces from beyond and above. How could religion adjust itself into such an attitude as at least to make the opposition less ?

The first and most natural thing to do was to

conceive Christian life and experience in evolutionary terms. That process of moral change
which acceptance of the great Christian ideas
entailed might at least be represented as carrying
on the process of development whereof the
evolutionary philosophy spoke. True, it would
still be out of a supernatural revelation that the
great ideas had come; but the very fact that
doctrines, such as that of atonement, which
had touched upon " happenings " and " trans-
actions " *outside* the world and had made the
religious life in man depend in great part upon
these—the very fact that doctrines such as these
had dropped into the background eased the
situation from this point of view; and in any
case, by the adoption of the evolutionary methods
of speech the sense of break between the general
order and the religious order was toned down.
The publication of Drummond's *Natural Law
in the Spiritual World* (1884) may be taken as
marking the adoption of the method on an extensive scale. In a series of chapters on such
themes as " Degeneration," " Death," " Eternal
Life," " Conformity to Type," " Environment,"
and the like, Drummond contended that all the
laws of spiritual life and character were exactly
the same laws as those which prevailed throughout
the organic kingdom, the processes of religious
life being thus looked upon as a repetition, so to
say in different material, of the processes on the
lower plane. Life is " harmony with environment," and the opposite of " harmony with
environment " is death—the " environment "
which is in question when we are dealing with

religion being God. So, again, spiritual degeneration sets in because the spiritual faculty is
allowed to lie unused, just as in nature living
creatures lose the use of organs—as moles their
sight—which they steadfastly refuse to employ.
And the Christian doctrine of new life through
Christ is only a re-statement of the law of
" biogenesis," or the law that " life can only
come from life." In this last respect (though of
course the scientific law on which Drummond
based himself is by no means universally accepted,
is indeed scientifically strongly suspect) Drummond actually came near to the suggestion of a
veritable life-dynamic in Christ as we have seen
others come near it, and missed it as we have seen
others do—the explanation probably being that
in his passion for bringing the spiritual and natural
worlds into absolute unity Drummond instinc-
tively sheered off from what would have compelled him to speak of something whereby that
unity was broken through.[1] But the matter of
immediate interest and importance, so far as
Liberal Orthodoxy's passage from point to point
in its progress is concerned, is that Drummond
sought to translate all the phenomena of Christian
experience into terms gathered from the evolutionary list. The procedure has become familiar
enough since; and not a few have found in it a
new door through which, unable to pass the doors
where theological formularies mount guard, they
have made their entrance into the realm of faith.

---

[1] It should be said that Drummond subsequently withdrew—at any rate in part, though it is difficult to say how
far—from the book's positions.

Nor is any depreciation of the procedure intended by what is here said. All that is implied
in the way of criticism is that the " something "
was lacking which would really have given to the
method the large value it was supposed to have.
And one has to add " O the little less, and what
worlds away ! " But in the present context we
have only to mark the adoption of the procedure
as being the first shifting of theology's position
(of an already attenuated theology's position, be
it remembered) at the sound of evolutionary
philosophy's challenging voice.

But this was no touching of the real difficulty
after all; for between Christ Himself and the
evolutionary process no connection had yet been
made; and if evolution's challenge was to be
averted rather than fought out, this must in some
way be done. Drummond, indeed, had rested
content without making any pronouncement
whatever about Christ's nature and Christ's
cosmic relationships; and just as *Essays and
Reviews* surprises us, when we look upon it now,
because it had no paper on the Person of Christ,
so in regard to *Natural Law in the Spiritual World*
one is surprised that upon this supreme topic it
had no single word. The tacit assumption, in
fact, was still that the Incarnation marked an
absolute break in the world-order, the alighting
upon the world's levels of One quite unconnected
in any organic sense with the human family in
whose midst He cast His lot. Not even the
humanity of Christ was realised as rooted in the
same soil with that of man. And the next step,
as the evolutionary challenge went on, and the

listeners came more and more to understand
what it meant and what it required, was to
correct this error by linking up Christ on His
human side with the human family as a whole.
The conception of Christ as the " ideal man,"
" the Head of the race "—the conception which
had meant so much to Erskine and Maurice—
re-entered from another direction than that
whence these thinkers had drawn it, coming
now not so much because it was chosen as because
it was forced upon those who desired to harmonise
religion with evolutionary thought.   In Christ,
man sees what man was meant to be, and what
the forces operative from history's beginning
had tended to make him; and he sees it, not
simply because he is looking upon an example,
but because he gazes upon the maturity of the
spiritual nature which is embryonic within himself : the incarnate Christ is in one sense a fulfilment, the fulfilment of all the aspirations, upward
strivings, soul-movements, which had been stirring in humanity's deeps, and in another sense
a prophecy, the prophecy of what humanity may
become when at last all its possibilities shall be
worked out and all its closed buds shall have
opened out and grown to fulness of their flower-
ing.   Christ was the ideal, thrown up at a given
point of the historical process out of the forces
which were moulding man (yet only because those
forces were interpenetrated by a special divine
activity), and thereafter giving straightness and
direction and purposefulness to that spiritual
effort which had been like groping in the dark
before.   In some of the essays contained in *Lux*

Mundi—a collection of theological papers by different writers published in 1889—particularly in the essay on " The Incarnation and Development " by Dr. Illingworth, this conception appears, as also in the Bampton Lectures on *The Incarnation of the Son of God* delivered two years later by *Lux Mundi's* editor, Dr. Gore. And as the years went on, the idea came to be more thoroughly worked and applied. Dr. Griffith-Jones's *Ascent through Christ* may be instanced as a re-reading of the entire idea of salvation—its need, its meaning, its process— and of all its associated or contrasted ideas in the light of that one interpretative idea; and Dr. Fairbairn (1838–1912) specially in *The Philosophy of the Christian Religion* and in *Christ in Modern Theology*, working from a more strictly historical standpoint, contrasting Christ and Christianity with all other moral ideals and powers to which the process of development has given birth and yet relating Christ and Christianity to these as the topmost to the lower stairs, came to Christ as development's crown, and consequently to Christ as Himself determinative for all man's thoughts both of man and of God, at the end. It must be borne in mind, however, in view of what falls to be said directly, that for the writers named the Incarnation of God in Christ was still a wholly special thing : it was not the actual process of Incarnation *itself*, whatever that may have been, but the Christ whom the Incarnation gave us, *on His human side*, that stood as the pattern whereto humanity was to be conformed; and Christ was still One in whom God had given a self-revelation never to be given elsewhere, a Saviour who, when all His work was completely consummated, would still possess a divineness different from whatever divineness man even as perfected could claim. It was the Incarnation which gave the perfect Man to the world, but the perfecting of man which would follow upon the appearance of the perfect Man did not mean that in *every* man a *similar* Incarnation was to be wrought. One may perhaps put it that in order (of course among other things) to show what *every* man might become, God made Christ to be what *no* other man could ever be. God became man to give the complete revelation of humanity; but it was not in that actual *becoming* that the revelation was to be found. That becoming, the actual Incarnation, was the *prius* of the revelation of the ideal Man; but the revelation was given by means of the Incarnation, not as identical with it. If the ideas lying upon the pages of such writers as those who have been named in any wise led on to ideas they did *not* entertain, it was only because Liberal Orthodoxy, being what it was and standing where it did, did not know how to use their gift; and their service will some day—when Liberal Orthodoxy has steadied itself by a return upon some things forgotten too long —be used without incurring any risk of being turned to harm. Returning to our immediate topic and to our survey of Liberal Orthodoxy's progress, we have only to observe how along these lines of thinking the evolutionary challenge was more fully met than it had previously been, since Christ was in some sort linked up with the general

evolutionary process, though at the same time
remaining in the fullest sense divinely special
and unique.

So far the supernatural Christ remains. But
now the danger involved in that theological
" reducing " process before spoken of—the process
of resolving theology into two or three great
ideas which, great as they may be, scarcely
appear to demand a *specially* supernatural
Revealer as their source—begins to make itself
felt. For of course the claims of the full evolutionary philosophy are not satisfied yet, even
though Christ has been in a manner fastened
down upon the evolutionary scheme. There is
still so much of Him, if one may thus put it,
outside. The most important thing about Him
and about His work for man constitutes an
interruption in or a superimposition upon the
development out of which man has come and in
which man is still embedded : the act of God
which makes Him what in the most essential
aspects of His being He is remains isolated,
implies a new beginning on God's part, does not
indeed even imply a new beginning, since it is
done but once : it is not so to say the historic
process produced, but something threaded into
it at a given point—nay, not even something
threaded into it, but something that alights upon
it and then takes wing never to return; so that
unity is not complete after all. Cannot Liberal
Orthodoxy come to a more satisfactory arrangement with what it has already so far met ? Moving on under the instinctive feeling that insistence
on too exceptional a quality in its Christ was not

worth while—now that Christ's revelation has
been minimised down to a few inspiring ideas
and His work reduced to the application of these
ideas, by word and example, to the lives of men—
if peace could be purchased by letting insistence
grow slack, Liberal Orthodoxy shifted the emphasis from the *special* character of the Incarnation to its *similarity* with the incarnation possible
to all mankind, held Christ *as incarnate* to be the
" ideal man," and the Incarnation *itself* as giving
the standard whereto the experience of all shall
reach. The incarnation of God in Christ was
nothing else than the incarnation of God in all
men carried up to its superlative degree—to
which same superlative degree the incarnation
of God in all men was also to be carried up at last.
Those who have made themselves familiar with
the theological literature of recent years will
recognise this at once as giving the note not
seldom struck. " The realisation of this union
in mankind, as it was once realised in Christ, is
the far-off Divine event towards which the whole
creation moves. The Incarnation of the Word
of God is not only an event in the past; it is the
ideal which the world at large is striving to
realise, and which is also in a sense the meaning
of salvation for each of us." So writes Dean
Inge in *Contentio Veritatis* [1] (1902). That is a
typical utterance. That there was something
special in the Incarnation of God in Christ is not
denied by writers of this school, nor is the historic
Christ robbed of the powers which the Gospel
narratives ascribe to Him. But the special

[1] P. 64.

elements in the Incarnation and the exceptional
elements in the historic Christ, pass to the rear.
It is not these that have most value for man's
salvation. The tendency—one might say the
deliberate effort—is to level up the *possibilities*
of our nature to the *actualities* of Christ's. The
Incarnation was an anticipation, a prophetic
fore-showing, of the evolutionary goal. The
consequence—obvious enough one would think,
though never really faced—is of course that for
the perfectly-evolved man of by-and-by there
will be nothing special left about Christ at all :
the distance which separates Him from us now
only indicates how far we have to go before our
own greatness is attained; and once the distance
is over-passed, we shall hail Him as brother
rather than as Lord. At the most, He will
appear *then* as the One who held out a helping
hand when the race could not walk alone. One
can hardly say of such a Christ as this that of the
increase of His kingdom and of His government
there shall be no end. But leaving this criticism
to stand for what it may be worth, we note that
to make the Incarnation merely an anticipation
of what the evolution of humanity is in the end
to reach—that this was the next natural step for
a Liberal Orthodoxy which had " reduced " its
theology and wanted besides to make friends with
the evolutionary idea. And the step was taken
at any rate by many in Liberal Orthodoxy's
ranks.

Further than this it was impossible for Liberal
Orthodoxy to go if it was to keep any right to its
name. But it was easy to pass the line into the

region where right to the name was lost. For by this time a fairly close approach had been made to that form of Christianity which had for years been gathering strength—that form of it which divorced itself entirely from faith in the Christ of the New Testament and from the creeds of the Church, and which, following Hegelian methods, explained Christian doctrine as having necessarily appeared when it did in that world-history which is the progressive self-unfolding of God, but as having no absolute validity and affording, as to its alleged miraculous facts, no access to objective truth. Thomas Hill Green (1836–1882)—fine intellect and pure heart—had taught a spiritualised Hegelianism at Oxford in the middle nineteenth century; Matthew Arnold (1822–1888) with his " Eternal not ourselves who makes for righteousness," and his Jesus who proclaimed a " method of inwardness " and a " secret of self-renouncement," had popularised the neo-Hegelian Christianity for the wider world; and it had come to be taken for granted by many that this sort of Christianity was the only sort possible to cultured men. The spirit and the great moral ideas of Christianity remained : the alleged facts and the doctrines founded upon them disappeared. The emergence of this spirit and of these great ideas itself constituted the incarnation of God; and other incarnation there was none. It is small wonder that some of Liberal Orthodoxy's followers, looking over the barrier on which, in the stage whereat we left them a moment ago, they were leaning, should be drawn. They could see how in this other

formulation of things what they most valued—
the great ideas of Christianity and the conception
of a divineness unfolding itself in and through
man—was included, while at the same time the
difficulty which yet beset them by reason of their
still imperfect reconciliation with the evolutionary
idea was overcome. It is small wonder that
some should leap the barrier and settle upon the
apparently inviting ground. And the leap was
made by at least a few. Upon the point of fact,
at any rate, there can be no controversy—that
among those who claim to be so far within
Christianity's limits that Liberal Orthodoxy
should have no special quarrel with them, have
been some for whom there is no supernatural
Christ, no miracle, no Incarnation save that
which takes place in every member of the human
family; some for whom there is even no personal
God; some for whom no Jesus of Nazareth ever
walked Palestine's holy fields.[1]

Nowhere has there been any violent break,
nowhere any wide leap. It has all been gradual,
smoothly-slipping, imperceptible. Nor is it that
Liberal Orthodoxy has at any stage (except in
the final capitulation just spoken of) been wholly
wrong. It has made ideas regulative which
should have been only contributory and so has
rendered them destructive instead of enriching,

---

[1] Certain English writers—for instance, Dr. K. C. Anderson
and Rev. R. Roberts—have recently adopted the " Christ-
myth " theory of Drews. In a recent book by one of the
younger Congregational ministers the author states that
even if Jesus never existed (though he does not himself
take that view) it makes no vital difference to the Christian
religion. Probably such an attitude is not common, but
one has to reckon with the fact that it is found.

as they might have been. And the whole
descent has been made, and has led to this final
issue, in natural consequence from the initial
error of taking Christianity as a system of ideas
(which Liberal Orthodoxy, no less than Conservative Orthodoxy, has itself done even when
it has most vigorously fulminated against the
folly and wrong of doing any such thing), through
failure to make the central thing realisation of
and submission to a living force acting from a
living Christ. True, there have been voices
raised more than once or twice on behalf of a
better conception; and such voices still are
heard. Dale, in *The Living Christ and the Four
Gospels* contended for the direct action of such a
force from such a Christ upon men to-day. But
he left the nature and method of action of the
Christ-originated force too vague. Dr. Moberly
in *Atonement and Personality,* and in the doctrine
of the Holy Spirit he there set forth, came near
to the idea of a real communication of life from
Christ to His own. And Dr. Forsyth, in all his
books, seeks to recall the Church to the idea of
revelation as " the free, final and effective act
of God's self-communication in Jesus Christ for
man's redemption." " It is not simply," he
proceeds, " an act of manifestation, or even of
impressive representation, but it is a historic
and eternal act of deliverance, prolonged in an
infinite number of acts *ejusdem generis* in the
experience by Christian people of their redemption
in Christ." [1] But such voices have a hard task

[1] Essay on " Revelation and the Person of Christ " in
Faith and Criticism, p. 116. This book (1893) consisted

U

to get deeper than the ear. For the moment,
the idea of revelation as the communication of
ideas possesses at any rate the greater part of
the field—with such consequences for Liberal
Orthodoxy as we have seen.

There, for the present, the matter rests. In
Britain, as in Germany, the permanent building
of theological doctrine has to be waited for still.
Admittedly, it is unsatisfactory to leave it so.
It is no rounded ending to the tale. But a
historian must take the last fact and position as
he finds them, even though they make no striking
climax from the artistic platform of criticism.
And it is therefore on the interrogative note of
" What next ? " that the story of Liberal Orthodoxy has to close.

[*Addendum*.—We may speak of America as
we spoke of European countries other than
Germany at the previous chapter's ending.
While in its theology all the various shades of
thought alluded to in this chapter are ably
represented, it can hardly be said that it has had
a " native " school of its own. Probably the
most original recent theologian there is Dr. Du
Bose. His thinking ranges round the idea of
Christ's headship of the race, but the idea is
applied in quite fresh directions. Thus Jesus
passed through an experience of *acquiring* holi-

---

of a collection of theological essays by Congregational
writers (with one exception). I have quoted these sentences because my eye chanced to light on them. But
they can be paralleled from all Dr. Forsyth's books. See
particularly *The Person and Place of Jesus Christ* and *The
Principle of Authority in relation to Certainty, Sanctity, and
Society*.

ness, and in our union with Him that experience is reproduced in us. Of course the doctrine is so formulated as to safeguard Christ's sinlessness. But there is scarcely need for special mention of any other name.]

EPILOGUE

AT more than one point in the course of the foregoing study it has been suggested that, if the conception of a veritable " life-dynamic " in Christ had been central for Liberal Orthodoxy, some of its stumbles might have been escaped, a more definite theological construction accomplished, and the final slip over (on to the ground where Liberal Orthodoxy becomes so " liberal " that it is " orthodoxy " no more) avoided. It is no chief part of my purpose in this historical *résumé* to advocate opinions of my own; but as the very making of the above criticism implies a positive idea on which it is based, it may be well—lest the matter be left as a mere perplexing question upon the reader's mind—to set down a few paragraphs by way of rendering the idea somewhat more plain. If they sound somewhat assertive, let it be pleaded that this is only because they are explanatory, not argumentative at all. And the paragraphs may take the form of a reply to the enquiry, " What is the real meaning and character of revelation as given by God in Jesus Christ ? "

We may begin with a statement obvious enough, however its implications may sometimes be unperceived. The revelation given in Jesus

Christ was not merely the supply of information to the mind. It was not merely the bringing to man of new information concerning God, God's nature, God's man-ward dispositions, God's will—information wherefrom man was to derive new encouragements, in the light of which man was to direct his spiritual strivings more success-fully and correct his spiritual adjustments to the true standard, from which man was to benefit in various ways. It was not merely new light on facts—it was an addition to the total sum of facts. Suppose that there is some topic into whose secret mysteries I have penetrated far more deeply than have most, and suppose that in virtue of my greater understanding I become the instructor of the less favoured, telling them what they have never known and, if you like, what they never could or would have known without my aid. I am a revealer in a sense, of course. But still I do not, in the imparting of my knowledge, exclusive as it may be—I do not interfere with actualities, or alter them, or add to them, in the slightest degree. I simply stand among them, out of the central mystery to which I have been privileged to win my passage describing and explaining them, and transferring the lessons of them from my own mind to the minds of those who hear me. The whole thing is a communication *of* thought to thought, and *from* thought to thought. There may be, of course—if my special knowledge is of a kind that has any bearing on conduct or character— there may be all manner of practical effects in a quickening of conscience and a heightening of

morality and a purifying of general spirit in
those who learn what I have to teach. But in
its essence, my revelation is just that—a communication *of* thought to thought, and *from*
thought to thought. From revelation in that
ordinary and limited sense revelation in Jesus
Christ is entirely distinct—so distinct that while
it includes the descriptions and the impressions
and the lessons, the essence and substantiality
of the revelation is of a quite different order and
on a quite different plane. That a new revelation came in Jesus Christ means something more
than that Jesus Christ was the supreme spiritual
specialist of all the ages. So long as we only
take Him so, we have not really—whatever
clauses as to His special divine nature we may
incorporate in our doctrinal scheme—we have
not really got beyond the Unitarian conception
of Him. It is not enough to take such revelation
as I should be giving under those hypothetical
circumstances I have just described, transfer
it to the spiritual realm, multiply it a thousand
or a hundred thousand times, and say " *That*
is revelation as given in Christ ! " It is not.
To stop at drawing parallels of the kind is to
miss one of Christianity's chief points, however
far beyond its fellow one of the parallel lines be
produced. Instead of drawing parallels, and
adding a few thousand extra lengths when we
draw the line standing for revelation in Christ,
we must draw distinctions. For we get much
nearer to the heart of the matter so. Revelation
in Jesus Christ was not, as my revelation of
specialised knowledge would be, a voice issuing

forth from remote regions which the speaker was the first or only one to explore. Revelation in Jesus Christ was as truly the emergence of a new actuality from God as was the first creation of the world. Revelation in Christ is distinct from the mere specialist's revelation in that while the revelation of the specialist is simply a movement in the specialist's own mind, revelation in Christ was a movement in *reality*, in the sum total of things—a movement first of all in God, the source and ground of things, and afterwards or concurrently (this of course in the earth-known Christ Himself) a movement introducing itself among and pressing itself into the facts and forces of the world and of world-history—so that in the end, when revelation in Christ had been given, there was not only more knowledge, but there was veritably something more to know. Revelation in Christ is distinct from the specialist's revelation in that while the specialist's revelation makes nothing, but only reports, revelation in Christ was a making, a literal making, of something non-existent before. Revelation in Christ is distinct from the specialist's revelation in that while, after the specialist has spoken, nothing is true in regard to the universe at large that was not true before he spoke, the coming of revelation in Christ did actually make something freshly true both of God and of the world. The Christian idea of revelation includes what we may dare to call (of course one speaks after the manner of men) an actual " event " in the life and being of God Himself, an " event " which, taking place in God, shows itself, even as

and while it happens, through Jesus Christ
to the eyes of man. In Jesus Christ God made
an actual new fact, simultaneously within Himself and within the history and order of the world.
And the making of this new fact, together with the
necessary implications concerning man's appreciation of it and use of it, was and is—in itself
constitutes—the revelation given in Christ.

This new movement in the sum total of things
—in God and in the world—was a definite new
planting-out (that word is one which Martineau
uses in another context, and is just the word
which for our present purposes we require) of
God's creative power in the midst of the world-
order, so that man, instead of merely improving
and accentuating those processes of spiritual
development and culture which he had carried
on till now, might attach himself to and sink
himself into that creative power, and thus be
morally and spiritually created afresh. For
Jesus Christ came to bring and to be *life* to men—
not merely to talk about it or to explain it or to
indicate how and where it might be found, but
to *be* it; and God's revelation in Jesus Christ
is God moving, not something which He has
created, but His actual creativeness itself, down
to the earthly plane, and offering it there for
the uses of mankind. God reveals Himself in
Jesus Christ because in Jesus Christ the whole
of God (not of course quantitatively, for you
cannot talk quantitatively about the Infinite,
but qualitatively)—the whole of God, including
that creativeness which, since it is inherent in
and diffuses itself from every one of God's

qualities and attributes, is really another name for God Himself, makes its entry upon the world-stage. At the first beginning of things in the remote past, when God created the heavens and the earth, when He said "Let there be light" and there was light, when He set going that long evolution of things which came to its crown of glory in man, God had flung forth something *out of* His creativeness; and He had thereafter, with worlds on worlds hanging on His hand, sustained by the breath of His power and by the ceaseless pressing out of the forces of His will the universe He had made. But God had never, from the earliest day to which the first chapter of Genesis looks back up to the day when there was born in Bethlehem of Judæa One who was to be the life and the light of men— God had never put His own creative power forth out of Himself and planted it among the facts and forces of the temporal order, the facts and forces which made direct appeal to and were immediately usable by the family of mankind. This is what He did in Jesus Christ; so that as the Father had life in Himself it was given to the Son to have life in Himself—to have life in Himself, note the force of the saying—*to have life in Himself*, a thing which could have been said of no one else in all the centuries gone by. The new fact in the sum total of facts and realities, the new fact constituting the new revelation, was this—a movement, not of something *out of* God's creativeness, but a movement *of* God's creativeness from its eternal hiding-place in the infinite divine Personality to its temporal (but

not temporary), to its temporal and thereafter
permanent dwelling in that Jesus whom it is
eternal life to know. It was the coming of
God's creative power to join, and necessarily in
great part to supersede, the moral and spiritual
forces already at man's command. God's revelation in Jesus Christ was God putting Himself
as Creator—potential Creator, if it be so preferred,
since this is a matter of re-creation rather than
of creation, and until man surrenders himself
the re-creative work cannot be done—God putting
Himself as potential Creator in Jesus Christ
alongside of man : it was a veritable approach
of one of the component elements in a projected
vital relationship to meet and seek out the other :
it was the planting of the eternal and inexhaustible
spring of life right down upon the path where
human feet were travelling, so that men, instead
of digging deeper such springs of life as they
already possessed and improving the existing
channels whereby the scanty streams were reaching them, had but to stoop and drink, with no
fear that they need ever thirst again : it was the
whole of God offering Himself from a new source
and from a new direction for the acceptance of
every one who was willing to receive and submit
and be re-made. Having sent forth from Himself, and supported through all its successive
steps, that long and curving process of things
which ended in man, God now in Jesus Christ—
it is not enough to say sends forth from Himself
something He had not sent before—God now in
Jesus Christ takes one step which at once brings
Him over, as if by some other and swifter and

straighter path, from the point at which the
process started to the point which the process
has attained, presents Himself there in that
creativeness which is in truth the whole of God,
and arrests man thus : " All this that has been—
the growing world and all the run of its history—
did indeed come forth from Me; but now I
Myself am here in this My Son, so that henceforth, if you will have it so, and will maintain
your side of the relationship between us as I
offer and maintain Mine, it shall be no more you
that live, but I that live in you." God's revelation in Christ is God moving, not something which
He has created, but His actual creativeness
itself, down to the earthly plane, and offering
it there for the uses of mankind.

In doing this, God of course provides a new
revelation in that narrower and smaller sense
in which the term is commonly employed, but
He does much more. Of course fresh knowledge
of God comes to man when God thus sets Himself by a fresh movement among the actualities
of the world-order, enters at a fresh door. God
cannot so stand there, with His own creative
life palpitating at a newly-established centre,
without telling to those who care to learn many
secrets about Himself which they could not
know before. But while fresh knowledge comes,
its coming is almost an incidental thing, and
certainly does not exhaust the significance of
the tremendous and transcendent event. We
set the emphasis wrongly if it is upon the new
knowledge about God we concentrate our thought.
This planting-out of God's creative power in

the world is the advent of a new fact added to the world's total sum of facts, and moreover, the advent of a new fact which is in itself a new *dynamic*—not in any metaphorical or semi-metaphorical sense like to that in which the sudden out-starting of a great idea or a great hope or a great purpose may be a dynamic, but in a sense entirely literal and exact. I drew just now a sort of negative parallel—indicated, perhaps it is better to say, how no parallel holds good—between God's revelation through Jesus Christ and the revelation given through any human specialist in any department of human thought. It may be worth while to indicate at this point what, if it ever happened, would afford some sort of analogy, though a faint one, to the greater thing. Imagine, then, what it would be, what it would mean, if electricity were to-day, not discovered, but actually *created*, for the first time—if we could say that yesterday it was not, but that to-day it is. Of course the suggestion is grotesque, but let it stand. Would it not be a real addition to the sum total of the actualities of our world, a new fact, and more-over, the addition of a veritable dynamic in the strictest sense of the word? It would mean the entrance among, the superimposing upon, those physical forces which had hitherto energised the physical development of the world, of a new force which would work according to its own nature and along its own lines : it would signalise the presence, not so much of a new product as of a new producer; and it would be a breaking into the hitherto closed circle of powers of a fresh power from out of an eternal and boundless deep of powers lying outside and beyond. And all the formulæ as to the method of the world's working and development would require re-stating now, because that method would itself have changed. In some feeble way the poor imagination may serve as an analogy to the advent of the new life-dynamic in Jesus Christ. God's revelation in Jesus Christ was God in His creativeness putting Himself afresh among the moral and spiritual forces at the disposal of man; and this life-force it was which was meant thenceforward to take the moral and spiritual progress of man into its charge, all the other moral and spiritual forces adjusting themselves to the sway of this, grouping themselves round it and having still their own work to do, but occupying now a quite secondary place. It is not by teaching and illuminating and revealing in the ordinary sense (though by its very presence it necessarily does all these things), but by work-ing, and working creatively, that the creativeness of God, set in Jesus Christ in among the actualities of the temporal world, must fulfil itself. To take added knowledge as the chief matter is in this case to mistake a subordinate member of the retinue for the King. It is as veritable, literal dynamic, life-dynamic, life-force whereby and wherefrom man is meant henceforward to live, that God's revelation in Jesus Christ must—because that revelation is God Himself coming in His creative power—be viewed.

The sense of being in this way a revelation of God—a true apocalypse *of* God, not merely a

communication *from* God—the depositary of God's
true creative power—this it was that moved
ceaselessly through the consciousness of Jesus
Christ Himself. And the idea of revelation here
suggested gains support when this is perceived.
If you take the conception of an incarnation
of God's own veritable creativeness, and hold
it up against the inner consciousness of Christ
as the records of His earthly life enable us in
part to discern it, you find that the conception
corresponds with all the deepest words wherein
that inner consciousness of His expressed itself,
and with that indefinable atmosphere—so won-
drous, so majestic, so charged with influences
which yielded their secret to no known test in
the laboratory of men, and withal so ineffably
sacred that halo rather than atmosphere is the
name whereby it ought to be called—with that
indefinable atmosphere which ceaselessly diffused
itself out of that inner consciousness of His as
He passed to and fro. I have quoted already
that central word of Christ's—that word which
surely no man of spiritual sensitiveness can
read without seeming to see doors opened in
Heaven and God himself coming through—
that as the Father hath life in Himself, so hath
He given to the Son to have life in Himself.
And you can crowd words together for witness,
if you like—there are so many of them. If,
indeed, Christ felt the veritable creative power
of God dwelling in Him, then I know how He
could say, " I *am* " (not " I talk about," not
" I teach " but " I *am* ") " I *am* the Way, and
the Truth, and the Life "; I know how He

could say that He had come in order that men
might have life and might have it more abun-
dantly; I know how He could say that to know
Him (implying by the very manner of putting
it that to know Him was really to know the only
true God) was in itself eternal life. There are
words enough. But it is not only nor mainly
a matter of words. Such words stand in the
Fourth Gospel alone, some tell us—and they tell
us, too, that the Fourth Gospel is suspect.
Well, such words do not stand in the Fourth
Gospel alone; but let that pass. Go to the
other three Gospels; and you find in them a
Christ who, if He does not utter so profusely
there the profundities of the Fourth, is in Himself
and in His view of Himself as baptized with
uniqueness, as endowed with something for which
earthly vocabularies have no adequate name, as
the Fourth Gospel displays Him. Certainly it
is He Himself—His own personality with the
mystic forces that circulate within and radiate
from it—that is the central point in the system,
if we care to call it so, which He proclaims; and
certainly it is by penetrating to, and resting in,
the depths of His nature, so far as they can,
that men are to find rest unto their souls; and
certainly this Christ is conscious, not that out
of those common sources within the ordinary
system of things whence men draw their endow-
ments of nature He has been more lavishly
endowed than the rest, but that from sources
far outside the ordinary system of things all that
He is has taken its rise and is still sustained;
and that which is in Him has somehow shared

a glory with God before the foundation of the world. What shall we say of this that He felt to be in Him? How can any—I will not say explanation, but any approach to explanation—be made? If we take the conception of an incarnation of God's actual creativeness in Christ, and lay it close against that consciousness of Christ's which the Gospels reveal, we begin at any rate to see as in a glass darkly. Revelation in Christ—yes, but not merely a fuller revelation *about* God! That is not how He read Himself. He could not have spoken of Himself as He did speak—could not have felt within Himself and about Himself as He did feel—would have had to put off that robe of majesty which He wears in such fashion as to show that He realised Himself to be, not the highest of a class but One standing absolutely alone—had that been all. I would almost prefer to say that the advent of Jesus Christ signalised the cessation of revelation, and the substitution of immediate personal contact for it; for when I seek after some form of speech sufficient for telling wherein the supremacy of Christ's revelation, as He Himself in His own inmost consciousness conceived it, really consists, I am driven back upon the formula which I have employed more than once before, and can only repeat that God's revelation in Jesus Christ is God moving His actual creativeness itself down to the earthly plane and offering it there for the uses of mankind.

If this conception of revelation—a conception which makes the coming of revelation in Christ

a continuous and dynamic fact as real to-day
as it was when it was first flung into the sum
total of realities centuries ago—if this be taken
as central for Christian theology, it will of course
need to be vindicated for philosophic thought.
That is, the possibility of the advent of such a
life-dynamic as that spoken of and its harmony
with the general scheme of things; the way in
which its advent and, thereafter, its constant
working, form at the same time an addition to
and a continuation of a world-process which was
being worked out before it came but which could
not be fully worked out without it; these things
will have to be shown. True, the primary test
and proof will lie in the actual experience of the
life-force itself. But in order that he who has
the experience may be able to assure himself
that in his interpretation of the experience he has
not gone astray, and in order that he may be
able to answer, and perchance persuade to make
trial for themselves, those who sceptically enquire
concerning a reason for the faith that is in him,
he will require to incorporate his central Christian
doctrine with his general world-view, at least
to adjust the first into harmonious relation with
the second.[1] But this once done, the question

[1] I trust I shall not be charged with egotism if I say that
I have tried to deal—in a preliminary and tentative fashion
—with some of the matters mentioned in this paragraph
in several articles in various Reviews. (*Philosophy and
Theology*, in *Holborn Review*, Jan. 1907; *Christianity as
Doctrine and as Dynamic*, in *Expository Times*, Jan. 1911;
Rational Mysticism and New Testament Christianity, in
Harvard Theological Review, July 1911; *Religious History
and the Idea of Immanence*, in the *Review and Expositor*,
Jan. 1913. The last two are of course American periodicals.)

x

of doctrine as a whole—the extent of its reach, the limits within which it may change—will be closed. Doctrine will have its place; for it will speak of what the Christ out of whom the life-force issues must have been and of what He still must be, of the human soul's self-adjustment to the offered power, of all those things which follow from and are indeed involved in the central fact. Christianity will be not doctrine, but dynamic; yet just because it is dynamic, the great doctrines will re-assert their place and right; for they will tell how the dynamic is offered, how it may be appropriated, how its gift may be won. The doctrine of atonement will tell how Christ's cross enabled Him to become the life of men in ways not possible before : the doctrine of faith will indicate the attitude into which man's nature must set itself in order that the approaching life-power may find an open door; and so with the rest. Thus it is in the central fact that every doctrine will find its regulative measure : thus it is some aspect of that central fact that every doctrine will show, and back upon that central fact that every doctrine will return : thus every doctrine will be " practical " in that it will prescribe a real " activity " of the soul correspondent to the " activity " of the life-giving Christ : thus the " moralising of dogma " will be achieved. And at the same time no necessary change will be barred. What the development of thought and the enlightenment of conscience (always with the life-giving Christ before them) find untenable will be given up; though for that matter, since all doctrine will be held, not in detachment nor for its own sake, but in its relation to one primary fact whose validity has been established once for all, the old clash of war between Christian doctrine and knowledge which has its centre elsewhere than in that fact can be heard no more. By its concentration upon the fact of a life-giving Christ—by its resolve to formulate, so far as is possible, *all* that the fact involves and yet to formulate *no more*—the Christian faith must grow simultaneously rich and secure. Still, what change is needed will rouse no fear, since the primary fact—found reasonable by the mind and re-given in the Christian experience of each recurring day and in that experience's understanding of itself—will abide, and since by the existence of that fact the limits of possible change will be fixed. And of course no " drift," like that on which we have seen Liberal Orthodoxy floating slowly down till its vessel passed the point where the supernatural Christ was suddenly found to have disappeared, will be possible. The historic Christ as the New Testament portrays Him will remain, the starting-point in history of the new life-offer, all the more real in that far-off past because on the present He *is* what the history declares Him to have been. And the supernatural Christ, given not merely as a truth to the mind, but as a dynamic reality to the inner experience—the experience of Him being actually an experience of His supernaturalness in that it is an experience of His constant creative power—remains the same yesterday and to-day and for evermore.

x 2

But to pursue these things would take us too far. Whether the suggestion here made points in the direction of a helpful theological reconstruction only the future can show. Our study of the past has at least shown the direction whence such a reconstruction will *not* come—perhaps a little more. Meanwhile, the suggestion may be tentatively made—if only to call out, and perhaps to tinge even as it loses itself in, suggestions happier than itself.

INDEX

RICHARD CLAY & SONS, LIMITED,
BRUNSWICK STREET, STAMFORD STREET, S.E.
AND BUNGAY, SUFFOLK.